# GATLEY

## ON

# LIBEL

# AND

# SLANDER

First Supplement
to the
Twelfth Edition

Up-to-date until September 2015

SWEET & MAXWELL        THOMSON REUTERS

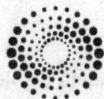

Published in 2015 by Thomson Reuters (Professional) UK Limited,
trading as Sweet & Maxwell, Friars House,
160 Blackfriars Road, London SE1 8EZ
part of thomson Reuters (Professional) UK Limited
(Registered in England & Wales, Company No 1679046.
Registered Office and address for service:
2nd floor, 1 Mark Square, Leonard Street, London EC2A 4EG

Typeset by Wright and Round Ltd, Gloucester

Printed and bound in Great Britain by CPI Group (UK) Ltd, Croydon, CR0 4YY

For further information on our products and services, visit:
www.sweetandmaxwell.co.uk

No natural forests were destroyed to make this product. Only farmed timber was used and
replanted.

**A CIP catalogue record for this book is available from the British Library**

| | |
|---|---|
| ISBN Main Work | 978–0–41402–843–2 |
| ISBN Supplement | 978–0–41405–2628 |

# JOINT EDITORS

Professor Alastair Mullis

LLB (Lond), LLM (Cantab)
Head of the School of Law,
University of Leeds

Richard Parkes Q.C., M.A. (Cantab)

Bencher of Gray's Inn,
a circuit judge and a
deputy High Court judge

## SENIOR CONTRIBUTING EDITOR
Godwin Busuttil, M.A., M.Phil. (Cantab), of Lincoln's Inn, Barrister

## CONTRIBUTING EDITORS
Andrew Scott, LLB MPhil (Belfast) PhD (Wales)
Associate Professor of Law, London School of Economics
Adam Speker, B.A., of Middle Temple, Barrister

## PRECEDENTS AND DAMAGES AWARDS
Chloe Strong, LLB (LSE), of the Middle Temple, Barrister

# HOW TO USE THIS SUPPLEMENT

This is the First Supplement to the Twelfth Edition of *Gatley on Libel and Slander* and has been compiled according to the structure of the main volume.

At the beginning of each chapter of this Supplement the mini table of contents from the main volume has been included.
Where a heading in this table of contents has been marked with a square pointer (■), this indicates that there is material that is new to the work in the Supplement to which the reader should refer.

Within each chapter, updating information is referenced to the relevant paragraph in the main volume. New paragraphs which have been introduced in this Supplement have been identified as, e.g. 25.19A. This enables references contained within these paragraphs to be identified in the tables included in this Supplement.

# PREFACE

The two years since the publication of the 12th edition have seen the coming into force of the Defamation Act 2013. The Act was the culmination of several years of campaigning for wide-ranging and radical reform in the law of defamation. While ultimately the Act did not go as far as many of the campaigners would have wished, it nevertheless sought in a number of ways to shift the balance struck by the law of defamation between free speech and reputation towards greater protection for the former.

It will take time before the full impact of the legislation is felt. So far, it has received surprisingly little judicial consideration. Nevertheless, one aspect of the Act which has had an impact is the new 'serious harm' threshold created by s.1. There have been a number of first instance cases considering the proper interpretation of s.1 (in particular *Cooke v MGN Ltd, Ames v The Spamhaus Project Ltd and Lachaux v Independent Print Ltd*). These cases indicate that the effect of the provision is to stiffen and transform the existing threshold requirement of actionability, remove the common law presumption of damage and require the claimant to prove actual, or likely, serious harm to reputation. The ramifications are fascinating. For instance, it appears that a full apology may draw the sting of harm to the claimant to the remarkable extent that what was at first a defamatory allegation may then cease to be so.

Other areas of interest include these: at which point is harm to be judged to have occurred or to be likely to occur? If serious harm is likely but has not yet occurred, when does time start running for limitation purposes? Will it be open to the claimant to rely for evidence of serious harm on the reactions of the public on social media? And if *cyber-vox pop* is indeed to be admissible, how is it to be reconciled with long established notions of single meaning and the standard set by right-thinking people? One might almost be tempted to suppose that Parliament did not fully realise what a Pandora's box it was opening

In terms of practice, the coming into force of s.11 has had the result that the jury ceases to be the presumptive tribunal of fact. Consequently, the trend towards the trial of preliminary issues (particularly of meaning) continues. 'Threshold' issues under s.1 will demand prompt application, usually before service of Defence. Full trials will surely become even rarer than they were before the Act. That, at least, is something that Parliament must have hoped to achieve.

The general editors have read the whole text of this supplement. They have been assisted by Godwin Busuttil, whose observations—often acerbic, always highly focused—have been invaluable. Subject to this, the responsibility for writing was as follows: Godwin Busuttil, Chapters 25, and 29-31; Alastair Mullis, Chapters 2-10, 13 & 14, 16-21 and 23; Richard Parkes, Chapters 24 and 32-35; Andrew Scott, Chapters 1, 11 & 1, 15 and 22; Adam Speker, Chapters

26-28 and 36. The appendix of damages awards was prepared by Chloe
Strong.

Alastair Mullis would like to offer his particular thanks to Richard Parkes for
his patience and guidance. He would also like to apologise to his family for
another lost summer.

**Alastair Mullis**                                          **Richard Parkes**
Leeds                                                        Salisbury Plain

# TABLE OF CASES

TABLE OF CASES

TABLE OF CASES

TABLE OF CASES

TABLE OF CASES

TABLE OF CASES

# TABLE OF STATUTES

# TABLE OF STATUTORY INSTRUMENTS

# TABLE OF CIVIL PROCEDURE RULES

# TABLE OF EUROPEAN AND INTERNATIONAL CONVENTIONS AND TREATIES

# TABLE OF EUROPEAN DIRECTIVES

# TABLE OF EUROPEAN REGULATIONS

# TABLE OF PRACTICE DIRECTIONS

CHAPTER 1

# INTRODUCTION

SECTION 1. INTRODUCTORY

**Reputation and Defamation.** *Add at end of paragraph*:                                    **1.1**

The Defamation Act 2013 is now in force: see Defamation Act 2013 (Commencement) (England and Wales) Order 2013 SI 2013/3027. Whether the Act will prove to have any profound impact on the nature and extent of defamation proceedings remains an open question.

Judicial statistics for 2014 showed a 60 per cent increase in the number of defamation claims being brought before the court relative to 2013 (227 claims compared with 142). This was the highest annual figure since 2009. Moreover, a much larger percentage of these claims than normal were for damages in excess of £50,000. It may be that in future these figures will be seen as a short-term "blip" in an ongoing decline in the number of defamation proceedings brought. Alternatively, it may signal a shift in the nature of claims reaching court: an increasing proportion of claims involved "social media" defendants.

One area in which the 2013 Act has clearly had a significant impact is that generated by s.1 of the Act: the serious harm threshold. The proper interpretation of the provision has been considered by the courts on a number of occasions: see *Cooke v MGN Ltd* [2014] EWHC 2831 (QB); [2015] 1 W.L.R. 895; *Ames v The Spamhaus Project Ltd* [2015] EWHC 127 (QB); [2015] 1 W.L.R. 3409; *Lachaux v Independent Print Ltd* [2015] EWHC 2242 (QB); [2015] E.M.L.R. 28. These cases indicate that the new test requires claimants to plead evidence of the harm—whether direct or inferential—they have suffered or will likely suffer if the claim is to progress beyond a preliminary stage: "It is now necessary to prove as a fact on the balance of probabilities that serious reputational harm has been caused by, or is likely to result in future from, the publication complained of"—see *Lachaux*, at [45] (per Warby J.). The practical ramifications of the emergent judicial interpretation of the test may not prove to be enormously significant—see *Lachaux* at [57]-[59]. A number of questions regarding the operation of the test remain open, however, and further litigation on the point can be expected. There is a risk that this change may "[defeat] Parliament's intention by making litigation in this area more not less expensive and complex", although such concerns have been described judicially as "alarmist and ill-founded" (see *Lachaux* at [56] (per Warby J.). One clear effect of the introduction of the s.1 test would appear to be that the common law presumption of damage has been significantly, perhaps entirely, undermined—see *Lachaux* at [60]: see the discussion at 2.5ff below.

SECTION 2. OVERVIEW OF DEFAMATION LAW

**1.7**     **The meaning of defamatory.** *Add after ", . . . although not unlawful" in the first paragraph*:

See *Barron v Vines* [2015] EWHC 1161 (QB) at [14] (per Warby J.): "the belief that words are not defamatory if they are true is a common misconception".

*Add at end of final paragraph*:

With the coming into force of s.1 of the Defamation Act 2013, the legal appreciation of when published words are defamatory has been limited to circumstances in which a statement "has caused or is likely to cause serious harm to the reputation of the claimant". In respect of corporate claimants, such serious harm must comprise "serious harm to the reputation of the claimant". In respect of corporate claimants, such serious harm must comprise "serious financial loss" (s.1(2), Defamation Act 2013). Furthermore, the presumption of damage in libel proceedings may "cease to play any significant role" in libel proceedings: *Lachaux v Independent Print Ltd* [2015] EWHC 2242 (QB); [2015] E.M.L.R. 28 at [60] (per Warby J.). See generally the discussion at 2.8 below.

SECTION 3. DEFAMATION AND THE RIGHTS CONTEXT

**1.11**     **Introduction: the rights context.** *Add after " . . . reputation that is protected by art.8", four lines from end of the paragraph*:

The right to a fair and impartial tribunal protected by article 6 can also play a role. For instance, in *Garcia v Associated Newspapers Ltd* [2014] EWHC 3137 (QB) at [302], Dingemans J noted that "the proper defence of an action is not to be taken into account in aggravation of damages in libel proceedings. Any other approach would be an impermissible interference with the vital right of the free press to defend itself, and would therefore be wrong". See also, *Weller v Associated Newspapers* [2014] EWHC 1163 (QB); [2014] E.M.L.R. 24 at [186] for a similar point made in the context of the claim for misuse of private information.

*Add at end of paragraph*:

See, for example, *Yeo v Times Newspapers Limited* [2014] EWHC 2853 (QB); [2015] 1 W.L.R. 971 at [14] per Warby J: "there is a human rights context . . . to which attention must be paid. On one side are the rights [the publisher] and its readers under Article 10(1) of the Convention to impart and receive information and ideas, which may only be interfered with to the extent necessary in a democratic society in pursuit of one of the legitimate aims recognised by Article 10(2). On the other side of the equation is the protection of reputation. Not only is this one of the legitimate aims identified in Article 10(2), it is also now recognised that an attack on reputation may engage Article 8(1) of the Convention, if serious enough in its effects on the enjoyment of private life: see, for instance, *Axel Springer v Germany* [2012] E.M.L.R.15. Human rights are therefore engaged, and may be engaged on both sides. There is a need for a careful and sensitive assessment. The common law and relevant statutory provisions must be interpreted and applied in a way consistent with the appropriate balance between the competing rights".

**Recognition of the rights—value of reputation.** *Add*: In *Building Register* **1.14** *Ltd v Weston* [2014] EWHC 784 (QB), Dingemans J. reflected the common ground between the parties that corporate claimants have "no article 8 rights, although article 1 protocol 1 rights might apply". Interestingly, however, in *Firma EDV* the Sectional court left open the question of whether the reputation of a company falls within article 8 and proceeded on the basis that it did so (*Firma EDV für Sie, EfS Elektronische Datenverarbeitung Dienstleistungs GmbH v Germany* app no 32783/08, unreported decision of Fifth Section, 2 September 2014). See further the discussion at 2.3 below.

# CHAPTER 2

# DEFAMATORY IMPUTATIONS

## SECTION 1. WHAT IS DEFAMATORY

**2.1**    *Replace third paragraph (starting "When the Defamation Act 2013 comes into force" with the following:* **The defamatory imputation.** s.1 of the Defamation Act 2013, which is now in force, requires the claimant to show that publication of the defamatory statement "has caused or is likely to cause serious harm to the reputation of the claimant". (*note 9*) Where the claimant is a "body that trades for profit", harm to its reputation is not "serious harm" unless "it has caused or is likely to cause the body serious financial loss". (*note 10*) Section 1 is clearly not intended as a wholesale replacement for the common law definition of what is defamatory. The language adopted in the provision—that a publication "is not defamatory unless'—is simply not apt to create a new definition and had Parliament intended to replace the existing, well-established definition, one would have expected that to have been done expressly (*new note 10A*). Instead, as the Explanatory Notes to the Defamation Act 2013 explain in para.11, s.1 is intended to build on the consideration given by the courts in a series of cases to the question of what is sufficient to establish that a statement is defamatory.

At common law, the courts had developed a twin-track approach to the elimination of trivial claims. They might fail on the ground that they did not meet the threshold of seriousness test that Tugendhat J. held in *Thornton v Telegraph Media Group* (*new note 10B*) was part of the test of what is defamatory; or they might be struck out as an abuse of process pursuant to *Jameel (Yousef) v Dow Jones & Co. Inc.* (*new note 10C*) Under the latter jurisdiction, a claim might be struck out on the basis that no real and substantial tort had been committed such that it would be disproportionate to allow the claim to proceed any further (*new note 10D*). This was the context in which s.1 was enacted and according to Warby J. in *Lachaux*, the language used in the provision was consistent with an intention to simplify the law:

> "The use in s.1(1) of the new language, "has caused or is likely to cause" is consistent with an intention to simplify the law by drawing together the strands, and subsuming all or most of the Jameel jurisdiction into a new and stiffer statutory test requiring consideration of actual harm." (*new note 10E*)

In other words, s.1(1) "stiffens" the existing common law test by raising the *Thornton* "threshold of seriousness" and by requiring that the claimant must prove actual harm to reputation. It is consequently no longer the case, as it was at common law, that the court should only consider whether the words complained of have the tendency adversely to affect a person's reputation: the court must now consider whether actual harm to reputation has been caused or is likely. That is not to say however that s.1 of the Act wholly supersedes the *Jameel* abuse jurisdiction. As Warby J. explained in *Ames v The Spamhaus Project Ltd.* (*new note 10F*):

> "There may be defamation cases in which the pursuit, or continued pursuit, of the claim cannot be justified as a necessary and proportionate interference with freedom of expression even though the publication has caused serious harm to reputation, or such harm is likely. *Lait v Evening Standard Ltd.* [2011] EWCA Civ 849; [2011] 1 W.L.R. 2973 could be an example of such a case."

Such cases are however likely to be very rare and the courts should now first consider whether the serious harm test is met and only then ask whether, notwithstanding that serious harm has been or is likely to be caused, the claim should be struck out as an abuse of process (*new note 10G*).

*New Note 10A: Lachaux v Independent Print Limited* [2015] EWHC 2242 (QB); [2015] E.M.L.R. 28 at [46].

*New Note 10B:* [2010] EWHC 1414 (QB); [2011] 1 W.L.R. 1985.

*New Note 10C:* [2005] EWCA Civ 75; [2005] Q.B. 946 CA.

*New Note 10D:* See further para.30.48 below.

*New Note 10E:* [2015] EWHC 2242 (QB); [2015] E.M.L.R. 28 at [50].

*New Note 10F:* [2015] EWHC 127 (QB); [2015] 1 W.L.R. 3409 at [51].

*New Note 10G: Ames v The Spamhaus Project Ltd.* [2015] EWHC 127 (QB); [2015] 1 W.L.R. 3409, at [51].

**The impact of the Human Rights Act.** *Note 23, add,* See also *Uppal v Endemol UK Limited* [2014] EWHC 1063 (QB). **2.2**

**Business and personal defamation.** *Insert the following at the end of para.2.3:* **2.3**

While English courts have not regarded attacks on corporate reputation as engaging art.8, the Fifth Section of the European Court of Human Rights in *Firma EDV für Sie, EfS Elektronische Datenverarbeitung Dienstleistungs GmbH v Germany* (*new note 37A*) was prepared to proceed on the basis that a company did have such rights. The Strasbourg Court has held in a number of cases that the legal premises (*new note 37B*) of a company and its correspondence (*new note 37C*) may be protected under art.8, and that protection of a company's reputation may be the legitimate aim of a restriction under art.10(2) (*new note 37D*), but it had not previously held that a company has a right to reputation. Reputation is of course not expressly protected within art.8 but protection has been said to arise because a person's reputation forms part of their psychological integrity and therefore their private life (*new note 37E*). While this reasoning might justify extending art.8 protection to natural persons, it is not easy to see how it justifies extending it to companies which have no psychological integrity. To say, as the Court in *Firma* did, that the outcome of any application should not, in principle, vary according to whether it has been lodged with the Court under art.10 of the Convention by the publisher of the offending article or under art.8 of the Convention by the person who was the subject of that article (at [22]), may be correct. It however begs the question whether a company has an art.8 right to reputation in the first place. While there may be merit in analysing these cases in the same way, bringing corporate reputation within art.8 would amount to a significant, as yet not clearly justified, extension of art.8's ambit. In the absence of compelling reasoning from the Court, it seems unlikely that English courts will adopt the same approach.

*New Note 37A:* Application no.32783/08 (2014).

*New Note 37B: Buck v Germany*, Application no.41604/98, at 31, ECHR 2005 IV; *Niemietz v Germany*, (1993) 16 EHRR 97.

*New Note 37C: Wieser and Bicos Beteiligungen GmbH v Austria*, no.74336/01.

*New Note 37D*: *Heinisch v Germany*, no.28274/08 2011 2011; *Steel and Morris v. the United Kingdom*, no.68416/01.

*New Note 37E*: See para.1.14 above.

*Delete existing para.2.5 and replace with the following*

**2.5**   *Insert this after 2.5* **Defamation Act 2013, s.1: introduction.** Defamation Act 2013, s.1(1) provides that: "A statement is not defamatory unless its publication has caused or is likely to cause serious harm to the reputation of the claimant." Where the claimant is a "body that trades for profit", harm to reputation is not, by virtue of s.1(2), "serious harm" unless it "has caused or is likely to cause serious financial harm." (*note 55*). As is explained in para.2.1 above, the effect of s.1 is to "stiffen" the existing common law test for what is defamatory. It does this in two ways. First, it raises the threshold for defamation set out in *Thornton v Telegraph Media Group* (*new note 55A*) from a tendency to cause "substantial" to "serious" reputational harm (*new note 55B*). Secondly, and most significantly, the claimant must now prove on a balance of probabilities that serious reputational harm has been caused by, or is likely to result in the future from, the publication complained of (*new note 55C*).

So far as the first of these effects is concerned, while the word "serious" is plainly intended to raise the bar above that set by the common law "substantial" test, how much higher the bar is raised is not clear. Bean J. accepted in *Cooke v*

*MGN Limited* that "serious harm" involves a higher threshold than "substantial harm" would have done (*new note 55D*) but declined to admit as an aid to construction a statement by Lord McNally, the Minister of State in charge of the Bill, to the effect that the serious harm test raises the bar "to a modest extent above the requirement of the common law": "Serious" is an ordinary word in common usage and I do not consider that it creates an ambiguity so as to bring *Pepper v Hart* into play." (*new note 55E*).

In determining whether "serious harm" has been caused or is likely, the court may consider all the relevant circumstances of the case, including evidence of what has happened after publication, the meaning of the words complained of and the harmful tendency of that meaning (*new note 55F*). Whether the threshold is met is a multi-factorial question that will require a consideration of such factors as the gravity of the allegation, the extent to which readers will have identified the claimant as the person referred to (*new note 55G*), whether the publication was oral or written, the status and number of publishees and the extent to which the allegations were believed, the status of the publisher and whether that makes it more likely that the allegation was believed, the likelihood that the readership may have been augmented by viral or "grapevine" publication, whether an apology has been offered or made (*new note 55H*), and the permanence of the publication. In appropriate cases, serious harm may be proved by inference (*new note 55I*).

At common law, in the case of defamation actionable per se, the cause of action is complete on the publication of the words to a third person. The test of what is defamatory can be answered by determining whether the words have a tendency to cause harm to reputation. If they do, a cause of action arises at the moment of publication. The position is different in respect of slanders not actionable per se. In relation to these, the cause of action is not complete until special damage is sustained (*new note 55J*). As Defamation Act 2013 s.1 has been held to abolish the presumption of damage and to require that serious harm to reputation be proved or be a likely consequence of the defamatory statement, it would appear that the cause of action may not be complete on the date of publication but instead only when serious harm to reputation is sustained or is likely to be. At least two issues of importance arise from this.

First, at what time does the cause of action accrue for limitation purposes? As a general rule, the moment of accrual of the cause of action for limitation purposes is the time at which the cause of action is complete (*new note 55K*). Determining what this time is may now be problematic, because it is often likely be a matter for the judgment of the claimant and his advisers to decide if and when serious harm has been, or is likely to be, caused. The second issue concerns the time at which the court should assess whether serious harm to reputation has in fact been, or is likely to be, caused for the purposes of determining whether the s.1 threshold has been met. Should the serious harm requirement be tested at the time of publication, the time of issue of proceedings, the time of determination of the issue, or some other time? These issues are considered below.

*"Serious harm" and limitation*: For limitation purposes, the cause of action does not accrue until the tort is complete. Where the claim is brought on the basis that the words complained of have caused serious harm to reputation, the cause of action will not be complete and, accordingly time will not start to run, until

such harm has occurred. This will frequently not be easy to identify with precision.

There may be cases, perhaps involving the most serious libels, where the cause of action will be complete at the moment of publication or at least a short period of time afterwards. If, for example, a public figure is accused in a national newspaper of being a paedophile, it is highly likely that a court would draw an inference of serious harm almost from the moment of publication (*new note 55L*). Where, however, a grave allegation is published but the publication is more limited, say on a blog which has a small number of readers, and (for instance) the claimant is not named or is not a public figure, determining the time at which the cause of action is complete may be much more difficult. Obviously, if the claimant could establish they had lost their job as a result of the allegation, that would be sufficient to prove serious harm and time might run from then. What if, however, no such "concrete" harm can be shown? How many unique views of the blog, for example, would have to be established before the threshold was met? Uncertainty about the time of accrual of a cause of action is highly undesirable and likely to give rise to considerable difficulties in advising clients when to issue the claim but this seems to be an inevitable consequence of treating proof of serious harm to reputation as the trigger for the accrual of the cause of action.

An additional issue arises in respect of limitation as a result of Defamation Act 2013, s.8 (*new note 55M*). Section 8 provides that in a case in which a person publishes a statement to the public and subsequently re-publishes the same, or similar, statement (whether or not to the public), any cause of action in respect of the later publication is to be treated as having accrued on the date of first publication (Defamation Act 2013, s.8(3)). This appears to be the case even if the cause of action for the first publication did not in fact (thanks to s.1) accrue at that time. Thus, if a statement is published on 1 January and republished on 1 June, the cause of action for the republication is treated as having accrued on 1 January. This will be so even if serious harm to reputation from the first publication did not result until 1 March. Of course, if serious harm to reputation from the first publication was not caused until 1 March, there would be the rather curious result that the limitation period would expire in respect of the republication before it did for the first publication. This can hardly be what Parliament had in mind in enacting s.8, yet it appears to follow from the interpretation that has been given by the courts to s.1. It is worth underlining the fact that by s.8(3) Parliament envisages the cause of action for the first publication as accruing "on the date of the first publication". That appears to be the old test for accrual of a cause of action in defamation, namely publication of (defamatory) words to a third party. It is doubly curious that there should be one test for the purposes of s.8 and another for s.1.

Similar difficulties are likely to arise in determining the date of accrual of any claim where a claim is based not on serious harm to reputation having been caused but instead on the likelihood of it being caused. The first time at which it may be shown that serious harm is likely to be caused must be the time of publication. It is at that moment that a statement has been put in circulation that has the potential to cause serious harm to the claimant. However, there may of course be cases where it would not be possible to show at that time that serious harm was more likely than not to result from the statement. Where this is so the judge will have to find on the facts of each particular case when the cause of action has accrued.

*"Serious harm" and the time at which harm should be assessed*: The second issue is at which time the court should assess whether serious harm to reputation has in fact been caused, or is likely to be caused, for the purposes of determining whether the s.1 threshold has been met. The point is an important one because conduct by the defendant or claimant after publication, or a change in circumstances, may have the effect of decreasing or even eliminating the serious harm that might otherwise have been suffered as a consequence of the statement. Thus, the prompt apology in *Cooke v MGN Limited* was treated as sufficient to eliminate or at least minimise any unfavourable impression that might have been caused by the original article in the mind of the hypothetical reasonable reader (*new note 55N*).

In *Cooke v MGN Limited* Bean J. ruled out the time of publication as the appropriate time:

> "The words "has caused" involve looking backwards in time, the words "or is likely to cause" involve looking forwards. The Act does not make clear the moment which marks the dividing line between past and future. It cannot be the moment of publication, since at that moment no harm "has been caused"." (*new note 55O*).

The judge went on to conclude, although it was not necessary for the decision, that the appropriate time was the time of issue of the writ, as this corresponded with the common law rule that, subject to certain exceptions, slander is not actionable unless by the date on which the writ was issued, special damage had already occurred (*new note 55P*). Warby J. in *Lachaux v Independent Print Limited* stated that he preferred the time at which the issue is determined (which may be the trial of the action or, more usually, the trial of a preliminary issue): "If the [time of issue of the claim form] is adopted a claim would fail if actual damage had been caused at the time of the determination, but was not likely at the time of publication; and a claim would succeed if damage was likely at the time of publication even if it turned out that none was caused." (*new note 55Q*).

Of the two suggested dates for the assessment of damages, the time at which the issue is determined is the preferable one. Both, as Bean J. pointed out in *Cooke v MGN Limited,* have "the curious effect that whether a statement is held to have been defamatory on the day it was published might depend respectively on the timing of the issue of proceedings, or the timing of the trial" (*new note 55R*). Warby J's reasons for choosing the date of determination are persuasive. But even his choice is not without its problems. An action may start as a perfectly viable claim, on the basis that there is at the date of issue a likelihood of serious harm; but if no actual harm is suffered in the interim, the court may determine at the hearing of the preliminary issue that there is in fact no likelihood of serious harm being caused. Or (as in *Cooke*) there may have been an apology which draws the sting, in which case the claimant may fail the determination of a s.1 test which at the date of publication and of issue he would probably have passed. In either event, the claimant starts out with a complete and viable claim which, because no harm has been suffered in the interim or because an apology has drawn the sting, is found not to be defamatory at all, and is struck out with costs. In *Lachaux*, Warby J. said that there would be nothing novel about that: the action would 'lie inchoate', like a slander claim awaiting the actual damage which makes it viable (*new note 55S*). That is questionable. On the hypothesis advanced here, there actually is a likelihood of serious harm at the time of publication and the time of issue: it is then a complete cause of action, not an inchoate one, which distinguishes it from slander actionable only on proof of damage.

*New Note 55A:* [2010] EWHC 1414 (QB); [2011] 1 W.L.R. 1985.

*New Note 55B: Lachaux v Independent Print Limited* [2015] EWHC 2242 (QB); [2015] E.M.L.R.28, at [45].

*New Note 55C*: At [45]. See also, per Bean J. in *Cooke v MGN Limited* [2014] EWHC 2831 (QB); [2015] 1 W.L.R. 895, at [30]-[33]; *Ames v The Spamhaus Project Ltd* [2015] EWHC 127 (QB); [2015] 1 W.L.R. 3409 at [49].

*New Note 55D:* [2014] EWHC 2831 (QB); [2015] 1 W.L.R. 895, at [37].

*New Note 55E:* Ibid, at [39]. See also *Lachaux v Independent Print Limited* [2015] EWHC 2242 (QB); [2015] E.M.L.R.28, at [29]; *Brett Wilson LLP v Persons Unknown* [2015] EWHC 2628, at [30].

*New Note 55F: Lachaux,* above, at [65].

*New Note 55G: Lachaux,* above, at [121].

*New Note 55H:* See, e.g., *Cooke v MGN Limited* [2014] EWHC 2831 (QB); [2015] 1 W.L.R. 895, at [44].

*New Note 55I:* See e.g. *Cooke* (above) at [43] and para.2.6 below. See also *Brett Wilson.*

*New Note 55J*: See, e.g., *Saunders v Edwards* (1663) 1 Sid. 95. See further para.19.13 below.

*New Note 55K:* See further Ch.19, s.4 below.

*New Note 55L:* In *Cooke v MGN Limited* [2014] EWHC 2831 (QB); [2015] 1 W.L.R. 895 Bean J. pointed out at [31] that the Act did not make clear which moment marked the dividing line between past ("has caused") and future ("likely to cause"), and ruled out the moment of publication, since at the time of publication no harm could be said to have been caused. That may be questionable. In many of the most serious cases (such as in the example above) serious harm will surely have been suffered at precisely the moment of publication, which is the moment when the damaging statement is read.

*New Note 55M:* See further, paras.6.6-6.9 below.

*New Note 55N: Cooke v MGN Limited* [2014] EWHC 2831 (QB); [2015] 1 W.L.R. 895, at [21].

*New Note 55O*: Ibid, at [31].

*New Note 55P:* Ibid, at [32].

*New Note 55Q: Lachaux v Independent Print Limited* [2015] EWHC 2242
(QB); [2015] E.M.L.R.28, at [67].

*New Note 55R: Cooke v MGN Limited* [2014] EWHC 2831 (QB); [2015] 1
W.L.R. 895, at [31].

*New Note 55S: Lachaux v Independent Print Limited* [2015] EWHC 2242
(QB); [2015] E.M.L.R.28, at [68].

*Delete existing para.2.6 and replace with the following:* **Proving serious**  **2.6**
**harm or likely serious harm to reputation.** The second effect of s.1(1) is that
the claimant must now prove, on the balance of probabilities, that serious
reputational harm has been caused by, or is likely to result in the future from, the
publication complained of (*new note 55T*). "Likely to" has the same meaning
here as it does in *Cream Holdings Ltd v Banerjee* (*new note 55U*), that is to say
"more probable than not" (*new note 55V*). Where it is claimed that serious harm
is likely to happen in the future, unless an inference will suffice, the claimant
must call evidence which demonstrates that likelihood (*new note 55W*).
    It is likely that in most cases, especially where the claimant is identified and
the libel has been published in a newspaper or other mass media, the claimant
will be able to rely on an inference of serious harm (*new note 55X*).
    However, in other cases the claimant's task will be more difficult. Reputation,
as the sum of the estimations of a person by other people, is not something that
can be measured with any degree of accuracy. Determining the real extent of a
publication and its impact is likely to be all but impossible. In many cases, the
claimant will not know, and will be unable to find out, who has read the
publication, and how the attitude of any publishees towards him has changed.
Proof of serious harm is consequently replete with difficulty. That said, proof that
the libel caused the claimant's employer to terminate his employment or that
several clients left the claimant's business following the libel would be both
admissible and highly relevant to the question whether the publication had
caused serious harm to the claimant's reputation. So too, is evidence that the
claimant was shunned or avoided by others or that people's behaviour to him
altered after the libel. In appropriate cases, expert evidence may be admissible,
for example, as to the extent of publication via electronic means. In this respect
evidence of viral or "grapevine" publication may be highly relevant (*new note
55Y*).
    In *Cooke*, Bean J seemed to suggest that an opinion poll or selection of
comments from the so-called "blogosphere" might be of some use in appropriate
cases but there is clearly a risk that such evidence would be highly unrepresentative of the population of "right-thinking" people (*new note 55Z*). Whether the
responses of unreasonable or prejudiced people should be taken into account is
not without difficulty. At common law, the court considered only whether right
thinking people would think less well of the claimant. Following the enactment
of s.1, it appears that provided right thinking people would have thought

adversely of the claimant on the basis of the single meaning that the court finds the words to carry, evidence of how others treated the claimant should be admissible even if their response was unreasoning or prejudiced and not how a reasonable person would have responded. The serious harm must however be to the claimant's reputation. Thus, while evidence that the claimant was shunned by his friends or subjected to hostile emails and phone calls would clearly be admissible to prove harm to his reputation, it is not enough to show that the publication has caused or is likely to cause serious distress or injury to feelings. (*new note 55AA*).

At common law, proof that those who had read the allegation did not believe it could not defeat the claim entirely, albeit that this could be relied upon in mitigation of damages (See, e.g., *Hough v London Express Newspapers Ltd.* [1940] 2 K.B. 507, at 515). However, under s.1(1) if the claimant can only prove that the words complained of were published to people who did not believe them, his claim will fail. In such a case, he will not be able to establish that serious harm to his reputation either has been caused or is likely to result from the publication (*Lachaux*, above, at [59]).

*New Note 55T: Lachaux v Independent Print Limited* [2015] EWHC 2242 (QB); [2015] E.M.L.R.28, at [45].

*New Note 55U:* [2004] UKHL 44, [2005] 1 A.C. 253.

*New Note 55V: Lachaux v Independent Print Limited* [2015] EWHC 2242 (QB), at [47]-[49], [65].

*New Note 55W: Lachaux*, above, at [30], [86]; *Ames v The Spamhaus Project Ltd* [2015] EWHC 127 (QB); [2015] 1 W.L.R. 3409, at [55].

*New Note 55X:* As to which, see *Cooke v MGN Ltd* [2014] EWHC 2831 (QB); [2015] 1 W.L.R. 895, at [43], *Lachaux* (above) at [36] and [86], and para 2.7 below. See also, *Brett Wilson LLP v Persons Unknown* [2015] EWHC 2628 (QB).

*New Note 55Y: Lachaux*, above, at [101]. See also, *Brett Wilson* in which probable loss of future business was, inter alia, treated as evidence of serious financial loss (at [29]).

*New Note 55Z: Cooke v MGN Ltd* [2014] EWHC 2831 (QB); [2015] 1 W.L.R. 895, at [43]. Similarly, in *Lachaux*, above, at [86] Warby J. suggests that evidence of adverse social media responses, name-calling or similar events is admissible.

*New Note 55AA: Cooke*, above, at [30]). It should be noted that in *Lachaux*, Warby J. did consider (at [123]-[127]) the claimant's distress and upset, and the steps he took and how fast he took them on becoming aware of the alleged libel, as part of his analysis of whether serious harm to reputation had been caused. That the claimant does not appear to be taking the words complained of very seriously may well indicate that he does not consider that he has suffered serious harm to his reputation and, as such, may make it difficult for him to make out his case. In that regard, a judge may be justified in taking account of how the claimant behaved after the statement was published. However, it does not follow from this that evidence that the claimant was upset and distressed can be used to establish that serious harm to reputation has been caused.

*Delete existing para.2.7 Defamation Act 2013, s.1: A "raised" threshold and replace with the following:*

**Proof of serious harm by inference**. While evidence may now be led on the    **2.7** question whether serious harm has been, or is likely to be, caused, it does not follow that a claim will necessarily fail if the claimant cannot adduce evidence to prove that the publication caused serious harm to his reputation. There may be circumstances in which one would expect to see tangible evidence "but as practitioners in this field are well aware, it is generally impractical for a claimant to seek out witnesses to say that they read the words complained of and thought the worse of the claimant" *(new note 55BB)*. Consequently, the "serious harm" requirement can be met, in appropriate cases, by an inferential case, based on the gravity of the imputation and the extent and nature of its readership or audience *(new note 55CC)*.

How readily the courts will draw inferences of serious harm will inevitably have a significant effect on the height of the hurdle to be overcome by a claimant under s.1(1). In *Cooke v MGN Limited*, Bean J. accepted that some statements are so obviously likely to cause serious harm to reputation that this likelihood can be inferred:

> "If a national newspaper with a large circulation wrongly accuses someone of being a terrorist or a paedophile, then in either case (putting to one side for the moment the question of a prompt and prominent apology) the likelihood of serious harm to reputation is plain, even if the individual's family and friends knew the allegation to be untrue. In such a case the matter would be taken no further by requiring the claimant to incur the expense of commissioning an opinion poll survey, or to produce a selection of comments from the blogosphere which might in any event be unrepresentative of the population of 'right thinking people' generally" *(new note 55DD)*.

However, Mrs Cooke's case did not come anywhere near that threshold. Although the publication complained of was made in a national Sunday newspaper, it was withdrawn in its online version one day later and an apology was printed in the following week's paper edition. The meanings found were not very serious. The judge found that the apology was likely to have eradicated or at least minimised the adverse effect created by the original article in the mind of the hypothetical reasonable reader who had read both *(new note 55EE)*. There was likely to be a residual group who had not read the apology but the claimants had not offered any evidence that the article had caused serious harm to their reputations and there was no room for inference that serious harm had been caused or was likely to be *(new note 55FF)*.

In *Lachaux v Independent Print Limited*, Warby J. was prepared to draw inferences of serious harm even though the claimant had only visited the UK on approximately five occasions and was known to at most a few hundred people. Two of the publications complained of were in national newspapers, and one in the *Evening Standard*, all with very significant readerships, and the allegations complained of were very serious. Similarly, the judge found serious harm had been caused by an online article with only a few thousand unique visitors, but which remained online for nine months. The judge concluded that the article had reached people who knew the claimant and whose opinion of him would have been seriously affected in an adverse way, and in addition that it had probably reached others whose opinion of him mattered (*new note 55GG*). This case suggests that where a claimant (even a person not widely known) is faced with seriously defamatory allegations published either in national media or to smaller but nonetheless substantial audiences online, and where there is no or no satisfactory apology, an inference of serious harm will readily be drawn.

*New Note 55BB*: Per Warby J. in *Ames v The Spamhaus Project Ltd* [2015] EWHC 127 (QB); [2015] 1 W.L.R. 3409 at [55].

*New Note 55CC: Lachaux*, above, at [57]; *Cooke v MGN Limited*, [2014] EWHC 2831 (QB); [2015] 1 W.L.R. 895, at [43]; *Ames v The Spamhaus Project Ltd*, above, at [55].

*New Note 55DD: Lachaux* (above) at [57]; *Cooke v MGN Limited*, above, at [43]; *Ames v The Spamhaus Project Ltd*, above, at [55]).

*New Note 55EE: Cooke v MGN Limited*, above, at [44].

*New Note 55FF*: Ibid, at [45].

*New Note 55GG: Lachaux*, above, at [144]-[145]. See also *Brett Wilson* in which Warby J. was prepared to draw an inference of serious financial loss in respect of a publication on the Solicitors From Hell website notwithstanding that there had been a relatively small number of *Google* searches for the claimant (276) during the relevant period. In *Umeyor v Nwakamma* [2015] EWHC 2980 (QB) Jay J. drew an inference that serious reputational harm to the claimant was likely in respect of an allegation of forgery made to 15 members of a community organisation and elders of the community.

*Delete existing para.2.8 Defamation Act 2013, s.1: Bodies that trade for profit and replace with the following:*

**2.8**     **Defamation Act 2013, s.1: Bodies that trade for profit.** So far as concerns claims brought by a "body that trades for profit", harm to reputation will not, by virtue of s.1(2) of the Act, be "serious harm" unless the statement has caused or is likely to cause serious financial loss. That will have to be fully pleaded. As is the case with natural persons, the claimant will also have to establish a causative link between the defamatory statement and the harm caused (*new note 55HH*). Clearly, proof that would meet the requirements of a claim for special damages would be sufficient to constitute serious harm provided that the loss was sufficiently significant. However, the requirement of "serious financial harm" might be satisfied notwithstanding that a claim for special damages would fail. Thus proof that the share price of a company had declined significantly as a result of the statement complained of might be sufficient evidence that serious financial harm had been caused notwithstanding that loss of share value has been held not to be recoverable as special damages (*new note 55II*). As serious harm may be established by inference (*new note 55JJ*) a court might be prepared to infer serious harm from a widespread publication of a sufficiently grave allegation that touched the core of the claimant's business.

While a trading corporation is clearly a "body that trades for profit", determining what entities beyond this will fall within the definition is not easy. On one view, s.1(2) may be read as encompassing any non-natural person that trades for profit whether that is their only or merely a minor part of their purpose. There is nothing in the Act that requires that trading for profit be the only or main purpose of the body. Thus, charities may fall within the provision, in so far as they are involved in trade for profit (*note 65*), as may non-governmental organisations, trade unions (*note 66*) and employers' associations. That said, for entities such as charities and NGOs, trading for profit is merely a part of what they do and such trade is carried on for the wider purposes of the organisation rather than for distribution to shareholders. During the passage of the Bill, attempts were made to exempt charities and other similar entities from the s.1(2) requirement. Though this did not happen, Lord McNally, in moving the Government amendment that became s.1(2), told the House of Lords (*new note 67A*).

" . . . the term that we have used to define those who will be subject to this requirement—"a body that trades for profit"—is a much clearer and simpler definition than that used in Amendment 2. These are the bodies that this House has expressed concern about, so we have phrased the amendment specifically and directly to meet those concerns. A vaguer formulation such as that in Amendment 2 would have risked inadvertently catching other bodies, such as charities, which are not the subject of concern. I believe that this effective and proportionate approach addresses the concerns that have been expressed in this House and elsewhere." (*new note 67B*).

No court has yet considered whether a charity or similar body falls within s.1(2). It is suggested however that the better view may be that if the activities of a charity or similar organisation include trading for profit they should be treated as falling within s.1(2). Bodies that trade for profit cannot sustain harm to their social relations nor suffer distress. The only real harm they can sustain is financial. Parliament recognised this by requiring in s.1(2) that they must prove serious financial harm as a condition of actionability. Charities and similar bodies are in a similar position. They have no immortal soul worthy of protection. Where they trade for profit, there is no reason why they should be treated any differently from trading bodies and as such why they should not be required to prove serious financial harm.

*New Note 55HH:* See e.g., *Tesla Motors Ltd. v BBC* [2013] EWCA Civ 152. See further paras.21.15, 26.32.

*New Note 55II: Collins Stewart Ltd v The Financial Times Ltd*. [2004] EWHC 2337 (QB), [2005] E.M.L.R. 64. See further para.8.16 below.

*New Note 55JJ: Lachaux v Independent Print Limited*, above, at [57]; *Cooke v MGN* Limited, above, at [43]; *Ames v The Spamhaus Project Ltd* [2015] EWHC

127 (QB); [2015] 1 W.L.R 3409 at [55]. See also *Brett Wilson LLP v Persons Unknown* [2015] EWHC 2628 (QB). There was also alternative evidence of a probable loss of an instruction.

*New Note 67A:* H.L.Col.1366, 23 April 2013.

*New Note 67B:* See also, Lord McNally's response to Lord Phillips of Sudbury (at col.1376, 1381).

SECTION 2. CATEGORIES OF DEFAMATORY IMPUTATION

**2.9**    **Introduction.** *Insert the following after the fourth sentence of first paragraph of para.2.9:*

It should also be noted that almost all of the decisions referred to in this section were decided before s.1 of the Defamation Act 2013 was passed. Given the construction placed on s.1(1) in *Lachaux v Independent Print Ltd* (*new note 68A*), the comment made above to the effect that imputations once held to be defamatory may no longer be treated as such applies with added force.

*New Note 68A:* [2015] EWHC 2242 (QB); [2015] E.M.LR. 28.

SECTION 3. STANDARD OF OPINION

**2.19**    **The community as a whole.** *Note 166, add*: See also *Modi v Clarke* [2011] EWCA Civ 937: It does not defame someone to say that he wishes to destroy the structure of world cricket, because that depends on the views of that section of the public interested in the sport on the current structure (at [30]). In *Moulay Hitcham v Elaph Publishing Limited* [2015] EWHC 2021 (QB) it was held that an allegation that the claimant, a cousin of the King of Morocco, was plotting, weaving machinations and scheming against the King, and that this was wrongful, was not capable of being defamatory because whether such conduct was wrongful depended on the views of that section of the public interested in the politics of Morocco, and it was not enough that the words should damage the claimant in the eyes of a section of the public only (at [4]). See also at [22].

**2.23**    **Anti-social views.** *Note 197, add*: See also *Rufus v Elliott* [2015] EWHC 807 (QB): Warby J. considered a press release issued by E that he held to mean that R, a former friend of E, had made public an SMS text message which E had sent him, in which E, a trustee of an anti-racism organisation, had abused R by calling him a 'nigger' and threatened him; and that as a result of this disclosure he had resigned his position with the organisation because, as he acknowledged, his use of the word was inappropriate and in conflict with his public position. The press release was held not defamatory. The conduct attributed to R would not lower him in the estimation of right-thinking members of society generally. The judge accepted that there was a "societal norm" not to betray or dishonour one's friends but:

"right-thinking members of the public generally would [not] disapprove of "blowing the whistle" publicly on the use of an unacceptable racially offensive term by . . . a public figure in his capacity as a trustee of an anti-racist organisation; and that is so, even though the message was sent to another black man and the disclosure (according to the words complained of) revealed details of a private message." (at [56])

SECTION 4. INSTANCES OF DEFAMATORY PUBLICATIONS

**Instances of defamatory words.** *Note 254, add,* See also *Ma v St George's*     **2.28**
*Healthcare Trust* [2015] EWHC 1866 (QB): imputation that the claimant was confrontational towards hospital staff, unjustifiably hit a member of staff, and was aggressive and loud.

*Note 271, add,* See also, *Starr v Ward* [2015] EWHC 1987 (QB). In *Jackson v Universal Music Operations Ltd* [2014] EWHC 882 (QB) Judge Mackie QC held that a statement on *Youtube* that "this video is no longer available due to a copyright claim" was not capable of being defamatory of the claimant as it did not amount to an allegation that the claimant had breached copyright but instead meant that there was an unresolved issue as to copyright which had caused *Youtube* to take the video down:

"The fact that a claim is made does not carry with it the implication that it is a good claim, nor does it necessarily imply a criticism of the person against whom the claim is made. If the approach of Mr Jackson were correct, news reports about claims would have to take a very different form. As I say, *YouTube* obviously carefully choose their words, possibly to anticipate claims like this. The fact that some might think the worse of Mr Jackson or anyone else for being on the receiving end of a copyright claim is nothing to the point, because the duty of the court is to apply the law of libel as it stands, and summarised in *Jeynes* . However upsetting all this was to Mr Jackson, he has no prospect of showing at trial that the words of which he complains have a defamatory meaning." (at [26])

In *Irvine v Sunday Newspapers Ltd (t/a The Sunday World)* [2013] NIQB 126 Gillen J. held that an imputation that the claimant had openly associated with and taken part in monitoring a parade conducted by members of an unlawful organisation (which subsequently sparked off three nights of orchestrated UVF violence) lowered the plaintiff in the estimation of right thinking people.

*Note 288, add,* In *Mughal v Telegraph Media Group Ltd.* [2014] EWHC 1371 (QB) Tugendhat J. held that words that were part of a public debate clearly identified as comment, or the opinion of the author, to the effect that the views that the claimant expressed, and for which he had received public honours, were not violent views, but were views which tended nevertheless to have dangerous consequences, were not defamatory of him. The criticism was as to the effect of his views. It was not of his character (at [29]) In so deciding, the judge emphasised that the article which contained the words complained of came within the scope of the principle that there is "little scope . . . for restrictions on political speech or on debate on questions of public interest." (at [27])

**2.29** **Sexual conduct.**

*Insert after first sentence of para.2.29:*

So too, any imputation of sexual conduct that would amount to a criminal offence is likely to be treated as defamatory (see, e.g., *Starr v Ward* (*new note 289A*): slander alleging that the claimant had sexually molested the defendant was actionable per se as imputing an allegation of sexual assault).

*New Note 289A:* [2015] EWHC 1987 (QB).

*Note 292, add,* In *Appleyard v Wilby* [2014] EWHC 2770 (QB) it was held to be defamatory of a police officer to allege that that he befriended and protected people he knew to be paedophiles and rapists, misused his position as a police officer in so doing and was himself a threat to children.

*Note 304, add,* In *Uppal v Endemol UK Ltd* [2014] EWHC 1063 (QB), Dingemans J. held that even if (contrary to his view of the matter) the words complained of meant that X wished to engage in lewd sexual activity with the claimant, this could not be defamatory of her as no reasonable viewer could possibly conclude that the claimant would have been a willing participant in any such activity (at [25]).

*Note 305, add,* In *Krause v Newsquest Media Group Ltd* [2013] EWHC 3400 (QB) a statement that the claimant "is now legally a woman but used to be a man" was held not to be defamatory. According to the judge:

" . . . the words complained of in that passage are incapable of lowering the reputation of the Claimant in the minds of right thinking people, and, even if they were, there is no dispute that the words are true." (at [19])

*Note 310, add,* In *Simpson v MGN Ltd.* [2015] EWHC 77 (QB), it was held to be defamatory to allege that a premier league footballer had, by his infidelity, broken up a committed long-term relationship and the family unit. The judge treated both the allegation of infidelity and the wrecking of a committed, family unit as defamatory (at [32]). See also, *Contostavlos v News Group Newspapers Ltd* [2014] EWHC 1339 (QB).

**2.35** **Reputation in business, trade or profession.** *Note 363, add,* In *RBOS Shareholders Action Group Ltd v News Group Newspapers Ltd* [2014] EWHC 130 (QB); [2014] E.M.L.R. 15, Tugendhat J. held that the words complained of meant that the claimant company was being controlled and used by one GW as a conduit for the fraudulent misappropriation for his own personal benefit of funds contributed by its members (at [33]) and that, even though it portrayed the company as a victim, that did not preclude a finding that the words were defamatory:

"Such a meaning has a tendency to deter third parties from dealing with, or being associated with the Claimant. In my judgment the hypothetical reasonable reader of the newspaper in question would not be being avid for scandal in understanding that this was the meaning. On the contrary, such a reader would be being over analytical in taking the view that, as a victim, the Claimant's reputation was not damaged." (at [35])

See also *Prince Al Saud v Forbes LLC* [2014] EWHC 3823 (QB).

**Dismissals.** *Note 410, add,* In *Briggs v Jordan* [2013] EWHC 3205 (QB), **2.39** Tugendhat J. held that it was plainly not defamatory to say of someone that they had been sacked (at [17]), nor that he sent "pompous emails" (at [21]).

**The law.** *Note 430,* See also *Bussey Law Firm PC v Page* [2015] EWHC 563 **2.41** (QB): allegation that lawyer paid for false reviews of his lawyering skills and lost 80 per cent of his cases. See also, *Brett Wilson LLP v Persons Unknown* [2015] EWHC 2628 (QB).

**Politics.** *New Note 446a after "corruption" in the first sentence on p.86:* In **2.42** *Thompson v James* [2014] EWCA Civ 600; [2014] B.L.G.R. 664 the Court of Appeal upheld Tugendhat J.'s decision that an allegation that the claimant, Chief Executive of Carmarthenshire County Council, had established a "slush fund" for himself and his cronies was defamatory in that it meant that he had unlawfully and corruptly used public money for the benefit of himself and his cronies.

*Note 447, add,* In *McEvoy v Michael* [2014] EWHC 701 (QB) allegations that the claimant councillor had taken "jollies abroad" and had claimed more in allowances than his predecessors were imputations of hypocrisy amounting to defamatory comment (at [68]-[69]). However, an allegation that the claimant was prone to unrealistic fantasies and improbable business ideas was the stuff of political disagreement and was not defamatory (at [84]). Nor was it defamatory to accuse the claimant of being a money-loving and money-seeking entrepreneur (at [83]).

*Note 449, add,* However, in *Yeo v Times Newspapers Ltd* [2014] EWHC 2853 (QB); [2015] 1 W.L.R. 971, Warby J. held that words imputing a willingness to act in a way that was in breach of the Code of Conduct of the House of Commons by acting as a paid Parliamentary advocate who would: a. push for new laws to benefit the business of a client for a fee of £7,000 a day; and b. approach Ministers, civil servants and other MPs to promote a client's private agenda in return for cash was defamatory. He also held that it was defamatory, albeit a comment, to accuse an MP of having acted scandalously, and having shown himself willing to abuse his position in Parliament to further his own financial and business interests in preference to the public interest (at [121]). See also *Cruddas v Calvert* [2013] EWCA Civ 748; [2014] E.M.L.R. 5: there were defamatory meanings that the claimant had corruptly offered for sale the opportunity to influence government policy, and acted in breach of UK electoral law on foreign donations.

*Insert after third sentence on page 86 the following:*

So too it was held in *Barron v* Collins [2015] EWHC 1125 (QB) to be a defamatory statement of fact to allege that three MPs knew many details of the scandalous child sexual exploitation that had taken place in their constituencies over a period of sixteen years, in the course of which an estimated 1,400 children were raped, beaten, plied with alcohol and drugs, and threatened with violence by men of Asian origin, yet deliberately chose not to intervene but rather to allow the abuse to continue. Statements that the MPs "acted in this way for motives of political correctness, political cowardice, or political selfishness", and that each "was thereby guilty of misconduct so grave that it was or should be criminal, as it aided and abetted the perpetrators and made the Claimants just as culpable as the perpetrators" were also defamatory but were opinions (at [32]-[33]).

**2.43**  **Doctors and other medical people.** *Note 463, add,* See also *Garcia v Associated Newspapers* [2014] EWHC 3137 (QB); imputations that a doctor had been seriously incompetent in his dealings with a patient by reporting him to the DVLA (without evidence to justify doing so) and that he had breached patient confidentiality in so doing, were held to be defamatory (at [19]-[28]).

**2.44**  **Entertainment.** *Note 477, add,* See also, *Johnson v League Publications* [2014] EWHC 874 (QB): imputations against the chairman of professional rugby league club that he had acted dishonestly by telling the police something he knew to be false, withheld salary from a player in breach of contract, threatened to fine a player even though he knew that there was nothing in the contract allowing him to do so, threatened a player with deportation without any lawful basis, behaved unprofessionally and rudely towards a player and made unlawful demands for reimbursement of money, were held to be defamatory.

*Note 478, add,* See also *White v Express Newspapers* [2014] EWHC 657 (QB): words imputing that there were reasonable grounds to suspect that the claimant, a professional snooker player, had communicated insider information to his friend, who had used it to place winning bets, and so reasonable grounds to support that both men had acted dishonestly, were defamatory allegations of fact.

**2.46**  **Defamation in relation to trade.** *Note 514, add,* See also, *Donovan v Gibbons* [2014] EWHC 3406 (QB): sale of dangerous pony.

# CHAPTER 3

# THE FORM AND MEANING OF THE DEFAMATORY STATEMENT

SECTION 2. THE DISTINCTION BETWEEN LIBEL AND SLANDER

**The consequences of the distinction.** *Delete the first paragraph of para.3.6* **3.6**
*and replace with the following:*

Libel is committed when defamatory matter is published in a "permanent form" or in a form that is deemed to be permanent. Defamation published by spoken word or in some other transitory form is slander. At common law, libel is always actionable per se (*note 43*), that is to say that the claimant is not required to show any actual damage and substantial rather than nominal damages may be awarded even in the absence of such proof (*note 44*), whereas in slander, subject to certain exceptions, the cause of action is not complete unless there is special damage. The coming into effect of Defamation Act 2013, s.1, now requires, so far as English law is concerned, that in every claim, whether for libel or slander, the claimant must show that "serious harm" has been, or is likely to be, caused to his reputation by the defamatory publication. On the authority of *Lachaux v Independent Print Ltd* (*new note 44A*), libel is no longer actionable without proof of damage, and the legal presumption of damage will cease to play any significant role (*new note 44B*). It would also appear that slander, like libel, is not actionable without proof of serious harm to reputation, though the claim is still, save in two exceptional cases, not complete without proof of special damage. The two exceptional cases where slander is actionable only on proof of serious harm to reputation, are: (1) where the words impute a crime for which the claimant can be made to suffer physically by way of punishment (*note 46*); and (2) where the words are calculated to disparage the claimant in any office, profession, calling, trade or business held or carried on by him at the time of publication (*note 47*). Two further exceptions—concerning imputations of unchastity to a woman and imputations of a contagious or infectious disease— have been removed by Defamation Act 2013, s.14(1) and (2) (*new note 47A*).

*New Note 44A,* [2015] EWHC 2242 (QB); [2015] E.M.L.R 28.

*New Note 44B, Lachaux v Independent Print Ltd* [2015] EWHC 2242 (QB); [2015] E.M.L.R 28 at [60] *a*nd see further, paras.2.5-2.8 above.

*New Note 47A,* See paras.4.13-4.14 and 4.20-4.22 below.

*Add to the first sentence of the second paragraph of para.3.6 (starting "Damage is presumed"):*

By virtue of s.1 Defamation Act 2013, damage appears no longer to be presumed: see *Lachaux* (above) at [60]: " . . . the legal presumption of damage will cease to play any significant role".

**3.7**    **Defamation Act 2013, s.1 and presumed damage.** *Replace the first five sentences of para.3.7 with the following:*

Section 1 of the Defamation Act 2013 came into force on 1 January 2014. In *Lachaux v Independent Print Ltd (new note 57A)*, Warby J. held that its effect is to "stiffen" the existing common law test of what is defamatory by raising the *Thornton (new note 57B)* "threshold of seriousness" and by requiring that the claimant must prove actual harm to reputation. It is no longer the case, therefore, as it was at common law, that the court should only consider whether the words complained of have the tendency adversely to affect a person's reputation: the court must now consider whether actual harm to reputation has been caused or is likely. It follows from this that libel is no longer actionable without proof of damage to reputation and that the legal presumption of damage will cease to play any role *(new note 57C)*. However, while serious harm to reputation must now be proved, it is not the case that a libel claimant must prove that the statement has caused him actual financial loss. Once serious harm to reputation has been established, damages are "at large", in the sense that they cannot be assessed by reference to any mechanical, arithmetical or objective formula *(new note 57D)*, and substantial damages may still be awarded in the absence of any proof that the defamatory statement has caused the claimant any financial loss.

*New Note 57A:* [2015] EWHC 2242 (QB); [2015] E.M.L.R 28 and see further, paras.2.5-2.8 above.

*New Note 57B: Thornton v Telegraph Media Group* [2010] EWHC 1414 (QB); [2011] 1 W.L.R. 1985.

*New Note 57C:* [2015] EWHC 2242 (QB); [2015] E.M.L.R 28 at [60].

*New Note 57D:* See further, para.9.5 below.

Section 3. Interpretation

**3.13**    **The meaning of words.** *Note 136, insert into first sentence of note after "recent examples"*

*Donovan v Gibbons* [2014] EWHC 3406 (QB); *Barron v Collins* [2015] EWHC 1125 (QB); *Hamaizia v Commissioner of Police for the Metropolis* [2014] EWHC 3408 (QB); *Johnston v League Publications Limited* [2014] EWHC 874 (QB); *Al Saud v Forbes LLC* [2014] EWHC 3823 (QB); *Lachaux v Independent Print Limited* [2015] EWHC 620 (QB). For a full list, see para.30.14, *note 66A* below.

*Insert at end of after final sentence of the first paragraph of para.3.13:*

Now that the jury has ceased to be the presumptive tribunal of fact following the coming into force of s.11 of the Defamation Act 2013, there is now no inhibition on judges determining the actual meaning of words complained of at an early stage in the proceedings. It follows that the question of whether words are or are not capable of bearing a particular meaning is liable to become largely an academic one (*new note 139A*).

*New Note 139A,* See in this connection the remarks of Sharp L.J. in *Rufus v Elliott* [2015] EWCA Civ 121; [2015] E.M.L.R.17 at [28] and see para 30.2 below).

*Note 141, add,* It will also be relevant in determining whether the claimant has suffered or is likely to suffer serious harm to his reputation as required by Defamation Act 2013, s.1.

**The general approach.** *Note 149, add,* For a recent authoritative statement of **3.14** the principles, see *Rufus v Elliot* [2015] EWCA Civ 121; [2015] E.M.L.R.17. The principles are as applicable to slander claims as they are to libel. A helpful adaptation of the *Jeynes* principles for slander cases can be found in *Meadows Care Limited v Lambert* [2014] EWHC 1226 (QB), at [15].

*Note 150, add,* See also *Simpson v MGN Limited* [2015] EWHC 77 (QB), at [10].

*Note 151, add,* In *Johnston v League Publications Limited* [2014] EWHC 874 (QB), Eady J. stated (at [4]) that where a judge is called upon to determine meaning:

" . . . it will generally be helpful . . . to read the words complained of untrammelled by any gloss put upon them by the parties, and before addressing any legal submissions, since it should be easier to approach the task as an ordinary fair-minded reader—with an open and fresh mind. Also, one has to recognise that a judge is faced with something of a dilemma when resolving issues as to meaning. It is necessary to give reasons, as in any judgment, for the conclusions arrived at. On the other hand, the assessment of meaning is essentially a matter of impression and it is important for a judge (or, for that matter, a jury) embarking on such a task not to be over-analytical about it: see *Charman v Orion Publishing Group Ltd* [2005] EWHC 2187 (QB) at [11]."

See also, *Building Register Limited v Weston* [2014] EWHC 784 (QB), at [14] where Dingemans J. noted that a judge should not engage in over-elaborate analysis of the various passages relied on by the respective protagonists:

"The meaning is to be determined from the viewpoint of the layman, not by the techniques of a lawyer . . . . The exercise has been described as one of ascertaining the broad impression made on the hypothetical reader by the words taken as a whole. The natural and ordinary meaning of words includes what the reasonable man will infer from the words, see *Gatley on Libel and Slander*, 12th Edition, at 3.18. The Court is entitled to reach its own conclusions on meaning, and is not required to adopt meanings advanced by either party." (at [14])

*Insert the following at the end of the penultimate paragraph:*

A judge called upon to determine meaning is not limited to the pleaded meanings of the parties (*new note 151A*) but "that is not to say, of course, that if the judge's meanings ultimately correspond in substance with those of the relevant party, he should nonetheless strive to find different words to express them, merely for the purpose of emphasising his independence". (*new note 151B*).

New Note 151A: *Slim v Daily Telegraph* [1968] 2 Q.B. 157 CA; *Lachaux v Independent Print Limited* [2015] EWHC 620 (QB), at [6].

New Note 151B: *Lachaux v Independent Print Limited* [2015] EWHC 620 (QB), at [6].

*Note 152, add,* In *Thompson v James* [2014] EWCA Civ 600; [2014] B.L.G.R. 664, the Court of Appeal considered whether the principles in *Jeynes* needed amplification in cases where local authority officers (or indeed servants of central government) bring defamation proceedings because of the importance given by the Convention to the need for healthy debate in a democratic society. Counsel had proposed adding a ninth principle in the following terms: "Where the choice of meaning is evenly balanced and in cases where the publication is critical of local or central government, the court should regard Article 10 of the Human Rights Convention as a final grain of sand tipping the balance in favour of the non-defamatory meaning." The court held that the principle proposed was not necessary:

> "It says no more than the second principle of *Jeynes* that a court should not select one bad meaning where other non defamatory meanings are available and it offends the third principle that over-elaborate analysis is best avoided. Article 10 has already been taken into account in the formulation of the principles in *Jeynes* and need not be taken into account in some separate or different way when government officials are defamed. Of course the court should not be too astute to assume defamation of a government officer when it is the government itself that is being criticised but that is a different matter . . . " (at [28]).

While the approach to meaning has not changed as a result of incorporation of the ECHR into English law, Warby J. noted in *Barron v Collins* [2015] EWHC 1125 (QB) that freedom of political expression is one of the most important freedoms and: "A consequence [of this] is, as Laws LJ observed in *Waterson v Lloyd* [2013] E.M.L.R. 17, at [66] that the third principle [of *Jeynes*]—that the court should avoid over-elaborate analysis when determining meaning —has particular resonance in the context of political speech. The seventh principle is also of particular importance in such a context." (at [12]) See also, *Mughal v Telegraph Media Group Limited* [2014] EWHC 1371 (QB), at [15]-[16].

**3.18    Ordinary meanings and implications.**

*Note 206,* In *Thompson v James* [2014] EWCA Civ 600; [2014] B.L.G.R. 664, the Court of Appeal held that Tugendhat J. at first instance ([2013] EWHC 515 (QB)) had been correct to conclude that use of the term "slush fund" imputed that the provider of the funds was acting corruptly. In colloquial terms the word "slush", as part of the term "slush fund", implied that the money was dirty money.

**Knowledge of extrinsic facts: (2) Relied on by the defendant.** *Note 260,* **3.23** *add,* In *Johnston v League Publications Limited* [2014] EWHC 874 (QB), Eady J. considered that the law stated above was correct and disapproved of a statement at para.27.10 in which it had been suggested that a defendant wishing to meet a claim based on a legal innuendo meaning must confine himself to the innuendo meaning contended for by the claimant (at [39]-[44]).

**More than one meaning possible.** *Note 263, add,* See also *Rufus v Elliot,* **3.24** [2015] EWCA Civ 121; [2015] E.M.L.R.17:

" ... the words "should not select one bad meaning where other non-defamatory meanings are available" are apt to be misleading without fuller explanation. They obviously do not mean in a case such as this one, where it is open to a defendant to contend either on a capability application or indeed at trial that the words complained of are not defamatory of the claimant, that the tribunal adjudicating on the question must then select the non-defamatory meaning for which the defendant contends. Instead, those words are "part of the description of the hypothetical reasonable reader, rather than (as) a prescription of how such a reader should attribute meanings to words complained of as defamatory": see *McAlpine v Bercow* [2013] EWHC 1342 (QB), at [63]-[66]" (per Sharp L.J., at [11])

See also, *Donovan v Gibbons* [2014] EWHC 3406 (QB), at [20]-[21].

**The ordinary person: temperament.** *Note 296, add,* See also, *Uppal v* **3.26** *Endemol UK Ltd* [2014] EWHC 1063 (QB), at [18].

**The ordinary person: knowledge.** *Note 310, add,* In *Barron v Collins* [2015] **3.27** EWHC 1125 (QB) the words complained of were said during a speech at a political party's conference. In determining the meaning of the words, Warby J. accepted that reasonable members of the audience would understand, and make allowances for the fact, that political expression will often include opinion, passion, exaggeration, and even inaccuracy of expression. However, they would also understand that unlike an impromptu speech, where words may be chosen in the heat of the moment, a speech delivered to a conference audience will have been prepared and the words chosen with care (at [29]-[30]).

It was accepted in *Al Alaoui v Elaph Publishing Limited* [2015] EWHC 1084 (QB) that the hypothetical reasonable reader of an article published in Arabic on the defendant's news website would know, as a matter of general knowledge, that there is a monarchical regime in Morocco and that the King is the ruler of Morocco.

**"Levels" of defamatory meaning.** *Replace the second sentence of the first* **3.28** *paragraph of para.3.28 with the following:*

The issue is obviously relevant on damages for a "man's reputation can suffer if it can truly be said of him that although innocent he behaved in a suspicious way; but it will truly suffer much more if it is said he is not innocent" (*note 314*) and it is also relevant in determining the seriousness of the libel for the purposes of s.1 of the Defamation Act 2013 (*new note 314A*) but it also frequently arises at an interlocutory stage in relation to a defendant's plea of justification.

*New Note 314A*: See, for example, *RBOS Shareholders Action Group Ltd v News Group Newspapers Ltd.* [2014] EWHC 130 (QB); [2014] E.M.L.R. 15, in which Tugendhat J. commented that:

" . . . in the circumstances of this case (and perhaps most cases) the court is required to determine the meaning of the words complained for the purpose (amongst others) of establishing the level of gravity, whether on the three tiers identified in *Chase* or somewhere in between, and to do this without evidence. There is a distinction to be drawn between the level of seriousness or gravity of a meaning (which is largely dependent on the words complained of and the identity of the claimant) and the seriousness of a libel (which embraces additional factors, such as the extent of the publication and the identity of the publishee(s) or their relationship to the claimant). This is illustrated by *Jameel v Dow Jones* where the meaning complained of was of the utmost gravity (funding terrorism) but the libel within the jurisdiction was not, because the allegation was published to only five publishees, three of whom were "in the claimant's camp", and two of whom had never heard of the Claimant (*Jameel v Dow Jones* at [18] and [68])" (at [21]).

*Note 324, add,* See also, *Al Saud v Forbes LLC* [2014] EWHC 3823 (QB).

*Note 330, add,* In *White v Express Newspapers* [2014] EWHC 657 (QB) Tugendhat J. commented (at [9]) that courts commonly refer to various (usually three) levels of possible meanings but noted that:

"It does not follow that all words complained of must be fitted into one or other of these categories. And there may be meanings which are less serious than level 3, but if there are, then a dispute may arise as to whether such lower meanings are defamatory at all. The court is not bound to choose between the contentions of the parties as to what the words complained of mean. Judges must make up their own minds." (at [10])

See also, *RBOS Shareholders Action Group Ltd. v News Group Newspapers Ltd* [2014] EWHC 130 (QB); [2014] E.M.L.R. 15, at [13]-[14].

**3.30**    **Context and circumstances of the publication.** *Note 364, add,* See also *Barron v Collins* [2015] EWHC 1125 (QB).

**3.31**    **Publication must be taken as a whole.** *Note 370, add,* In *Stokes v Sunday Newspapers Limited* [2015] NIQB 53 Stephens J. considered that the words complained of could give rise to a number of different meanings but stated that:

" . . . the range of permissible meanings is to be taken on the basis that the reasonable reader has read the article as a whole with the ability to consider whether some of the later words are literal or metaphorical or whether taken in the round they affect the overall meaning." (at [26])

For a decision in which it was held that exculpatory or explanatory remarks were not capable of removing the sting, see *RBOS Shareholders Action Group*

*Ltd v News Group Newspapers Ltd* [2014] EWHC 130 (QB); [2014] E.M.L.R. 15.

*Note 375, add,* See also, *Hamaizia v Commissioner of Police for the Metropolis* [2014] EWHC 3408 (QB).

**Vulgar abuse.** *Note 427, add to end of first sentence of note, Uppal v Endemol* **3.37** *UK Ltd* [2014] EWHC 1063 (QB) ("piece of shit").

CHAPTER 4

## SLANDERS ACTIONABLE PER SE

SECTION 1. GENERAL.

**4.1**   **Libel and slander.** *Replace the the first two sentences of para.4.1 with the following*:

The distinction between libel and slander has already been considered *(note 1)*. At common law, libel has always been actionable per se *(note 2)*. However, the position has now changed as a consequence of Defamation Act 2013, s.1, which requires the claimant to prove that the publication complained of has caused or is likely to cause serious harm to reputation. On the authority of *Lachaux v Independent Print Ltd (new note 2A)*, libel is no longer actionable without proof of damage, and the legal presumption of damage will cease to play any significant role *(new note 2A)*.

*New Note 2A:* [2015] EWHC 2242 (QB); [2015] E.M.L.R 28.

*New Note* 2B: See *Lachaux*, above, at [60] and see further paras.2.5-2.8 above.

**4.2**   **The four categories of slander actionable per se.** *Insert after heading*: In the light of Defamation Act 2013 s.1: It appears that slander, like libel, is now no longer actionable without proof of serious harm to reputation *(new note 5A)*. However, that does not mean that s.1 has impliedly repealed s.2, Defamation Act 1952:

"All that s.1(1) has done is to add" [to s.2] "a requirement that a claimant prove actual or likely serious damage to reputation." *(new note 5B)*

*New Note 5A:* See 4.1 above.

*New Note 5B: Lachaux*, above, at [62].

*Note 7, add*: Defamation Act 2013, s.14(2) is now in force.

*Note 10, add*: Defamation Act 2013, s.14(1) is now in force.

*Insert the following at the end of para.4.2:*

On the coming into force of s.14 of the Defamation Act 2013 on 1 January 2014, only slanders imputing a crime for which the claimant can be made to suffer physically by way of punishment and slanders calculated to disparage the claimant in any office, profession, calling, trade or business held or carried on by him at the time of publication are actionable without the need to prove special damage. However, in both cases, s.1 of the 2013 Act requires that serious harm to reputation must have been or be likely to be caused by the defamatory statement.

Section 2. Criminal Offences

**Crime need not be indictable.** *Note 26, add*: *Bedi v Karim* [2013] EWHC    **4.5**
4280 (QB): imputation that the claimant had made illegal use of a Disabled parking badge not actionable per se as it was an offence punishable only by a fine (at [10]).

**Charge need not be specific.** *Note 46, add*: In *Starr v Ward* [2015] EWHC    **4.7**
1987 (QB) Warby J. gave permission to amend the Particulars of Claim to allege that the slanders complained of were actionable per se. In respect of the allegation that the claimant had "groped" the defendant it was plainly arguable that this imputed behaviour amounting to a criminal offence punishable by imprisonment (at [59]-[64]).

**Judge and Jury.** *Note 66*: Defamation Act 2013, s.11 is now in force for all    **4.12**
actions begun on or after 1 January 2014. It has the effect that the right to jury trial in England and Wales is abolished: see Ch 34 above. Issues of meaning are now as a rule determined by the judge as a preliminary issue: see 30.2 above.

Section 3. Words Imputing a Contagious Disease

*Note 67, add*, Defamation Act 2013, s.14(2) is now in force.

Section 4. Words Calculated to Disparage in any Office, Profession,<br>calling Trade or Business

**Development of the law: the Defamation Act 1952.** *Note 88, add*, The    **4.15**
common law also continues to apply in the Bahamas and in *Bethel v Cable Bahamas Ltd.* [2014] 2 L.R.C. 397 (Bahamas Court of Appeal) the court held that imputations relating to the claimant's conduct as Attorney General would only be actionable per se if they had been made at a time when he still held the office. As he had ceased to hold office at the material time, he had no cause of action in the absence of proof of special damage.

*Insert at end of para.4.15*:

However, following the coming into force of Defamation Act 2013, s.1, slander, like libel, is now no longer actionable without proof of serious harm to reputation . However, that does not mean that s.1 has impliedly repealed s.2, Defamation Act 1952: "All that s.1(1) has done is to add" [to s.2] "a requirement that a claimant prove actual or likely serious damage to reputation." (*new note 91A*)

*New Note 91A: Lachaux v Independent Print Ltd* [2015] EWHC 2242 (QB); [2015] E.M.L.R.28, at [62].

**4.16**     **Calculated to disparage.** *Note 95, add*, In *Starr v Ward* [2015] EWHC 1987 (QB), Warby J. stated that he could see no reason why the test of "calculated to disparage" in Defamation Act 1952, s.2 could not be satisfied by showing that it was likely that the imputation complained of would be republished and so seen by a much wider audience. In this respect, Defamation Act 1952, s.2 should be viewed in the same way as a claim for special damages where the damage can arise from the repetition of the slander by others (at [65] referring with approval to para.5.9 below).

**4.18**     **Callings.** *New Note 113A to be inserted after the word "business" in the first sentence:*

In *Reachlocal UK Ltd. v Bennett* [2014] EWHC 3405 (QB) it was held that statements imputing that the claimant company had mis-sold to its customers were calculated to disparage the claimant and were therefore actionable without proof of special damage (at [21]).

*Note 116, add*, In *Starr v Ward* [2015] EWHC 1987 (QB) it was accepted that "entertainer and comedian" were professions that came within the Act.

**4.19**     **Offices of profit and honour.** *Note 120, add*, In *Barron v Vines* [2015] EWHC 1161 (QB) it was agreed that the office of MP falls within Defamation Act 1952, s.2.

*Note 125*, add, In *Bedi v Karim* [2013] EWHC 4280 (QB) H.H.J. Moloney QC refused to strike out a claim for slander in respect of an allegation that the claimant was not fit to be Chairman of the Residents' Association of a substantial public housing estate. The judge held that it was at least arguable that the position of Chairman of the Residents' Association of a substantial public housing estate was an "office" of the kind protected under Defamation Act 1952, s.2 (at [10]). There was no discussion in the decision of whether the distinction between offices of profit and offices of honour had survived the Act.

SECTION 5. WORDS IMPUTING UNCHASTITY TO A FEMALE

*Note 126, add*, Defamation Act 2013, s.14(1) is now in force.

**Defamation Act 2013.** *Replace first sentence with the following*:     **4.22**

Defamation Act 2013, s.14(1) repeals for England and Wales the Slander of Women Act 1891.

# CHAPTER 5

## SLANDER ACTIONABLE ONLY ON PROOF OF SPECIAL DAMAGE

**5.1    Special damage necessary to maintain action.**

*Insert at the end of para.5.1:*

On the authority of *Lachaux v Independent Print Ltd* (*new note 1A*), in the light of s.1 Defamation Act 2013, defamation is no longer actionable without proof of actual or likely serious harm to reputation, and the legal presumption of damage will cease to play any significant role (*new note 1B*). In *Lachaux*, the judge rejected an argument that s.1 of the 2013 Act had impliedly repealed s.2, Defamation Act 1952, saying at [62] that 'All that s.1(1) has done is to add' [to s.2] "a requirement that a claimant prove actual or likely serious damage to reputation". (*new note 1C*) Presumably it follows that in a case of slander actionable only on proof of special damage, the claimant must now show both special damage and also actual or likely serious harm to reputation. Of course, a claimant who is in a position to prove substantial special damage should not have much difficulty in persuading the court that serious harm to reputation has been suffered.

*New Note 1A:* [2015] EWHC 2242 (QB); [2015] E.M.L.R 28.

*New Note 1B:* See *Lachaux* at [60] and see further paras.2.5-2.8 above.

*New Note 1C*: *Lachaux*, above, at [62].

**5.3    Accrual of special damage.** *New Note 16a: to be inserted after first sentence:*

"If the slander is of a kind that requires proof of special damage the cause of action is not complete unless and until the special damage is suffered." Warby J. in *Lachaux v Independent Print Ltd.* [2015] EWHC 2242 (QB); [2015] E.M.L.R. 28 at [15].

*Note 26, add*: In *Reachlocal UK Ltd. v Bennett* [2014] EWHC 3405 (QB) H.H.J. Parkes QC allowed, as special damages, costs incurred by the claimant in mitigating its loss. The claimant had taken a number of steps in mitigation including: (1) giving credits to customers planning to cancel their contracts as a result of the slanders; (2) giving refunds to disgruntled customers who had decided to leave the claimant to reduce hostility to the company; and, (3) employing a public relations consultant to manage damage to the company's reputation caused by the slanders. The judge allowed the claimant to recover losses under (1) and (3) above but not (2). While the standard of reasonableness to which the victim of loss will be held in seeking to mitigate is not a high one (at [50]) and there may have been commercial sense in making refunds to leaving customers, such payments could not be characterised as reasonable steps in mitigating the loss suffered. Such payments were going to have no effect whatever in mitigation of the loss suffered, at least for the immediate future, and any effect which it was likely to have in the longer term, in terms of softening hearts towards ReachLocal, was almost entirely speculative (at [52]).

**Loss of custom.** *Note 31, add*: In *Reachlocal UK Ltd. v Bennett* [2014] EWHC **5.4** 3405 (QB) the claimant recovered special damage for proved losses suffered as a result of decisions by customers not to proceed with cycles of advertising that had been booked but not paid for. So too, loss of theatrical bookings by an entertainer as a consequence of a slander may constitute special damage if proved (in *Starr v Ward* [2015] EWHC 1987 (QB), the claim for special damage failed as the claimant had not proved that the withdrawal of bookings resulted from the publications complained of).

**Causation.** *Note 47, add*: So too in *Reachlocal UK Ltd. v Bennett* [2014] **5.6** EWHC 3405 (QB) three reasons were given for customers cancelling contracts with the claimant: (1) they felt harassed by the defendants and wanted to cancel to avoid further harassment; (2) they doubted the claimant's credibility, in that they did not want to be associated with a company of bad reputation which might cheat them, and wanted their advertising handled professionally; and, (3) they had learned that the defendants had obtained a customer list from an internet marketing consultant who had recently left the claimant, which led them to re-evaluate their contacts with the claimant out of concern for the security of their business. H.H.J. Parkes QC noted that all three reasons flowed from the contacts that the defendants had had with the claimant's customers. However, only the second of the three reasons was caused by the publication of the defamatory material. The judge held, nevertheless, that of the three reasons it was:

> "little more than common sense to suppose that loss of confidence in the honesty and trustworthiness of the . . . claimant will have been the main factor which led customers to make their decision . . . concerns about harassment or about confidentiality seem to me, viewed objectively, to be distinctly less likely to have been causative, and perhaps likely to have been mentioned as a tactful way to explain the decision." (at [47])

Inevitably it was impossible to be precise and therefore the judge discounted the sum claimed by 20 per cent to allow for those customers who decided not to have further dealings with the claimant for reasons other than loss of trust in it by reason of defamatory communications.

CHAPTER 6

# PUBLICATION

SECTION 1. GENERAL PRINCIPLES

**6.1** **General principles: publication.** *Second paragraph of 6.1*: Section 1 of the Defamation Act 2013 is now in force for all actions where the cause of action accrued on or after 1 January 2014.

**6.2** **General principles: limited publication.** *Note 29, add,* See also, *Liberty Fashion Wears Ltd. v Primark Ethical Trading Limited* [2015] EWHC 415 (QB): claim brought by Bangladeshi company in respect of allegedly defamatory statements published within English jurisdiction. H.H.J. Parkes QC struck out the claim pursuant to *Jameel* on the basis that publication within the jurisdiction was limited and the timing of the page views gave rise to a strong inference that most were published to the parties and their lawyers and not third parties. Given the likely cost and time that would be involved in litigating the claim there was no realistic prospect of a trial yielding any tangible or legitimate advantage such as to outweigh the disadvantages for the parties in terms of expense, and the wider public in terms of court resources (at 54]-[55]).

*Note 37, add,* See also, *Vaughan v Lewisham LBC* [2013] EWHC 4118 (QB).

*Note 38, add,* See also, *Decker v Hopcraft* [2015] EWHC 1170 (QB). Claim was struck out by Warby J. on the basis that the persons to whom the publication was made did not believe them and consequently the claimant could not establish that serious harm to his reputation had been caused by the publication as required by s.1(1) of the Defamation Act 2013. Further the claim could not be salvaged by an allegation that it was likely that the defendant had repeated the publication to others. This was entirely speculative and insufficient to satisfy s.1(1) (at [60]).

*Note 39, add,* See also, *Starr v Ward* [2015] EWHC 1987 (QB) in which Warby J. stated that, had he not found that the words were true, he would have struck out the claim in respect of the eBook publication given "(at most) the very small number of copies sold in the jurisdiction" (at [121]).

*Note 42, add,* See also, *Subotic v Knezevic* [2013] EWHC 3011 (QB) at [60]. In *Otuo v Morley* [2015] EWHC 1839 (QB) Eady J. dismissed an appeal against Master Leslie's refusal to grant the defendants summary judgment in a slander claim. Although the publication was only to three people, if the words meant that the claimant had been guilty of fraud, the allegation was one that was at least capable of causing serious reputational damage. Consequently the judge held that it would be unduly "robust" to strike the claim out (at [11]-[14]). In *Ma v St George's Healthcare Trust,* 8 May, 2015 (unrep), H.H.J. Moloney QC refused an application to strike out the claim as a *Jameel* abuse notwithstanding that publication was limited and almost all within the Hospital Trust and related bodies. See also, *Owens v Grose* [2015] EWHC 839 (QB): judge refused to strike out claim by Mr Owens notwithstanding limited publication because words complained of imputed serious wrongdoing (at [45]).

*Note 45, add,* See also, *Ansari v Knowles* [2013] EWCA Civ 1448: the publication was limited to a small number of people but the nature of the allegations and the identities of the persons to whom it was communicated made it potentially very serious.

**Publication and Defamation Act 2013, s.1** *Add*: Defamation Act 2013 s.1 is **6.3** in force and applies to actions in which the cause of action accrued on or after 1 January 2014.

*New Note 50A to be inserted at the end of the third sentence of para.6.3:*

Serious harm may, in appropriate cases, be inferred: *Ames v The Spamhaus Project Ltd* [2015] EWHC 127 (QB); [2015] E.M.L.R. 13 at [55]; *Lachaux v Independent Print Limited* [2015] EWHC 2242 (QB); [2015] E.M.L.R 28, at [57]. In *Ames,* Warby J. refused to strike out a claim brought in respect of online publications as it was not possible to establish that the extent of the publication was insufficiently substantial to satisfy s.1. Moreover, the words complained of had foreseeably been republished by other authoritative websites and that would undoubtedly have added to the harm caused (at [92]).

**Defamation Act 2013, s.8—single publication rule.** Section 8 of the Defama- **6.6** tion Act 2013 is now in force.

**Defamation Act, s.8—limitation.** *Insert after first sentence of para.6.9:* **6.9**

This appears to be the case even if the cause of action for the first publication did not in fact (as a result of Defamation Act 2013, s.1) accrue at that time. Thus, if a statement is published on 1 January and republished on 1 June, the cause of action for the republication is treated as having accrued on 1 January. This will be so even if serious harm to reputation from the first publication did not result until 1 March. In that event, there would be the curious result that the limitation period would expire in respect of the republication before it did for the first publication. This can hardly be what Parliament had in mind in enacting s.8, yet it appears to follow from the interpretation that has been given by the courts to s.1. It is worth underlining the fact that by s.8(3) Parliament envisages the cause of action for the first publication as accruing "on the date of the first publication". That appears to be the old test for accrual of a cause of action in defamation, namely publication of (defamatory) words to a third party. It is doubly curious that there should be one test for the purposes of s.8 and another for s.1.

**6.10**   **General principles: responsibility for publication.** Section 10 of the Defamation Act 2013 is now in force for all proceedings in which the cause of action accrued on or after 1 January 2014.

*Note 76, add,* In *Brett Wilson LLP v Persons Unknown* [2015] EWHC 2628 (QB), Warby J. was prepared to conclude that persons unknown who were the defendants in the case were persons within the definition of "editor" in s.1(2) of the Defamation Act 1996.

**6.11**   **Joint and several liability.** Note 84, add, See also *McEvoy v Michael* [2014] EWHC 701 (QB) H.H.J. Keyser QC accepted as correct the principles contained in paras.6.10-6.11 above and held the defendant, as the chairman of a local branch of the Labour Party, liable for defamatory statements contained in political leaflets notwithstanding that he was not the author of them. The leaflets had been written to implement a branch decision and the author of the leaflet gave effect to that decision by producing drafts to the members, including the defendant, for approval. The judge found that the defendant had played an active part in the approval process but also said that had he not done so the process was such that his approval would have been inferred by silence.

SECTION 2. PUBLICATION

**6.13**   **Acts amounting to publication—"hyperlinking".** *Note* 107, add, See also *Niemela v Malamas,* 2015 BCSC 1024 (British Columbia Supreme Court at [56]-[60].

**6.21**   **Proof of publication.** *Insert at end of para.6.21:*

It should be noted, however, that a failure to prove, whether by evidence or inference, that the words were published to more than an insignificant number of people, may mean that the claimant will be unable to establish that serious harm has been or is likely to be caused to his reputation under Defamation Act 2013, s.1.

SECTION 3. PARTICULAR PUBLISHERS AND DISTRIBUTORS

**6.28**   **Liability of internet search engine operators.** *Note 225, add,* The British Columbia Supreme Court in *Niemela v Malamas* 2015 BCSC 1024 held that Google was not a publisher of the "snippets" generated by its search engine, at least until it had notice of the defamatory content (at [107]-[108]). In so concluding, the court noted that the "tenor of *Crookes* and of recent jurisprudence in England is to narrow the test for who is a publisher of defamatory material to those who do deliberate acts" (at [95]).

*Insert the following at end of para.6.28:*

The same conclusion was reached by the Hong Kong High Court of First Instance in *Yeung v Google Inc.* [2014] HKCFI 1404; [2014] 4 HKLRD 493. Deputy High Court Judge Ng held that there was a good arguable case that *Google Inc.* was a publisher of defamatory "snippets" generated by their search engine. By generating objectively defamatory materials by its automated processes *Google* was a "publisher" within the meaning explained in *Oriental Press Group Ltd v Fevaworks Solutions Ltd* [2014] E.M.L.R.11:

> "It is also arguable that *Google Inc* by creating and operating its automated systems that generate materials in the manner they and their staff intended satisfies the requisite mental element for the act of publication, i.e they provided the platform for dissemination and/or encouraged/facilitated or actively participated in the publication with intent to assist in the process of conveying the impugned words to publishees, and knowledge of defamatory content is not necessary (especially for an unwitting publisher who may in due course wish to invoke the defence of innocent dissemination if it can)." (at [103]).

However, in *Bleyer v Google* [2014] NSWSC 897, a case not referred to Judge Ng in *Yeung*, the Supreme Court of New South Wales adopted the reasoning of Eady J. in the *Metropolitan Schools* case. In staying a libel action against *Google Inc* based on defamatory snippets because the resources of the court and the parties that would be expended were disproportionate to the plaintiff's interest in obtaining vindication, McCallum J. held that Google was not a publisher of the "snippets" generated by its search engine:

> "The evidence before me establishes that there is no human input in the application of the *Google* search engine apart from the creation of the algorithm. I would respectfully disagree with the conclusion reached by Beach J in *Trkulja* that the performance of the function of the algorithm in that circumstance is capable of establishing liability as a publisher at common law. I would adopt the English line of authority to the effect that, at least prior to notification of a complaint (and on the strength of the evidence before me), *Google Inc* cannot be liable as a publisher of the results produced by its search engine" (at [83]).

**Applicable principles for internet publications.**                                 **6.29**

*Note 247, add,* See also, *Yeung v Google Inc.* [2014] HKCFI 1404; [2014] 4 HKLRD 493.

**Defamation Act 2013, s.5** Section 5 of the Defamation Act 2013 is now in   **6.39** force as regards actions in which the cause of action arose on or after 1 January 2014.

**Defamation Act 2013, s.5—where the defence is defeated.** *Insert the follow-*   **6.40** *ing after the first sentence in para.6.40:*

The relevant regulations are contained in The Defamation (Operators of Websites) Regulations 2013.

*Note 346, add,* It should be noted that the complainant does not have to set out in detail any steps he has taken to identify the poster or why this has not been possible. The provision simply requires the complainant to confirm that he does not have sufficient information to bring a claim.

*Delete the existing Note 349 and replace with the following*:

Section.5(7) of the Act provides that: "Regulations may make provision about the circumstances in which a notice which is not a notice of complaint is to be treated as a notice for the purposes of this section or any provision made under it."

The Defamation (Operators of Websites) Regulations 2013 are now in force. Regulation 2 provides as follows:

Subject to regulation 4, a notice of complaint must (as well as including the matters referred to in s.5(6)(a) to (c) of the Act):

(a) specify the electronic mail address at which the complainant can be contacted;
(b) set out the meaning which the complainant attributes to the statement referred to in the notice;
(c) set out the aspects of the statement which the complainant believes are:
    (i) factually inaccurate; or
    (ii) opinions not supported by fact.
(d) confirm that the complainant does not have sufficient information about the poster to bring proceedings against that person; and
(e) confirm whether the complainant consents to the operator providing the poster with:
    (i) the complainant's name; and
    (ii) the complainant's electronic mail address.

*Insert the following after the second sentence of the second paragraph of para.6.40*:

Under reg.2, the complainant must also: provide an email address at which he can be contacted; set out the meaning he attributes to the statement and any aspects of the statement that he believes to be inaccurate or, if an opinion, not supported by facts; confirm that he does not have sufficient information to bring proceedings against the person who posted the statement; and, confirm whether he consents to his name and address and / or email address being provided to the poster.

*Delete the existing note 351 and replace with the following:*

The Defamation (Operators of Websites) Regulations 2013 provide in reg.3 and the Schedule for the steps to be taken on receiving a valid notice of complaint in order to be able to rely on the defence in s.5. The operator is required within 48 hours of receiving the notice of complaint to send the poster:

(a) a copy of the notice of complaint;
(b) notification in writing that the statement complained of may be removed from the locations on the website specified in the notice of complaint unless the operator receives a response in writing from the poster including the information specified in (c) below, by midnight at the end of the 5th day after the day on which the notice of complaint was sent. The provision excluding non-business days does not apply to this period;

(c) the communication must indicate that the statement may be removed unless the poster: informs the operator whether or not the poster wishes the statement complained of to be removed from the locations on the website specified in the notice of complaint; if the poster does not wish the statement to be removed, provides the operator with the poster's full name and details of the postal address at which the poster resides or carries on business; and indicates whether the poster consents to the operator sending these details to the complainant; and,

(d) notification that, where the poster does not consent to the operator sending the poster's contact details to the complainant, the operator will not release them to the complainant under the s.5 process and will only release them where ordered to do so by a court.

(See further *Complaints about defamatory material posted on websites: Guidance on s.5 of the Defamation Act 2013 and Regulations* (Ministry of Justice January 2014)).

Should the notice of complaint be defective, the website operator can reject it provided that he does so within 48 hours of receipt. However, if the notice is compliant, to keep the defence, the operator must inform the complainant in writing within 48 hours of receiving the notice that he has received it and that he has notified the poster in accordance with the above requirements.

There are five main situations that can arise in relation to the poster's response. First, if the poster fails to respond, the website operator should remove the statement from the locations on the website which were specified in the notice of complaint and send the complainant notice in writing, within 48 hours, that the statement has been removed from the website (Sch. para.5).

Secondly, where the poster replies agreeing to removal of the statement, to keep the defence the operator must remove the statement from the website within 48 hours of receiving the poster's response; and send the complainant notice in writing, within 48 hours, that the statement has been removed (Sch. para.7).

Thirdly, if the poster replies within the specified time period, but does not provide all the information requested then, to keep the defence, the operator must remove the statement from the website within 48 hours of receiving the poster's response. The operator is not required to send any further communication to the poster (Sch.para.6).

Fourthly, if the poster does not wish the statement to be removed, provides the required contact details, and agrees to these being sent to the complainant, then, to keep the defence, the operator must contact the complainant in writing within 48 hours of receiving the poster's response. This communication must inform the complainant: (a) that the poster does not wish the statement to be removed; (b) that the statement has not been removed from the locations on the website specified in the notice of complaint; and, (c) provide the contact details given by the poster (Sch. para.8).

Finally, if the poster does not wish the statement to be removed but refuses to consent to the operator sending contact details to the complainant, then, to keep the defence, the operator must contact the complainant in writing within 48 hours of receiving the poster's response, such response to include notification of the fact that the poster has not consented to the operator sending him contact details.

If a defamatory statement has been removed after a complaint and the poster reposts the same or substantially similar material, the complainant must submit a further notice of complaint. On the first such occasion, the operator should comply with the steps set out above. However, if the same or substantially similar material is posted for a second or subsequent time after having been removed, the operator must on receipt of a notice of complaint, remove the statement from the website within 48 hours of receiving a notice of complaint.

*Insert the following at the end of the second paragraph of para.6.40:*

There is no obligation on the website operator to follow the process set out in the Regulations. Thus, he can on receiving a notice of complaint, choose to remove the posting at any point, add his own commentary or notice to the posting, or allow it to remain posted. Should he not follow the Regulations, the s.5 defence will not be available to him. However, this does not affect the availability of any other defences.

**6.45**     **Defamation Act 2013, s.10—claim against secondary publishers.** Defamation Act 2013, s.10 is now in force.

**6.46**     **Defamation Act 2013, s.13—order to remove.** Defamation Act 2013, s.13 is now in force.

SECTION 4. REPUBLICATION AND REPETITION

**6.49**     **Effect of Defamation Act 2013, s.8** Defamation Act 2013, s.8 is now in force.

*Note 376, add,* See *Brett Wilson LLP v Persons Unknown* [2015] EWHC 2628 (QB).

**6.52**     **General principle.** *Replace the third paragraph of para.6.52 with the following:*

It is clear that if the republication was by a person for whom the defendant is vicariously liable under the principles of master and servant or agency then the defendant is liable for that. Beyond this, a question has arisen as to the appropriate test to be applied where it is sought to make the original publisher liable as a *publisher* of the republication. There is some authority to the effect that the test of liability should be the same whether it is sought to make the defendant liable as publisher or for the republication by another. Thus, in *Broxton v McClelland* (*new note 423A*), a claim based on the defendant's liability as publishers in respect of the republication by another, the Court of Appeal appeared to treat the appropriate test as that contained in *Slipper v BBC* (*new note 423B*), namely whether the re-publication should have been within the reasonable contemplation of the defendant. However, it is suggested that the better view is that the defendant will only be liable as a *publisher* of the republication, if it is shown that he intended or authorised the republication As Laws L.J. pointed out in *Terluk v Berezovsky* (*new note 423C*), albeit that the court did not have to reach a conclusion on the issue, the effect of applying the test of reasonable contemplation to the liability of the original publisher would be to move defamation closer to the tort of negligence:

"That might be apt for the protection of reputation seen as akin to a right of property. But I incline to think that the modern law in this area should more visibly occupy the legal territory of privacy and free expression, and the tensions between them; and to that end the tort of defamation should excoriate not carelessness, but knowing or deliberate action." (*new note* 423D)

Laws L.J.'s view was accepted as correct by Nicol J. in *Starr v Ward* (*new note* 423E), albeit that again it was not necessary to reach a conclusion on the issue because on either test the claimant failed to establish that the defendant was liable for the republication. In *Starr*, the claimant was identified in a television broadcast by a combination of words spoken by the defendant during an interview and footage of the claimant broadcast immediately before the interview. The defendant did not intend the claimant to be identified in the broadcast and that was why she referred to him as "a famous person" rather than naming him. The question arose whether she would be liable for the publication. Nicol J. held that she was not liable for this publication. There was no evidence that she intended that the claimant be identified, nor had she impliedly or inferentially authorised the broadcaster to put out such a composite broadcast. Moreover, even if the correct test was one of reasonable foreseeability, the claimant could not prove that the composite broadcast was a reasonably foreseeable consequence of the interview that the defendant gave to the broadcaster:

"Far from it being reasonably foreseeable that the BBC would broadcast the Defendant's interview in such a way as to identify the Claimant, the exact opposite was the case. The Defendant [and others involved in conducting the interview] expected that, if the BBC words were broadcast, the Claimant would *not* be identified." (*new note* 423F).

*New Note 423A:* [1995] E.M.L.R. 485 CA.

*New Note 423B:* [1991] 1 Q.B. 283 CA.

*New Note 423C:* [2011] EWCA Civ 1534. See also *Asghar v Ahmed* [2015] EWHC 1118 (QB), at [158]).

*New Note 423D:* [2011] EWCA Civ 1534, per Laws L.J., at [28].

*New Note 423E:* [2015] EWHC 1987 (QB).

*New Note 423F:* Ibid, at [77].

# CHAPTER 7

# IDENTITY OF THE PERSON DEFAMED

SECTION 1. REFERENCE TO THE CLAIMANT

**7.1**    **Words must the published "of the claimant"** *Add after "would understand by them" in the second paragraph*:

Under Defamation Act 2013, s.1, however, a claim will fail unless publication of the statement has caused or is likely to cause serious harm to the reputation of the claimant. Consequently, a failure to prove, whether by evidence or inference, that some people to whom the words were published actually understood that the claimant was referred to by the words complained of will mean that the claim will now fail.

**7.2**    **Claimant need not be referred to by name.** *Insert the following at end of para.7.2*:

Reference may be established by a combination of facts. In *Starr v Ward* (*new note* 35A), the makers of a television programme showed footage of the claimant immediately before they broadcast an interview with the defendant during which she spoke of what a "famous person" had done to her. This was held by Nicol J. to be sufficient to identify the claimant as the person referred to (*note* 35B).

*New Note 35A:* [2015] EWHC 1987 (QB).

*New Note 35B:* Ibid, at [69]-[70].

**7.3**    **Statement capable of referring to the claimant: the position at common law.** *Replace the first sentence of para.7.3 with the following*:

At common law, the issue of identification is to be decided on the same principles as those which govern the question of whether the words are capable of a defamatory meaning (*note 36*).

*Note 36,* See *Barron v Collins* [2015] EWHC 1125 (QB) at [49] and *Lachaux v Independent Print Ltd.* [2015] EWHC 2242 (QB); [2015] E.M.L.R. 28 at [15](1),(2).

*Note 37, add,* In *Irvine v Sunday Newspapers Ltd (t/a The Sunday World)* [2013] NIQB 126 the defendant published an article under the heading "Fury over UVF's Nice Little Board's Earner". A small photograph accompanied the article in which four men had their heads circled. One was stated to be "Glen Irvine". Also named were Winston Irvine, the plaintiff's uncle, and Mark Vinton, both alleged members of the Ulster Volunteer Force. The plaintiff was not the man circled in the picture and he usually (but not always) spelled his name (Glenn) with two 'n's. Nonetheless, the court held that he had been understood to be the "Glen Irvine" referred to. His name was given and the person named as Glen Irvine and circled in the photograph was standing close to his uncle, Winston Irvine. The ordinary reader imbued with a certain amount of loose thinking forming no more than a general impression of the article would almost inevitably have concluded that reference to "Glen Irvine" was a reference to the plaintiff. The man in the photograph was not the plaintiff, but the casual reader would not scrutinise the picture to any great degree and would be more likely to have his attention arrested by the nomenclature.

*Note 39*, See also *Irvine v Sunday Newspapers Ltd (t/a The Sunday World)* [2013] NIQB 126 (fn.37 above).

*Note 40, add*, In *Barron v Collins* [2015] EWHC 1125 (QB), the defendant in a speech about sexual abuse of children in Rotherham said of "the three Labour MPs for the Rotherham area" that they "knew of the horrific sexual abuse of around 1,400 children in Rotherham over sixteen years but failed to act, keeping quiet and allowing the abuse to continue because it suited their political purposes". Reference to the first and second claimants was not disputed, but it was a live issue in the case of the third claimant. Warby J. held that the words referred to the three sitting MPs, including the third claimant. The judge accepted that there might have been people in the audience who knew: (a) the long duration of the child sex abuse scandal; (b) that the third Claimant had only recently been elected as an MP (c) what she had been doing before that; and (d) that her predecessor was Denis MacShane, also a Labour MP. However, these facts were not matters of general knowledge and nothing was said by the speaker to make clear she was targeting Denis McShane. To conclude that the ordinary reasonable reader would have taken the defendant to be targeting Denis McShane and not the third claimant would depend upon adding to the store of knowledge possessed by the audience which were not matters of general knowledge and which had not been established to be matters of special knowledge possessed by members of the audience.

> "The principles as to reference are . . . similar to those which apply to meaning. Both can be affected by the knowledge of the readership or audience. Words may be defamatory either in their natural and ordinary meaning, considered in the light of matters of general knowledge, or by way of true innuendo, that is, because of some particular special knowledge possessed by some or all of those to whom they are addressed. Equally, words may refer to a person on their face in the light of general knowledge, or by virtue of a "reference innuendo": because of some special knowledge possessed by some audience members. The same is true in reverse: special knowledge may cause words that are on their face defamatory to bear an innocent meaning (a "reverse innuendo"), or mean that words that appear to refer to A are taken instead to refer to B (a "reverse reference innuendo")" (at [49]).

*Insert after first sentence of second paragraph*:

At common law, it is not essential for the claimant to prove that at least one person understood the words complained of referred to the claimant (*new note 40A*).

*New Note 40A: Lachaux v Independent Print Ltd*, above, per Warby J. at [15](2).

*Insert new para.7.3A*

**7.3A**      **Reference to the claimant and Defamation Act 2013, s.1** By Defamation Act 2013, s.1(1), for a statement to be defamatory, the claimant must prove that the words complained of have caused or are likely to cause serious harm to his reputation. Although the provision appears, in terms, to deal only with the question whether a statement is defamatory, it seems clear that it is intended to make proof of serious harm to reputation, or the likelihood thereof, a condition of actionability. Thus, a claim may fail not only because it is insufficiently serious to cause harm to reputation but also because it is published to a small number of people or only a small number of people will have recognised that it was the claimant who was referred to (*new note 47A*). It follows that the question of how many readers would in fact have understood that the words complained of referred to the claimant is a relevant matter to be determined by evidence or inference in considering whether the statement complained of has caused, or is likely to cause, serious harm to the claimant's reputation (*new note 47B*). If the claimant cannot prove, whether by evidence or inference, that some readers understood the words as referring to the claimant, it would appear that the claim should fail on the basis that serious harm to reputation has not been established.

However, subject to the need in post 2013 Act cases to prove serious harm, it will not always be necessary to adduce evidence from readers in the relevant class. Thus, in *Yeo v Times Newspapers Limited* (*new note 47C*), the claimant sued in respect of two articles. The claimant was named in the first article and described, inter alia, as a select committee chairman. The second article, published two weeks after the first, did not name him but made allegations similar to those made in the first article against an MP identified as "the chairman of a Commons select committee". Warby J. refused to strike the case out on the basis of lack of identification:

"The essential issues for determination at a trial, on the pleaded case as it stands, will be (a) how many of those who read the [second] Sunday Times article of 23 June 2013 had read the articles of 9 June, and recalled enough of what had been published then to identify Mr Yeo as the "select committee chairman" referred to; (b) is the number of such readers sufficient to make the publication on 23 June a real and substantial tort? I do not accept that in order to sustain such a case it is necessary for a claimant to adduce evidence from readers in the relevant class. That may be so, if the inference that would otherwise have to be drawn is an inherently improbable one as, for instance, in *Fullam v Newcastle Chronicle & Journal Ltd*. But I see no reason why in this case the court may not proceed by way of inference, in the absence of evidence from such readers. This is a national newspaper with a very substantial circulation; it is well-known that newspaper readers are reasonably loyal to a given title; the articles of 9 June were prominent; and only a fortnight passed between the two articles. The inference cannot be said to be fanciful" (at [38]).

While s.1 now requires proof, whether by evidence or inference, that some readers did actually understand the words complained of to refer to the claimant, such proof cannot conclude the reference issue. If a reasonable reader would not have understood the words to refer to the claimant, then the claim will fail even if some readers did in fact understand it so to do. Consequently a court should first decide whether reasonable readers would have understood that the words referred to the claimant and if it concludes that they would, should then consider whether a sufficient number of people who read the words did in fact understand the words to refer to him such that serious harm to reputation had been, or was likely to be, caused. Such evidence might be provided by calling those who had read the words but may in appropriate cases be established by inference (*new note 47D*).

*New Note 47A:* See para.2.5 above.

*New Note 47B: Lachaux v Independent Print Ltd.* [2015] EWHC 2242 (QB); [2015] E.M.L.R. 28 at [100].

*New Note 47C:* [2015] EWHC 2132 (QB); [2015] 4 Costs L.R. 687 (a pre-2013 Act case).

*New Note 47D: Yeo v Times Newspapers* [[2015] EWHC 2132 (QB); [2015] 4 Costs L.R. 687, at [38].

**Identification from other material.** *Insert the following at the end of para.* **7.4**
*7.4:*

Whether s.1 of the Defamation Act 2013 will have any impact on these principles is not entirely clear. If a court decided, in a case similar to *Hayward v Thompson*, that the second statement was admissible because, for example, the first was defamatory on its face, a question must arise as to the date from which the cause of action accrued. At common law, the cause of action would presumably have been complete at the time of first publication. Because s.1 now requires serious harm to be proved or likely, the cause of action cannot be complete at the time of first publication: at that moment serious harm to reputation has not been caused, nor is it likely because the claimant has not been identified. Presumably therefore the first time at which the cause of action could possibly arise is the date of the second publication and it may not arise until after that (*new note 52A*).

*New Note 52A:* See further para.19.13 below.

SECTION 3. CLAIMANT MEMBER OF A CLASS

**Words referring to a class.** *Note 80, add,* See also *Mainstream v Staniford,* **7.9**
2012 BCSC 1433: a defamation claim against an environmental activist who led

a campaign against salmon farming and in particular against Norwegian inves-
tors' ownership of British Columbian salmon farms. The plaintiff, a Norwegian
owned salmon farming company, was the second largest producer of farmed
salmon in British Columbia. The court held that reference was established to the
plaintiff, which was one of only three Norwegian owned companies:

> "The group of Norwegian-owned salmon farming companies in B.C. is small, with only
> three members.While this is not conclusive when trying to decide whether comments
> ostensibly about a group are defamatory of individual members, it is an important
> factor. . . . the group of Norwegian owned salmon farming companies in B.C. is not
> only small, but—in the context of the statements alleged to be defamatory—
> homogeneous" (at [138]).

Cf. *Christian Advocacy Society of Greater Vancouver v Arthur* 2013 BCSC 1542:
defamatory allegations made against Crisis Pregnancy Centres in North America
(of which there were 4200) could not give rise to a claim by individual crisis
pregnancy centres. While the question of size was not determinative: "This group
is very large and I consider this factor alone to weigh heavily against the
plaintiffs" (at [83]).

**7.10** **Sufficient reference.** *Insert the following after second sentence of
para.7.10*:

In *Barron v* Collins (*new note 98A*) the defendant in a speech about sexual
abuse of children in Rotherham said of 'the three Labour MPs for the Rotherham
area" that they "knew of the horrific sexual abuse of around 1,400 children in
Rotherham over sixteen years but failed to act, keeping quiet and allowing the
abuse to continue because it suited their political purposes". Warby J. held (*new
note 98B*) this sufficiently identified all three sitting MPs even though the third
claimant had only just arrived on the political scene and that a major feature of
the Rotherham scandal was that it had gone on for many years until it attracted
national attention.

*New Note 98A:* [2015] EWHC 1125 (QB). See further, fn.40 above.

*New Note 98B:* Ibid, at [45]-[52].

CHAPTER 8

# PARTIES: WHO MAY SUE AND BE SUED

SECTION 2: DIPLOMATIC AGENTS AND FOREIGN SOVEREIGNS

**Foreign states.** *Note 24, add,* A helpful summary of the ambit of state **8.5** immunity can be found in the judgment of the Court of Appeal in *Belhaj v Straw* [2014] EWCA Civ 1394; [2015] 2 W.L.R. 1105 at [34]-[36].

*Note 29, add,* See also *Fogarty v United Kingdom* (2002) 34 E.H.R.R. 12, at [34]-[36]; *McElhinney v Ireland and United Kingdom* (2002) E.H.R.R. 13, *Cudak v Lithuania* (2010) 51 E.H.R.R. 15, at [54] ff; *Sabeh El Leil v France* (2012) 54 E.H.R.R. 14, at [46]-[54]; Application No. 156/04, *Wallishauser v Austria* at [59]-[60], *Oleynikov v Russia* [2013] 57 E.H.R.R. 15, at [60]-[61]; and *Jones v United Kingdom* [2014] 59 E.H.R.R. 1 at [186]-[189].

*Insert the following at the end of para 8.5:*

The apparent conflict between the reasoning of the House of Lords in *Holland v Lampen Wolfe* and the Strasbourg authorities has now been considered, albeit not determined, by the Court of Appeal in *Benkharbouche and Janah v Embassy of Republic of Sudan and Libya* [2015] EWCA Civ 33; [2015] 3 W.L.R. 301. The court noted that in *Holland v Lampen Wolfe* the House of Lords had concluded that art.6 was not engaged where the grant of immunity was required by international law. On the facts therefore it followed that there was no conflict between either the common law or State Immunity Act and the Convention. By way of contrast, the Strasbourg court has held that art. 6 is engaged even where the grant of immunity is required by international law, albeit that in such a case the restriction on the right to access to a court contained in art.6 will be treated as a proportionate means of achieving a legitimate aim. The Court of Appeal did not, on the facts of the case, consider it necessary to choose between the two approaches (at [16]), but nevertheless stated that if a state adopts a rule restricting access to the court which it is not required by international law to adopt, there will be a violation of art.6 ECHR unless the rule otherwise meets the requirements for a limitation on that right (at [20]).

That conclusion is not inconsistent with the decision of the House of Lords in *Holland v Lampen Wolfe* and of course opens up the possibility that a law granting immunity might be found to be inconsistent with the Convention unless it can be shown to be required by international law. In *Holland v Lampen Wolfe* the House of Lords was firmly of the view that international law required the grant of immunity in the circumstances of the case.

Yet the precise scope of immunities required by international law is often the subject of controversy and the line between immunity and non-immunity difficult to draw. Indeed in *Benkharbouche* the Court of Appeal concluded, in respect of employment claims by employees of the embassies of Sudan and Libya, that s.16(1) and 4(2) of the State Immunity Act 1978 were incompatible with Art. 6 of the ECHR and could not be read down and given an effect to in a way which was compatible with the ECHR pursuant to the interpretative obligation imposed by s.3(1) of the Human Rights Act. Accordingly the court made a declaration of incompatibility pursuant to s.4(2) of the Human Rights Act. The court also concluded that these sections violated the equivalent provision in the Charter of Fundamental Rights of the European Union (Art.47) and they should be disapplied where the claimants' claims were derived from EU law measures.

The consequences of this decision are potentially significant. In terms of effect, the court's decision is more significant in respect of Art.47. Art.47 has, according to the court, horizontal direct effect such that the claimants could rely on it against states which are not member states of the EU or EU institutions Consequently, the claims in the *Benkharbouche and Janah* case were allowed to proceed notwithstanding the immunity in the State Immunity Act. A declaration of incompatibility pursuant to s.4(2) is of course of less value to the individual claimants in that the State Immunity Act will remain in full force and effect unless and until Parliament takes further action.

While its general impact is potentially significant, it is unlikely that this element of the decision will have much effect on the law of defamation as there are currently few situations in which breaches of EU law measures might give rise to such a claim.

SECTION 3. FOREIGN SUBJECTS AND COMPANIES

**Capacity to sue or liability to be sued.** *Insert after first sentence*: **8.6**

While a foreign person, whether natural or juristic, is not subject to any disability with regard to capacity to sue, the Court may strike out a claim under the *Jameel* jurisdiction if the publications which took place in the jurisdiction do not (individually or collectively) establish a real and substantial tort within the jurisdiction (*new note 29A*). A foreign claimant unable to establish that he has a significant reputation in the jurisdiction is consequently likely to find that his claim will be struck out. However, a claimant may be able to show a reputation sufficient to establish a real and substantial tort notwithstanding that he had no reputation at the time the imputation complained of was published, where such a reputation was created and destroyed by the publication (*new note 29B*).

*New Note 29A:* See, e.g., *Karpov v Browder* [2013] EWHC 3071 (QB); [2014] E.M.L.R. 8; *Ames v The Spamhaus Project* [2015] EWHC 127 (QB); [2015] 1 W.L.R. 3409; *Subtonic v Knezevic* [2013] EWHC 3011 (QB).

*New Note 29B: Ames v The Spamhaus Project* (above), per Warby J. at [69]. See also Eady J in *Multigroup v Bulgaria Holding AD v Oxford Analytica Ltd* [2001] E.M.L.R. 28 at [19], [24].

SECTION 4. BANKRUPTS AND INSOLVENT COMPANIES

**Generally.** *Note 35, add*, In *Hayes v Butters* [2014] EWHC 4557 Nugee J. **8.7** held that a claim for damages for harassment under the Protection from Harassment Act 1997 could not be characterised as a purely personal claim in all circumstances (at [36]). Where the only claim that is or could be launched is a claim for distress and anxiety caused by the harassment then it is a purely personal claim. However, if the harassment has caused, in addition to distress and anxiety, financial loss (such as loss of earnings) or any other resulting loss then the claim falls to be treated as a hybrid one. As such, the claim will vest in the trustee but he holds damages for distress and anxiety on trust for the bankrupt.

*Note 37, add*, In *Vaughan v London Borough of Lewisham* [2013] EWHC 4118 (QB) Eady J. struck out for abuse of process a libel claim brought by a bankrupt person. To allow the claim to continue in the particular circumstances would amount to an abdication of the court's duty of case management (at [29]).

*Insert the following at end of para. 8.7*:

While it is probably the case that a trustee has no claim to the damages in a libel claim where the damages awarded are general, the position may be different in a slander claim where there is a successful claim for special damage or where in a libel claim the claimant is able to prove a specific financial loss was caused by the libel. In both such examples, it is arguable that the claim ought to be treated as hybrid in form so that where the claimant recovers general damages for the injury to his reputation and special damages for an identified financial loss, the claim vests in the trustee but he holds the general damages on constructive trust for the bankrupt.

SECTION 7. DECEASED PERSONS AND REPRESENTATIVES

**8.11**     **No defamation of the dead.** *Note 58, add,* The European Court of Human Rights has held (*Putistin v Ukraine* Application no 16882/03), in a claim brought by the applicant in respect of an article which he alleged defamed his father, that art.8 of the ECHR was engaged: "The reputation of a deceased member of the person's family may, in certain circumstances, affect that person's private life and identity, and thus come within the scope of Article 8" (at [33]).

The applicant's father had been a player for Dynamo Kiev football team before the Second World War. He was involved in the infamous "Death Match" between the Kiev city team, which included several former Dynamo Kiev players, and a team of German soldiers. The Kiev city team won but many in the team suffered reprisals. A Russian newspaper published an article about a film that was to be made of the match which, according to the applicant, defamed his father by implying that he had collaborated with the Germans. The applicant complained about the national courts' refusal to grant a rectification of the information about his father. Though the Strasbourg court held that damage to the reputation of an applicant's family could engage art.8, the applicant was affected only in an indirect manner and, in the particular circumstances the impact was quite remote (at [39]). Consequently his art.8 rights were only marginally affected and when weighed against the newspaper's right of freedom of expression, the court held that the domestic courts had not failed to strike the correct balance (at [40]).

See also, *Dzhugashvili v Russia* Application No. 41123/10, in which the ECtHR rejected the applicant's complaint in respect of a newspaper article about his grandfather, Joseph Stalin. While the court accepted that the applicant's reputation, as part and parcel of his family's reputation, fell within the scope of art.8, that had to be balanced against the great importance of historical events and figures remaining open to public historical scrutiny and criticism (at [32]). Accordingly the court held that the domestic courts had struck a fair balance between the journalist's right to freedom of expression and the applicant's right under art.8.

SECTION 8. MENTALLY DISORDERED AND DRUNKEN PERSONS

**8.14**     **Mentally disordered persons.** *Note 71, add,* In *Seal v Chief Constable of South Wales Police* [2007] UKHL 31; [2007] 1 W.L.R. 1910 (which involved a civil claim against the police for assault and false imprisonment) the House of Lords held, by a majority, that s.139(2) of the Mental Health Act 1983 did not infringe the claimant's right of access to a court under Art.6 ECHR. Lord Bingham explained the position thus:

"The European Court has accepted that the right of access to the court is not absolute, but may be subject to limitations: *Ashingdane v United Kingdom* (1985) 7 EHRR 528, para 57. The protection of those responsible for the care of mental patients from being harassed by litigation has been accepted as a legitimate objective: ibid, para 58; *M v United Kingdom* (1987) 52 DR 269, 270. What matters (*Ashingdane*, para 57) is that the limitations applied must not restrict or reduce the access left to the individual in such a way or to such an extent as to impair the very essence of the right. But the threshold for obtaining leave under s.139(2) has been set at a very unexacting level: *Winch v Jones* [1986] QB 296" (at [20]).

The claimant's application to the Strasbourg court (*Seal v United Kingdom* (2012) 54 E.H.R.R. 6) was also rejected, that court accepting that the restrictions on access to court were proportionate. The Court reiterated that the right of access to a court was not absolute and may be subject to limitations In this regard, Contracting States enjoy a certain margin of appreciation (at [76]). However, the Court must be satisfied that the limitations applied do not restrict or reduce the access left to the individual in such a way or to such an extent that the very essence of the right is impaired. Furthermore, a limitation will not be compatible with Article 6 if it does not pursue a legitimate aim and if there is not a reasonable relationship of proportionality between the means employed and the aim sought to be achieved. On the facts of the case the Court concluded that the requirement to obtain leave pursued a legitimate aim (of protecting those who exercise powers under that Act, including the police) and was proportionate (at [77]).

SECTION 9. CORPORATIONS AND GOVERNMENTAL BODIES

**Trading corporations.** *Delete in the third sentence of para.8.16 "when it* **8.16** *comes into force".*

*Note 81, add,* The question of whether a corporation is entitled to the protection of Art.8 is considered above at para.2.3. See *Firma EDV für Sie, EfS Elektronische Datenverarbeitung Dienstleistungs GmbH v Germany* Application no. 32783/08.

*Note 82, add,* In *Reachlocal UK Ltd v Bennett* [2014] EWHC 3405 (QB); [2015] E.M.L.R 7, which involved an application for final relief in consequence of judgment in default of defence, H.H.J. Parkes QC noted that while the first claimant traded within the jurisdiction, that was not the case with respect to the second claimant. Indeed the second claimant appeared to have no other function than as the headquarters and holding company of the European operations of the ReachLocal group and the judge thought it highly unlikely that anyone would have understood the words complained of as referring to it. Had the second claimant not had default judgment in its favour, it was difficult to see that it would have been able to establish that the threshold established in s.1(2) of the Defamation Act 2013 was crossed. Nevertheless, it followed from the fact that the second claimant had judgment that it had to be assumed that the threshold had been passed and the practical solution was therefore to award it a nominal sum by way of damages.

**8.19**     **Non-Trading corporations (other than governmental).** *Note 119, add*, See also *Otuo v Morley & Watch Tower Bible & Tract Society of Britain* [2015] EWHC 1839 (QB).

## Section 10. Trade Unions

*Note 163, add*, See also *Canadian Union of Postal Workers v Quebecor Media Inc.* 2015 ONSC 4511 in which the Ontario Superior Court refused to strike out a claim by a trade union on the ground that the issue of legal standing in an unincorporated association to sue in defamation is case specific and remains an unsettled and burgeoning area of the law. Accordingly, it was not plain and obvious that the pleadings disclosed no actionable cause of action (at [64]). See also *Gauthier v Toronto Star Daily Newspapers Ltd* 2003 CanLII 49328 (Ont SC), [2003] 228 D.L.R. (4th) 748 (Ont CA); *Northfield Capital Corp. v Aurelian Resources Inc.* [2007] 84 D.R. (3rd) 748 (SCJ); *Portuguese Canadian Credit Union Ltd. v Cumis General Insurance Co.* [2010] 104 O.R. (3rd) 16 (SCJ).

## Section 13. Vicarious Liability

*Note 204, add*, See also *Asghar v Ahmad* [2015] EWHC 1118 (QB): joint liability established in respect of material published on website run by fifth defendant on basis that the fourth defendant had provided defamatory material to the fifth defendant with the intention of encouraging him to publish the material on the website knowing that he had the proclivity to post material of a derogatory nature on his website (at [159]). See also, *McEvoy v Michael* [2014] EWHC 701 (QB).

CHAPTER 9

## REMEDIES

SECTION 1. COMPENSATORY (GENERAL) DAMAGES

**Vindication and reasoned judgment.** *Note 23, add*, See also, *Sloutsker v* **9.2**
*Romanova* [2015] EWHC 2053 (QB); [2015] E.M.L.R. 27, at [80].

*Note 25, add*, In *Rai v Bholowasia* [2015] EWHC 382 (QB) H.H.J. Parkes QC
gave little weight to the fact there had been a reasoned judgment of the court
because: "It seems to me that this is not a case where most people are likely to
read a detailed analysis of the judgment of the court, although it may be that there
will be some reporting of it in the local press." (at [174]). See also, *ReachLocal
UK Ltd. v Bennett* [2014] EWHC 3405 (QB); [2015] E.M.L.R. 7 in which the
judge held, in a case in which judgment was entered in default, that because this
was not a contested decision on the merits the effect on damages of any
vindication was marginal only (at [56]).

**General damages compensatory.** *Note 38, add*, In *Sloutsker v Romanova* **9.4**
[2015] EWHC 2053 (QB); [2015] E.M.L.R. 27, Warby J. stated that damages for
injury to feelings might be significant and the court: "must take account of what
the claimant "thinks other people are thinking of him" (at [76], quoting Lord
Diplock in *Cassell & Co. Ltd. v Broome* [1972] A.C. 1027, at 1125).

*Note 40, add*, In *Sloutsker v Romanova* [2015] EWHC 2053 (QB); [2015]
E.M.L.R. 27, Warby J. noted that vindication was sometimes identified as a
purpose of damages separate from compensation. However, he preferred to see it
as an intrinsic part of compensation for the tort, "the gist of which is the effect
on the claimant's reputation and standing in the eyes of others. Damages which
serve to restore the claimant's reputation to what it was by vindicating his
reputation serve a compensatory purpose. If the award fails to achieve vindication it fails properly to compensate. The correct analysis does not however
impact on the approach in the present case" (at [77]).
See also, *Hill v Church of Scientology of Toronto* [1995] 2 S.C.R. 1130, per
Cory J., at [166].

*Note 57, add,* In international libels, the court must be careful to ensure that it compensates only for damage that occurs within the relevant jurisdiction. Vindication in this context is only necessary so far as it is required to clear the claimant's name in that jurisdiction (see Warby J. in *Sloutsker v Romanova* [2015] EWHC 2053 (QB); [2015] E.M.L.R. 27, at [79].

*Note 58, add,* Note, however, as Warby J. made clear in *Sloutsker v Romanova* [2015] EWHC 2053 (QB); [2015] E.M.L.R. 27, while the maintenance of a plea of justification or failure to apologise may aggravate damages, the court should be careful not to treat assertions that an allegation is true as conduct that in itself increases harm to reputation, or otherwise aggravates damages: "Persistence in asserting the truth can aggravate injury to feelings, and is compensatable if the allegation is manifestly unsustainable" (per Warby J. in *Sloutsker v Romanova*, above, at [81]). See also, *Rai v Bholowasia* [2015] EWHC 382 (QB) per H.H.J. Parkes QC, at [177]. See further, para.9.21 below.

**9.5** **Matters affecting the level of the award.** *Note 67, add,* Where the claim is made in respect of foreign publication only, the stress of pursuing litigation in a foreign jurisdiction may be taken into account: *The Bussey Law Firm PC v Page* [2015] EWHC 563 (QB), at [13].

*Insert in second sentence of para.9.5 after "his credibility":* . . . the class of persons to whom publication is made.

*New Note 69A, to be inserted after "the class of persons to whom publication is made":* See, *ReachLocal UK Ltd. v Bennett* [2014] EWHC 3405 (QB); [2015] E.M.L.R. 7, in which H.H.J. Parkes QC held that the seriousness of the libel is likely to be increased where the libel is published to the claimant's customers or people professionally interested in the claimant's field of operation (at [58]).

In *Sharma v Sharma* [2014] EWHC 3349 (QB), H.H.J. Moloney QC stated that in having regard to the extent of publication "the court must have regard both to the number of people and their type (in terms of their influence and their closeness to the Claimant and his life) to whom the words have been published" (at [36]). Consequently, where, as in the *Sharma* case, the publication was to people influential in the Hindu faith, this served to increase the gravity of the libel. See also *Umeryor v Nwakamma* [2015] EWHC 2980 (QB).

*Note 70, add,* Where the claimant is a relatively newly established company or the person defamed someone new to a profession, this may be taken into account in assessing damages because such claimants are particularly vulnerable to attacks on their reputation: *ReachLocal UK Ltd. v Bennett* [2014] EWHC 3405 (QB); [2015] E.M.L.R. 7, at [63]. See also *Jon Richard v Gornall* [2013] EWHC 1357 (QB). In *Garcia v Associated Newspapers* [2014] EWHC 3137 (QB), Dingemans J. stated that in assessing damages a wide range of matters can properly be taken into account including the claimant's standing and position (at [298]). The standing of the defendant may also be relevant. Thus, in *Sharma v Sharma* [2014] EWHC 3349 (QB), H.H.J. Moloney QC held that the status of the defendant as someone who was well respected in the Hindu faith increased the severity of the libel because it made it more likely that others would believe what he said (at [42]).

*Note 73, add to end of penultimate paragraph in the note*, See also, *Sloutsker v Romanova* [2015] EWHC 2053 (QB); [2015] E.M.L.R. 27, at [75]; *The Bussey Law Firm PC v Page* [2015] EWHC 563 (QB) (damages awarded to take account to "some extent" of the "grapevine effect": at [14]); *Rai v Bholowasia* [2015] EWHC 382 (QB), at [173]; *ReachLocal UK Ltd. v Bennett* [2014] EWHC 3405 (QB); [2015] E.M.L.R. 7, at [60].

*Note 75, add after first sentence in the note.*, See also, *Flood v Times Newspapers Limited* [2013] EWHC 4075 (QB) in which Nicola Davies J. held that the defendant's unwillingness to publish exculpatory material when it became available for more than two years and its persistence in pursuit of evidence to contradict the exculpatory evidence gave rise to a proper need for vindication (at [73], [74]). So too, the aggressive behaviour of the defendant's lawyer was a matter that could be taken into account by the court.

*Note 77, add*, In *Cruddas v Calvert* [2015] EWCA Civ 171; [2015] E.M.L.R. 16, the Court of Appeal held, in reducing the damages award for meanings 2 and 3 (that the claimant was countenancing a criminal breach of the Political Parties, Elections and Referendums Act 2000, s.61 in respect of foreign donations), that the damages should be reduced by one third to take account of the fact that the defendant had justified meaning 1 (corruptly offering for sale, in exchange for donations to the Conservative Party, an opportunity to influence government policy) which meant that the claimant was to be treated as a man who had not conducted himself properly when talking to potential donors about the rewards available to them for political donations (at [135]-[138]). Aggravated damages were also reduced on a similar basis (at [140]).

**Damages awards and the European Court of Human Rights.** *Note 90, add,* **9.6**
*Rai v Bholowasia* [2015] EWHC 382 (QB), at [181]: means of the defendant irrelevant to the exercise of assessment.

**Role of the Court of Appeal.** *Replace first sentence of second paragraph of* **9.7** *para.9.7 with the following*: The level of damages for non-pecuniary loss in personal injury cases is now a relevant "comparator" for libel damages (*note 96*) and in that area the maximum, taking into account the Jackson reforms, is now of the order of £300,000 (*new note 96A*).

*New Note 96A:* See *Cairns v Modi* [2012] EWCA Civ 1382; [2013] 1 W.L.R. 1015, at [25] and *Simmons v Castle (No.2)* [2012] EWCA Civ 1288; [2013] 1 W.L.R. 1239. See also, *Rai v Bholowasia* [2015] EWHC 382 (QB), at [179].

**Relevance of personal injury damages.** *Replace third sentence of para.9.9* **9.9** *with the following*:

However, in the period since awards in personal injury cases have come to be assessed by judges, there has developed a broad judicial tariff of awards for different types of standard injuries, with a maximum of around £300,000 for the worst injuries (*note 109*).

*Note 109, add*, The Legal Aid, Sentencing and Punishment of Offenders Act 2012 (Commencement No. 5 and Saving Provision) Order 2013 brought fully into effect LASPO, ss.44-46, on 1 April 2013. However, by art.4(b), publication and privacy proceedings were expressly excluded. The Ministry of Justice conducted a consultation on "Costs protection in defamation and privacy claims" (https://consult.justice.gov.uk/digital-communications/costs-protection-in-defamation-and-privacy claims). A response to this was expected in early 2014 but has not yet been published. See also 35.13 below.

*Note 110, add,* The relevant edition of the Judicial Studies Board's Guidelines for the Assessment of General Damages in Personal Injury cases is now 13th edition, 2015.

*Note 128, add, Sloutsker v Romanova* [2015] EWHC 2053 (QB); [2015] E.M.L.R. 27 (£110,000 for allegations of corruption and conspiracy to murder against Russian senator published to audience running into high tens of thousands).

Section 2. Aggravated Damages

**9.18**    **Aggravated damages.** *New Note 169A to be inserted after "The conduct of the defendant" in the first sentence of para.9.18:*

In *Johnson v Steele* [2014] EWHC B24 (QB), Eady J. in awarding aggravated damages took into account the "extraordinary" conduct of the defendant who had done everything in his power to cause maximum damage to the claimant's reputation including: hiding behind a cloak of anonymity; persisting in publishing defamatory matter about the claimant over many months; reporting the claimant to the police; hiding computers; denying his own authorship of the publications complained of; setting up fake accounts in the claimant's name; and setting a up "copycat mirror website" in the United States two days after the claimant had managed to get some of the UK sites set up by the defendant suspended for defamatory publications.

*Note 172, add,* Aggravated damages are not available simply for anxiety and hurt feelings: "These are a natural consequence of a defamatory publication and do not aggravate damages" (per Nicola Davies J. in *Flood v Times Newspapers Limited* [2013] EWHC 4075 (QB), at [67]).

**9.21**    **Relationship of aggravated and other damages.** *Insert the following at the end of first paragraph of para.9.21:*

While the maintenance of a plea of justification or failure to apologise may aggravate damages, the court should be careful not to treat assertions that an allegation is true as conduct that in itself increases harm to reputation, or otherwise aggravates damages: "Persistence in asserting the truth can aggravate injury to feelings, and is compensatable if the allegation is manifestly unsustainable." (per Warby J. in *Sloutsker v Romanova* [2015] EWHC 2053 (QB); [2015] E.M.L.R. 27, at [81]).

*Note 202, add,* Somewhat surprisingly, Nicola Davies J. justified her award of aggravated damages in *Flood v Times Newspapers Limited* [2013] EWHC 4075 (QB) in part on the basis of the need for deterrence:

"To that figure I have awarded a further £15,000 to represent the aggravation of those damages by reason of the conduct of the defendant and to serve as a deterrent to those who embark upon public interest journalism but thereafter refuse to publish material which in whole, or in part, exculpates the subject of the investigation" (at [83]).

With respect, this appears to confuse the purpose of aggravated damages (which are compensatory only in intent) with exemplary damages.

**Crime and Courts Act 2013.** The Royal Charter on Self Regulation of the **9.22** Press was approved on 30 October 2013. The Charter establishes an Independent Recognition Panel which decides whether a self regulator meets pre-set criteria for regulatory independence and effectiveness. The Press Recognition Panel opened for applications on 10 September 2015 but has not yet received any applications. Should the Press Recognition Panel recognise a regulator as meeting the criteria established in the Leveson Report the provisions of ss.34-39 of the Crime and Courts Act 2013, which is now in force (23 April 2014) will be available to those subject to the regulatory regime.

SECTION 5. INJUNCTIONS

**Libel and slander actionable per se.** *Note 329, add,* In *Bell v Payne* [2015] **9.41** EWHC1714 (QB) H.H.J. Moloney QC refused to grant an injunction. The evidence given by the claimant was to the effect that the defendant (against whom judgment had been made on a default basis) was continuing to make allegations of assault against him though the only known communications had been between her and the police. The judge held that it would be entirely wrong to grant an injunction restraining the defendant from going to the police to make complaints and there was insufficient evidence of a real and substantial risk that the defendant would, absent an injunction, continue to publish the allegations. Consequently, the judge was not prepared to issue the injunction sought.

CHAPTER 11

# TRUTH (JUSTIFICATION)

SECTION 1. INTRODUCTION

**11.1**  **Terminology and policy.** Section 2 of the Defamation Act 2013 is now in force—see Defamation Act 2013 (Commencement) (England and Wales) Order 2013 SI 2013/3027. It applies to causes of action that accrued on or after 1 January 2014.

**11.2**  **The Defamation Act 2013.** Section 2 of the Defamation Act 2013 is now in force—see Defamation Act 2013 (Commencement) (England and Wales) Order 2013 SI 2013/3027.

**11.5**  **Determination of Meaning and the Defence of Truth**. *Add new note at line 9 after text " . . . in their natural and ordinary sense":*

The standard reference on the principles relevant to the determination of meaning is the judgment of Sir Anthony Clarke M.R. in *Jeynes v News Magazines Ltd* [2008] EWCA Civ 130 at [14]. See, further, paras.3.14ff. The judge is not bound by the parties' pleaded meanings: see, for example, *Johnson v League Publications* [2014] EWHC 874 (QB) at [5]; *Donovan v Gibbons* [2014] EWHC 3406 (QB) at [22]; *Rufus v Elliott* [2015] EWHC 807 (QB) at [23]; *Mughal v Telegraph Media Group Limited* [2014] EWHC 1371 (QB) at [3]; *White v Express Newspapers* [2014] EWHC 657 (QB) at [10]; *RBOS Shareholders Action Group Ltd v News Group Newspapers Ltd* [2014] EWHC 130 (QB); [2014] E.M.L.R. 15 at [14]. Neither is the judge bound to select the least defamatory meaning available: see *McAlpine v Bercow* [2013] EWHC 1342 (QB); [2014] E.M.L.R. 3 at [66]; to do so would be "unreasonable" and "naïve" (per Tugendhat J.) That the role of the judge in determining meaning is to put himself in the position of the lay person was emphasised by Dingemans J. in *Building Register Limited v Weston* [2014] EWHC 784 (QB) and *Garcia v Associated Newspapers Ltd* [2014] EWHC 3137 (QB). In the latter case, this point was illustrated by the interpretation afforded to the phrase "alcohol dependency". While the term has a technical medical meaning, the judge concluded that this would not be inferred by the lay person and so ascribed to the phrase the non-technical meaning "persistent abuse of alcohol" (at [21]).

*Note 31*: As envisaged in this paragraph, with the coming into force of the Defamation Act 2013 it has become commonplace for judges to be asked to determine meaning at a preliminary stage in proceedings. In *Yeo v Times Newspapers Ltd* [2014] EWHC 2853 [2015] 1 W.L.R. 971 at [82], Warby J. explained that "the right approach ... when ... a judge is adjudicating at an early stage on what meanings the words complained of actually bear ... [he] is not confined to the precise meanings advanced by the parties or to the wording of those meanings set out in the respective statements of case. The judge may find the words to bear some different meaning or meanings. But the judge should not normally make a finding of any meaning which is not either advanced to some extent in the statement of case or submissions of one or other party, or within the same class or range as a meaning so advanced". The determination as to whether the statement complained of comprises a statement of fact or comment should normally be dealt with at the same time (at [83], citing *Cammish v Hughes* [2012] EWCA Civ 1655; [2013] E.M.L.R. 13 at [43]). See further, paras 30.2 and 30.15.

*Add new note at the end of the second paragraph after text "... the evidence that each party adduces":*

In *Yeo v Times Newspapers Ltd* [2014] EWHC 2853 (QB); [2015] 1 W.L.R. 971 at [60], Warby J. noted that "it is possible to envisage a simple libel action concerning a single factual allegation in which meaning is not in dispute and the sole issue is truth ... such actions are rare in practice, however". He was speaking in the context of the desirability of a trial by judge alone and the concomitant provision of a reasoned judgment on meaning.

SECTION 2. BASIC REQUIREMENTS OF THE DEFENCE

**Truth of Particular Imputation**. *Note 46*: In *Karpov v Browder* [2013] **11.6** EWHC 3071 (QB); [2014] E.M.L.R. 8, Simon J. criticised the defendant's plea of justification as it "focuse[d] on the claimant's motive; and motive alone is not sufficient to support a plea of torture and murder ... the only overt act relied on is the claimant's involvement in the arrest and imprisonment ... the causal link which one would expect from such a serious charge is wholly lacking; and nothing is said about torture or murder".

**Substantial Truth of Particular Imputation**. *Add new note after text "... * **11.7** *can provide the basis for the defence of truth." At the end of the final paragraph*:

*New note 55A* See the reflection on the meaning of the words "to fleece" in *Euromoney Institutional Investor Plc v Aviation News Ltd* [2013] EWHC 1505 (QB) at [46] et seq (and also the hypothetical discussion of the phrase "to kill"—at [49]).

SECTION 3. PARTICULAR CASES AND THE DEFENCE OF TRUTH

**11.13**    **Defence of Truth and Levels of Meaning.** *Add to note 90*: Often there will be a dispute between the parties as to the level of meaning conveyed in the words published: see, for example, *Yeo v Times Newspapers Ltd* [2014] EWHC 2853 (QB); [2015] 1 W.L.R. 971.

*Add to note 91*: In *Karpov v Browder* [2013] EWHC 3071 (QB); [2014] E.M.L.R. 8 at [128], Simon J. criticised the defendant's plea of justification as it "focuse[d] on the claimant's motive; and motive alone is not sufficient to support a plea of torture and murder . . . the only overt act relied on is the claimant's involvement in the arrest and imprisonment . . . the causal link which one would expect from such a serious charge is wholly lacking; and nothing is said about torture or murder".

*Add to note 92*: In *Miller v Associated Newspapers Ltd* [2014] EWCA Civ 39 at [14]-[22], the Court of Appeal considered the argument that the judge at first instance had "imposed too stringent a test" such that the defendant was effectively required "to establish actual impropriety" (effectively a *Chase* level 1 obligation). The court saw some merit in the submissions, but concluded that it was "not persuaded that this very experienced judge lost sight of the important distinction between *Chase* Level 1 and *Chase* Level 2 imputations . . . it is clear from the passage as a whole that the judge was directing her mind to the need to establish reasonable grounds for suspicion" (at [22]).

*Add to note 96*: A principal complaint presented to the Court of Appeal in *Miller v Associated Newspapers Ltd* [2014] EWCA Civ 39 at [16] and [27] was that the judge at first instance had failed to abide by this "rule against hindsight". The court held, however, that "it is necessary to draw a distinction between events occurring after the date of publication and statements, whenever made, which tend to prove or disprove the existence of facts subsisting at the date of publication. The latter are admissible, but the former are not" (at [27] per Moore-Bick LJ).

SECTION 4. THE REPETITION RULE

**11.18**    **The Basic Rule.** The repetition rule would appear to have survived the Defamation Act 2013. Although the point was not argued, in *Lachaux v Independent Print Ltd* [2015] EWHC 620 (QB) at [42], Sir David Eady observed: "I see no reason to suppose that the long established (although only relatively recently named) "repetition rule" has been impliedly abrogated by the Defamation Act 2013. Accordingly, in so far as any of the defamatory imputations contained in these articles are attributed to [family members of a witness relied on by the defendants], a defence of truth will still require the substantive allegation to be proved—not merely that the allegation was so made: see e.g. *Gatley on Libel & Slander* (12th edn) at 11.18 and 30.8".

CHAPTER 12

# HONEST COMMENT

SECTION 1. INTRODUCTION

**The Basis of the Defence**. *Add to note 4*: See also, *Yeo v Times Newspapers*  **12.1**
*Limited* [2014] EWHC 2853 (QB); [2015] 1 W.L.R. 971 at [15] (per Warby J):
"The common law has always been fiercely protective of comment and opin-
ion."

**The Elements of the Defence**. *Add to note 11*: See also, *Donovan v Gibbons*  **12.2**
[2014] EWHC 3406 (QB) at [14] per HHJ Richard Parkes QC: "A fair balance
has to be struck between allowing a critic the freedom to express himself as he
will and requiring him to identify to his readers why it is that he is making that
criticism. That is particularly important on the internet, where people can make
public comment about matters which are far from generally known, and where it
will often be impossible for other readers to evaluate the views expressed".

**Reform: Section 3 of the Defamation Act 2013**. *Add text at end of first sub-*  **12.4**
*paragraph*: Section 3 of the Defamation Act 2013 is now in force and applies to
publications that occurred on or after 1 January 2014. (Defamation Act 2013
(Commencement) (England and Wales) Order 2013 SI 2013/3027). In some
cases, publication will have occurred both before and after the appointed date on
which the 2013 Act came into force. See, for example, *Donovan v Gibbons*
[2014] EWHC 3406 (QB) (*YouTube* video available online before and after the
appointed date); *Yeo v Times Newspapers Limited* [2014] EWHC 2853 (QB);
[2015] 1 W.L.R. 971 (newspaper articles published online before and after the
appointed date).

SECTION 2. RECOGNISABILITY AS COMMENT

**Centrality of Recognisability as Comment**. *Add*: As Warby J. commented in  **12.7**
*Yeo v Times Newspapers Limited*, however, "the requirement that comment be

[61]

recognisable as comment as distinct from a factual imputation is not as straightforward as at first it might seem" ([2014] EWHC 2853 (QB); [2015] 1 W.L.R. 971, at [89]).

**12.8**      **The Distinction Between Fact and Comment.** *Add new text after '. . . the question is in the first instance to be answered by the judge.' at the end of the second sentence*:

The issue is now commonly determined by way of preliminary hearing alongside such other themes as the determination of meaning, assessment as to whether the meaning is defamatory, and satisfaction of the s.1 threshold. (See, for example, *Euromoney Institutional Investor Plc v Aviation News Ltd* [2013] EWHC 1505 (QB); *Donovan v Gibbons* [2014] EWHC 3406 (QB)). Insofar as such questions are taken together at a preliminary stage, it is probably immaterial which question is answered first assuming that the impact that a decision on one may have on another is borne in mind—see *Donovan v Gibbons*, at [7]. Collectively, such determinations will indicate whether a substantive defence need be pleaded at all, and if so which defence or defences are appropriate. The desirability of ordering of the questions to be answered had been suggested by the Lord Chief Justice in *British Chiropractic Association v Singh* [2010] EWCA Civ 350; [2011] 1 W.L.R. 133 at [32]. The suggestion was considered in *Euromoney,* at [30]-[35]. In *Meadows Care v Lambert* [2014] EWHC 1226 (QB) at [12], Bean J. expressed the view that "a defendant cannot sensibly be expected to formulate a defence of honest comment in a slander case until it is proved what words he spoke".

**12.9**      **"Bare Comment".** *Add to note 60*: See also, *Yeo v Times Newspapers Limited* [2014] EWHC 2853 (QB); [2015] 1 W.L.R. 971, at [89]-[90].

**12.10**      **Inferences of Verifiable and Unverifiable Fact.** *Add note after "This is an issue ripe for judicial determination" at the end of the first line of the final paragraph:* For an interesting and intelligent reflection on this theme, and on the history and purposes of the defence, based on close attention to case law, see Bosland, Kenyon and Walker, "Protecting inferences of fact in defamation law: fair comment and honest opinion" (2015) *Cambridge Law Journal*, 74(2), 234-260. The theme was raised by counsel and recognised by Warby J., with reference to this paragraph, in *Barron v Collins* [2015] EWHC 1125 (QB) at [16]-[17], although it was not necessary for the judge to determine the issue in that case.

**12.11**      **Importance of Context**. *Add to note 73*: In *Yeo v Times Newspapers Limited* [2014] EWHC 2853 (QB); [2015] 1W.L.R. 971 at [97], Warby J. explained that "in seeking to place itself in the position of the ordinary reasonable reader the court should take as its starting point the general features of the article and the impact these are likely to have on how the words used strike the mind of the ordinary reader. It should bear in mind the positioning within the paper of the article under examination (for instance whether it is in the news section or in an "op ed" piece or magazine); the general nature of the subject matter dealt with in that article (news, political, social, financial or other); who has written the material, if this is apparent (is it for example the paper's political correspondent or an established commentator?); and the form of expression the reader would be likely to expect from an article on this subject matter, positioned as it is, and by this or these author(s). It is against that background that the court should consider the particular statements in the article and assess, as far as possible at the same time, what if any defamatory meaning it conveys and the extent to which this is factual or comment. In performing this last task the court should be alert to the importance of giving free rein to comment and wary of interpreting a statement as factual in nature, especially where ... it is made in the context of political issues. In drawing the distinction the court should consider what the words in their context indicate to the reader about the kind of statement the author intends to make". On the facts, the judge indicated that the expectation of "a reader of *The Sunday Times* (print or online), a serious-minded weekly newspaper, reading lengthy articles prominently positioned in the news section of the paper on a serious topic of evident political and public importance" would likely be that the article was "largely comprised of factual revelations" along with "some indication of the paper's viewpoint on what it had uncovered" (at [98]).

*Add at end of first paragraph*: The courts are also capable of appreciating the nature of different online publication platforms, and distinguishing one platform from another in terms of the tendency to publish comment or to make free-standing points. In *Donovan v Gibbons* [2014] EWHC 3406 (QB) at [15]-[16] counsel sought to draw an analogy between *YouTube* and popular online review sites such as *TripAdvisor*, and submitted on this basis that the online video publication in question thereby fell into the category of a review which by its nature is likely to involve opinion and comment. The judge, HHJ Richard Parkes QC, noted that *YouTube* is today broadly as familiar as the typical contents of a newspaper and rejected the analogy. Hence, there could be no starting assumption that the video comprised an expression of opinion. On the facts, the judge found that the publication included at least one defamatory allegation of fact (that the claimant had knowingly sold a dangerous pony as being suitable for use by children).

*Add after text above, in separate paragraph*: One dimension of the argument before the High Court in *Yeo v Times Newspapers Limited* concerned the general context of political speech and the influence of Strasbourg jurisprudence on the domestic courts' consideration of alleged defamation in that context ([2014] EWHC 2853 (QB); [2015] 1 W.L.R. 971 at [92]-[94]. For a review of the Strasbourg jurisprudence, see *Axel Springer AG v Germany (No 2)* App.no. 48311/2010 [2014] ECHR 745). Counsel for the defendant emphasised four themes: the essential role of the press in a democratic society and its duty to impart information and ideas on all matters of public interest; the principle that the scope for interference with freedom of expression is limited where political speech is concerned; the distinction between fact and value judgment in Convention jurisprudence and the associated need for care in approaching the task of categorisation, and the consistent jurisprudence of the Strasbourg court to the effect that statements impugning motive should be treated as value judgments, a point made repeatedly in the context of political speech. By detailed reference to the facts of the instant case, however, Warby J. explained at [115] that "It is not the law that an imputation of a state of mind amounts in all circumstances to a comment. It depends on the context", and that the facts of *Yeo* left it very different to those that had generated the Strasbourg jurisprudence ([116]). He also noted (at [92]) that it had not been suggested that the Strasbourg jurisprudence was "inconsistent with [the] rules of the common law" in this regard.

## SECTION 4. INDICATION OF FACTS

**12.24**     **Sufficient reference.** *Add at the end of the first sentence*:

It is accurate to say that "the rule that in order for a statement to be treated as comment it must identify the facts on which it is based is not . . . as exacting as at one stage it was thought to be": *Yeo v Times Newspapers Limited* [2014] EWHC 2853 (QB); [2015] 1 W.L.R. 971 at [91] (per Warby J).

## SECTION 7. MALICE

**12.36**     **Words Not the Defendant's Opinion.** *Add new text at end of penultimate paragraph*:

A pleading of malice with its implicit allegation of dishonesty was at issue in *Yeo v Times Newspapers Ltd (No2)* [2015] EWHC 209 (QB); [2015] 1 W.L.R. 3031. The defendants complained allegation of dishonesty was lacking in proper particularity. Warby J. explained at [30]-[31] that "clarity and precision are always required in statements of case, but never more so than when an allegation of dishonesty is being made. This is axiomatic. One reason is the obvious one that the ordinary requirements of fairness dictate that a person accused of acting dishonestly must be given a clear statement of the case against him, so that he can prepare to meet it . . . clarity and precision are also required in order that the party accused and the court can police the making of allegations of dishonesty, and weed out those which do not deserve to go to trial because the case cannot attain the high standard required".

The judge then referred to the discussion of the correct approach to be taken to the pleading and proof of allegations of dishonesty that was set out by Lord Hobhouse in *Three Rivers District Council v Bank of England* [2001] UKHL 16; [2003] 2 AC 1 at [161]: "The law quite rightly requires that questions of dishonesty be approached more rigorously than other questions of fault. The burden of proof remains the civil burden—the balance of probabilities—but the assessment of the evidence has to take account of the seriousness of the allegations and, if that be the case, any unlikelihood that the person accused of dishonesty would have acted in that way. Dishonesty is not to be inferred from evidence which is equally consistent with mere negligence. At the pleading stage the party making the allegation of dishonesty has to be prepared to particularise it and, if he is unable to do so, his allegation will be struck out . . . It is normally to be assumed that a party's pleaded case is the best case he can make (or wishes to make). Therefore, in the present case, the particulars given provide a true guide to the nature of the case being made by the plaintiffs (claimants)". (For the consequences of this for the pleading of malice in defamation claims, see paragraph 28.6 below). Warby J. emphasised that such principles represent an "important safeguard for freedom of expression": *Yeo*, above, at [35].

In *Henderson v London Borough of Hackney* [2010] EWHC 1651 (QB) at [35], Eady J. explained that "It is not appropriate merely to plead . . . absence of honest belief . . . . Unsupported by relevant factual averments, those are merely formulaic assertions. It is certainly not right that a judge should presume such assertions to be provable at trial. Otherwise, every plea of malice, however vague or optimistic, would survive to trial. It would be plainly inappropriate to move towards such an unbalanced regime, since it would tend to undermine the rights of defendants protected under Article 10 of the European Convention on Human Rights".

*Add new text at end of final paragraph*:

It is not necessary to demonstrate that a defendant had an ulterior motive when seeking to establish malice: *Makudi v Triesman* [2014] EWCA Civ 179; [2014] Q.B. 839 at [35].

**Defamation Act 2013: Retention of the Malice Issue** *Add*: In *Yeo v Times*    **12.38**
*Newspapers Ltd (No 2)*, Warby J. stated that with regard to publication on or after 1 January 2014, s.3(5) (by which the defence of honest opinion is defeated on proof that the defendant does not hold the opinion expressed) is to the same effect as the common law rule that the defendant who does not hold the opinion expressed is malicious: [2015] EWHC 209 (QB); [2015] 1 W.L.R. 3031 at [27].

# Chapter 13

## ABSOLUTE PRIVILEGE

## Section 2. Statements Made in or in Connection with Judicial Proceedings

**13.5**     **General rule.** *Insert the following at the end of para.13.5*:

While the immunity from suit for defamatory statements made in the course of judicial proceedings remains secure for the present, considerable damage to reputation can be caused by false allegations made in civil proceedings. This is particularly the case given the right of the public in most civil proceedings to inspect the pleadings which have to be filed, and of the media, without fear either of contempt of court or of the law of libel, fairly and accurately to report their contents even if defamatory. Where such proceedings are brought maliciously without reasonable or probable cause, the case for providing a remedy might be considered particularly strong. Yet the House of Lords in *Gregory v Portsmouth CC* [2000] 1 A.C. 419 held that the tort of malicious prosecution was not available beyond the limits of criminal proceedings and special instances of abuse of civil legal process. Lord Steyn, with whose speech the other members of the House of Lords agreed, declined the appellant's invitation to extend the tort to disciplinary proceedings (at 428-432) and, while recognising that there was a stronger case for extending the tort to civil actions, declined to do so for "essentially practical reasons", namely that:

"any manifest injustices arising from groundless and damaging civil proceedings are either already adequately protected under other torts or are capable of being addressed by any necessary and desirable extensions of other torts" (at 432-433).

Notwithstanding the decision of their Lordships in Gregory, the Privy Council held, by a majority, in *Crawford Adjusters v Sagicor General Insurance (Cayman) Limited* [2013] UKPC 17 that a claim for malicious prosecution of civil proceedings is available if the claimant can establish that he has suffered damage as a result of a civil claim which was brought against him maliciously and without reasonable cause, and which was determined in his favour.

While there is much to be said for the decision of the Privy Council in the *Crawford Adjusters* case, there were strong dissents from both Lords Sumption and Neuberger. Both highlighted concerns about the possibility of deterring parties from bringing legitimate claims and the uncertain ambit of the tort recognised by the majority (at [147], [194]). Moreover, there were very real risks of providing litigants with an occasion for prolonging disputes by way of secondary litigation. As Lord Sumption explained:

"It is no answer to these concerns to say that the bar can be set so high that few will succeed. Malice is far more often alleged than proved. The vice of secondary litigation is in the attempt. Litigation generates obsession and provokes resentment. It sharpens men's natural conviction of their own rightness and their suspicion of other men's motives. It turns indifference into antagonism and contempt. Whatever principle may be formulated for allowing secondary litigation in some circumstances, for every case in which an injustice is successfully corrected in subsequent proceedings, there will be many more which fail only after prolonged, disruptive, wasteful and ultimately unsuccessful attempts" (at [148]).

In light of these dissents and the decision of the House of Lords in *Gregory v Portsmouth CC* [2000] 1 A.C. 419, it is perhaps unsurprising that Amanda Tipples QC held in *Willers v Gubay* [2015] EWHC 1315 (Ch) that a claim for malicious prosecution of civil proceedings should be struck out. The judge held that she was bound by the decision in *Gregory* which she held had decided that the tort of malicious prosecution was not available in English law beyond the limits of criminal proceedings and special instances of abuse of civil legal process. Moreover, she was not in any event persuaded that it was a foregone conclusion that if the case went to the Supreme Court, the court would follow *Crawford Adjusters* in preference to *Gregory*. The decision in *Crawford Adjusters* involved a departure from the decision of the House of Lords and it did not seek to give guidance as to the proper interpretation to be placed on *Gregory* as a matter of English law. There was no overlap between the constitution of the two courts and the decision was by a majority. There were also two strong dissenting judgments and the difference between the majority and minority was very fundamental. Consequently, there was no justification for taking the exceptional course of departing from a decision of the House of Lords (at [71]).

(b) *Privilege of Witnesses*

*Note 113, add*, See also *Singh v Governing Body of Moorlands Primary School and Reading Borough Council* [2013] EWCA Civ 909; [2013] 1 W.L.R. 3052 for a helpful summary of the extent of witness privilege (at [66]).

**Extent of Privilege.** *Insert the following at the end of first paragraph* **13.12** *(p.477):*

While it is the case that absolute privilege extends beyond what is said in court by a witness, it should not be forgotten that the core immunity relates to the giving of evidence and its rationale is to ensure that persons who may be witnesses in other cases in the future will not be deterred from giving evidence by fear of being sued for what they say in court. Where, however, the basis of any claim is not the allegedly false statement itself, but instead matters that would not form part of the evidence in a judicial enquiry, there is no necessity to extend the immunity. Thus, in *Singh v Governing Body of Moorlands Primary School and Reading Borough Council* [2013] EWCA Civ 909; [2013] 1 W.L.R. 3052 (not a libel case), the Court of Appeal held that absolute immunity did not apply where the claimant's cause of action was based not on allegedly false evidence that the defendants intended to adduce in court but instead on the process by which the evidence was procured. Ms Singh had brought a claim against her employers for discrimination while she was still in their employment. After exchange of witness statements, she resigned complaining that the witness statement of one of her colleagues (SH), being untrue, was an act in breach of the duty of mutual trust and confidence. In particular, she sought to amend her employment tribunal claim to allege that the defendants had placed undue pressure on SH to produce a witness statement containing false or otherwise inaccurate evidence for the purpose of these proceedings. Both the employment tribunal and the employment appeal tribunal held that the amendment should not be permitted because judicial proceedings immunity covered all the Council's activities (whether proper or improper) in gathering evidence for the purpose of defending Ms Singh's claim of discrimination. The Court of Appeal allowed the appeal, holding that absolute immunity did not attach. Ms Singh's claim was not based on anything that SH might or might not say to the employment tribunal. Instead it was based on what was alleged to have gone on outside the tribunal and in particular on the process by which the defendants procured SH to give evidence:

"While alleged untruths in Mrs Heath's witness statement (and discrepancies between that statement and what Mrs Heath had previously said in interview) may help Ms Singh to prove the allegation that undue pressure was applied, the complaint is not about the content of the statement, but the means by which it was procured. The complaint that the Council is in breach of contract would be just as valid if [SH] had told Ms Singh about the alleged pressure but had stoutly resisted it. Thus the second fallacy in the Council's argument is the proposition that it is Mrs Heath's witness statement that is alleged to have caused the damage. That is not the allegation. The nub of the complaint is that the Council has done something calculated to destroy or damage the trust and confidence that is inherent in an employment relationship. If an employer, to the knowledge of an employee, is prepared to use underhand and improper means to defeat a claim of discrimination brought against it by the employee that is destructive of the requisite trust and confidence whether or not the employer succeeds" (at [71]).

*Note 115, add*, See also *CLG v Chief Constable of Merseyside Police* [2015] EWCA Civ 836. The statement of a police officer containing sensitive information about a vulnerable witness was disclosed by the CPS to the defendant in a criminal trial. In an action for negligence against the police, the Court of Appeal held that the police were immune from action in respect of the transmission of the statement to the CPS. This case fell squarely within Lord Hoffmann's statement in *Taylor v Director of the Serious Fraud Office* (set out below in the main text). The action was not based on the nature of the statement itself, as it would be if the claim were for defamation, but on the transmission by the police to the CPS of a statement required for the purposes of enabling the police officer to give evidence in court, as he subsequently did. In substance, the position was essentially the same as if the police officer had made his statement orally to a representative of the CPS. To hold the police liable for communicating its contents to the CPS would outflank the immunity to which they were entitled in relation to the evidence once given in court. See also, *Smart v Forensic Science Service Ltd* [2013] EWCA Civ 783; [2013] P.N.L.R. 32 in which a claim to immunity was not accepted.

*Note 118, add,* See also, *Decker v Hopcraft* [2015] EWHC 1170 (QB): a complaint to police about the "theft" of club keys was held to be protected by absolute privilege and accordingly a claim based on this allegation was struck out as clearly unwinnable as a matter of law (at [63]-[68]).

In *Crawford v Jenkins* [2014] EWCA Civ 1035, the Court of Appeal held, not agreeing with the reasoning of H.H.J. Seymour QC in *Halcyon House Ltd. v Baines* [2014] EWHC 2216 (QB), that immunity covered the Protection From Harassment Act 1997: "It seems to me that the policy of the immunity rules applies just as much to a claim in harassment based on such a statement as it does to a claim in defamation" (at [70]).

*Insert in main text after Note 122*:

However, in *Crawford v Jenkins* [2014] EWCA Civ 1035 the Court of Appeal has made clear that the immunity will not apply to a complaint made to the police if the wrongful complaint results in prosecutions or other court proceedings. It does however apply where the complaint does not lead to proceedings being brought. "If the interference with the claimants' liberty or his assets is the result of a court order or some kind . . . or is the ffect of the issue of proceedings . . . there can be no remedy by way of compensation to the claimant by recourse to the court which made the order . . . Accordingly it is right that there should be a distinct remedy, if necessary elements can be proved, against the person who invoked the court procedure . . . If, however, there are no court proceedings, the claimants' arrest not being followed by any proceedings whether civil or criminal, then there is no question of abuse of process of the court, no reason why . . . the person responsible for the arrest should not be answerable for the imprisonment and correspondingly no reason to treat a claim for compensation for arrest as one to which the witness immunity rule applies (at [54]-[67]).

*Note 126, add,* In *Chief Constable of South Wales Police v Daniels* [2015] EWCA Civ 680, the Court of Appeal emphasised that the mere fact that an activity may be intimately associated with the judicial phase of the criminal process, as distinct from the administrative or investigatory function, does not, in itself, necessarily give rise to immunity. Thus, not only will the immunity not apply where the defendant deliberately destroys evidence (*Darker v CC West Midlands* [2001] 1 A.C. 435), it will also not apply where evidence is deliberately withheld or concealed. In *Daniels*, which involved a claim for misfeasance in public office, the Chief Constable had argued that the service of the schedule of unused material on the respondents could be considered an express or implied statement to the court of compliance with the disclosure requirements in the Criminal Procedure and Investigations Act 1906, thus falling within the scope of the immunity as a statement intimately connected with the prosecution of the criminal proceedings. However, the court concluded that absolute immunity did not apply because the gist of the claim in misfeasance of public office was not founded on the content of any statement associated with service of the schedule of unused material but instead related to the way in which the disclosure exercise was conducted. The nature of the complaint was in essence that the respondents had deliberately or recklessly withheld documents that would have been helpful to the appellant's defence. In *Darker* all of the members of the House of Lords were agreed that the immunity did not extend to the fabrication of false evidence and a corollary of that must be that the deliberate destruction of documents which may be of assistance to the defence in a criminal prosecution must equally fall outside the scope of the absolute immunity. As Lloyd Jones L.J. noted:

> "It would be a surprising and unsatisfactory state of affairs if, notwithstanding that the deliberate destruction of potentially relevant documents does not attract immunity, their concealment or withholding, as alleged in the proposed amended pleading, were to do so. To my mind, the rationale which denies immunity to the fabrication or destruction of evidence applies equally to its concealment or withholding" (at [47]).

*Add to end of final paragraph*:

Whether a claim may lie for malicious prosecution of civil proceedings is less clear and is discussed at para.13.5 above The Privy Council in *Crawford Adjusters v Sagicor General Insurance (Cayman) Limited* [2013] UKPC 17; [2014] A.C. 366 held that such a claim was available if: (1) the prior proceedings had been determined in the claimant's favour; (2) the allegations made in the prior proceedings had been made without reasonable cause; (3) the allegations had been made maliciously; and, (4) as a result of the allegations the claimant had suffered substantial financial loss or other significant damage. However, this does not sit easily with the decision of the House of Lords in *Gregory v Portsmouth CC* [2000] 1 A.C. 419 in which it was held that the tort of malicious prosecution was not available beyond the limits of criminal proceedings and special instances of abuse of civil legal process. Unless and until the question reaches the Supreme Court, it seems likely that English Courts should continue to follow *Gregory* (see *Willers v Gubay* [2015] EWHC 1315 (Ch)).

**13.13**    **Limits of privilege.** *Note 138*: The case of *Iqbal* is properly cited as *Iqbal v Dean Manson Solicitors (No 2)*.

SECTION 3. STATEMENTS MADE BEFORE OTHER TRIBUNALS HAVING FUNCTIONS OF A JUDICIAL NATURE

**13.23**    **Examples: tribunals of a judicial nature.** *Note 218, add*, In *Halcyon House Limited v Baines* [2014] EWHC 2216 (QB) it was held that absolute immunity applied to statements made before a Leasehold Valuation Tribunal (at [292]).

SECTION 5. PROCEEDINGS IN PARLIAMENT

**Extent of the privilege.** *Insert at the beginning of para.13.30:* As the Court   **13.30**
of Appeal explained in *Makudi v Triesman* [2014] EWCA Civ 179; [2014] Q.B.
839: "Absolute privilege is a common law rule affording a defence in those
defamation cases to which it applies. Its scope is strictly defined by reference to
the setting in which the words complained of were uttered: Parliament; the
Queen's courts. Once publication in the prescribed setting is established, the
privilege attaches." (at [19]). So far as absolute privilege in the context of
Parliament is concerned, it has been said to apply to all "proceedings in Parliament". Erskine May states that the primary meaning of proceedings is:

> "some formal action, usually a decision, taken by the House in its collective capacity.
> While business which involves actions and decisions of the House are clearly proceed-
> ings, debate is an intrinsic part of that process which is recognised by its inclusion in
> the formulation of Article IX" (Erskine May, 24th edition (London, 2011),
> pp 235-236).

Clearly within the definition are speeches made within either chamber.

*Add:* Section 13 of the Defamation Act 1996 has now been repealed by
Schedule 23 paragraph 44 of the Deregulation Act 2015. However, in so far as
it stated in s.13(5) the proceedings to which it applied, it largely reflected the
common law position relating to the ambit of proceedings in Parliament. Consequently, the repeal of the provision is unlikely to have any effect on what
amounts to a proceeding in Parliament for the purposes of absolute privilege.

**Broader scope of Bill of Rights.** *Insert the following at end of para.13.31:*   **13.31**

The relationship between art.9 and absolute privilege was considered in detail
by the Court of Appeal in *Makudi v Triesman* [2014] EWCA Civ 179; [2014]
Q.B. 839. The respondent, then Chairman of the English Football Association
(FA), gave evidence on 11 May 2011 to the Culture Media and Sports Committee
of the House of Commons (CMSC). In his evidence, he alleged that the appellant, the head of Thailand's football federation, had requested the television
rights to a friendly match between England and Thailand in circumstances that
suggested that the *quid pro quo* would be support for England's bid for the World
Cup. Almost immediately after the hearing before the CMSC, the FA appointed
Mr Dingemans QC to conduct a review of the respondent's allegations. Mr
Dingemans invited the respondent to interview on 20 May 2011, during which he
declined to add anything to what he had said before the CMSC. The appellant
issued claims in defamation and malicious falsehood against the respondent in
respect of four publications made outside Parliament:

(1) the respondent's oral evidence given to Mr Dingemans on 20 May 2011;
(2) the respondent's witness statement published to Mr Dingemans; (3) and (4)
publications by Mr Dingemans himself to FIFA and the FA. At first instance
([2013] EWHC 142 (QB)), Tugendhat J found all four publications were made
on occasions of qualified privilege (though this had been common ground).
The judge also accepted two submissions advanced by counsel for the respondent: (1) that the court could not enquire into the respondent's state of mind

[71]

before Mr Dingemans (in order to test the appellant's claim of malice) without also enquiring into his state of mind before the CMSC; but that would violate Article 9; and (2) that an acceptance of the appellant's evidence at trial would not entail the conclusion that the respondent was dishonest: it would be equally consistent with his having been mistaken. The appellant appealed arguing, *inter alia*, that his claim did not constitute an affront to art.9 as it did not target anything stated in Parliament but what the respondent said (or conveyed by reference) to Mr Dingemans.

The Court of Appeal dismissed the appeal. Laws L.J. held that the reach of absolute privilege and art.9 was not the same and the two should not be conflated (as they had been by the Privy Council in *Buchanan v Jennings* [2005] 1 A.C. 115). "Absolute privilege is a common law rule affording a defence in those defamation cases to which it applies. Its scope is strictly defined by reference to the setting in which the words complained of were uttered: Parliament; the Queen's courts. Once publication in the prescribed setting is established, the privilege attaches." (at [19]) The reach of art.9 was less clear but in preventing any impeachment or questioning of freedom of speech and debates or proceedings in Parliament it sought to ensure members and witnesses speaking in either House or in Committee were not to be vexed by the fear of litigation. Such protection was afforded not for the sake of the individual member, but for the integrity of the legislature's democratic process (at [20]). It followed that if a Member of Parliament for his own purposes chose to repeat something he said in Parliament outside the House, whether by quotation or reference, he would not have the protection of art.9 (at [22]). However, there might be cases where extra-Parliamentary repetitions and references were not the gratuitous choice of the speaker and the protection of art.9 ought to be accorded to them. Such circumstances would, according to the court, vary on the facts:

" ... generally ... such cases will possess these two characteristics: (1) a public interest in repetition of the Parliamentary utterance which the speaker ought reasonably to serve, and (2) so close a nexus between the occasions of his speaking, in and then out of Parliament, that the prospect of his obligation to speak on the second occasion (or the expectation or promise that he would do so) is reasonably foreseeable at the time of the first and his purpose in speaking on both occasions is the same or very closely related".(at [25]).

Laws L.J. made clear that he did not intend to lay down an invariable rule and that there might be cases which justified the protection of art.9 which would not precisely demonstrate these characteristics: "As always, the common law will proceed case by case." (at [26]) Moreover no distinction ought to be drawn between repetition of what was said in Parliament and adoption of it without repetition for the purposes of determining the reach of art.9.

Applying these principles to the facts of the case, the court concluded that it did possess the necessary characteristics to fall within art.9. There was plainly a public interest in Mr Dingemans' inquiry which would be served by the respondent's contribution. So too there was a close nexus between his evidence to the CMSC and his interview with Mr Dingemans. The prospect that he might be called upon to speak was not only foreseeable but was actually foreseen. Consequently, art.9 prevented an examination of the respondent's statements to Mr Dingemans.

The precise consequences of the Court of Appeal's decision in *Makudi* are not entirely easy to anticipate. What is clear is that the reach of art.9 and absolute privilege are different and while extra Parliamentary speech is not protected by absolute privilege the same is not necessarily true of art.9. However, while there will be, as this case makes clear, occasions when extra-Parliamentary speech is protected under art.9, such occasions are likely to be infrequent. The judgment must be read in light of Laws L.J.'s statement that the courts will look for a very strong case on the facts if art.9 is to run:

"They will be concerned to see that the protection of the Article is not extended to speech outside Parliament more than is strictly necessary, given the high importance of the two other public interests which must take second place to the legislature's untrammelled freedom of debate: "the need to protect freedom of speech generally [and] the interests of justice in ensuring that all relevant evidence is available to the courts" as Lord Browne-Wilkinson described them in *Prebble.*" (at [27]).

**Defamation Act 1996, s.13.** *Add,* Section 13 of the Defamation Act 1996 was **13.32** intended to remedy the injustice perceived to exist in the *Hamilton v Guardian* type of case. In that case, an MP, Neil Hamilton, sued The *Guardian* newspaper over allegations that he had accepted money to ask parliamentary questions. In its defence, the newspaper argued that for a proper defence it would need to rely on parliamentary proceedings as evidence relating to Hamilton's conduct and motives in tabling parliamentary questions and early day motions. The judge found that this was contrary to art.9 and stayed the proceedings. Section 13 allowed a person in Neil Hamilton's position, whose conduct in, or in relation to, proceedings in Parliament was in issue in defamation proceedings, to waive the protection of privilege for the purposes of those proceedings. However, it proved controversial. It was considered by the Joint Committee on Parliamentary Privilege in 1999 and its repeal was recommended:

"A fundamental flaw is that it undermines the basis of the privilege: freedom of speech is the privilege of the House as a whole and not of the individual member in his own right, although an individual member can assert and rely on it. Application of the new provision could also be impracticable in complicated cases; for example, where two members, or a member and a non-member, are closely involved in the same action and one waives privilege and the other does not. Section 13 is also anomalous: it is available only in defamation proceedings. No similar waiver is available for any criminal action, or any other form of civil action. (Report of Joint Committee on Parliamentary Privilege (HL 43-I / HC 214-I (1999), at [68]).

In spite of the criticism, no steps were taken to repeal s.13 until 2013 when the Joint Committee on Parliamentary Privilege again recommended its repeal (HC Paper 30/ HC 100, 3 July 2013) on the grounds that the anomalies it created were more damaging than the injustice that it was intended to cure and there was no persuasive argument for granting either House a power of waiver or for restricting such a power to defamation cases alone (at [170]). The Government responded to the report in December 2013 (Cm 8771) and agreed that s.13 should go when parliamentary time permitted. The repeal of s.13 has now been achieved by Schedule 23 paragraph 44 of the Deregulation Act 2015 and consequently an MP can no longer waive the protection of privilege for the purpose of commencing or defending defamation proceedings.

*Note 302, add,* See also *Yeo v Times Newspapers Ltd* [2015] EWHC 2132 (QB); [2015] 1 W.L.R. 971. In that case journalists had posed as representatives of a company and had approached the claimant offering him cash in return for lobbying ministers. The journalists then wrote an article alleging that, in breach of the House of Commons' code of conduct, he had offered to act as a paid Parliamentary advocate. The MP brought libel proceedings. Objection was taken to the inclusion of complaints by the claimant that the defendant had withheld evidence or unreasonably delayed in providing evidence to the Parliamentary Standards Commissioner. The defendant argued that its case could not be advanced without infringing Parliamentary Privilege and in the circumstances of the case, it would be unfair to allow Mr Yeo to make this complaint, if TNL would be prevented or hampered by privilege from defending itself (at [42])). Warby J. accepted this submission and struck out the affected complaints.

**13.36**    **Defamation Act 2013, s.7** *Add*: Section 7 came into force with effect from 1 January 2014, and applies to all causes of action that accrued on or after that date.

SECTION 8. MISCELLANEOUS STATUTORY HEADS OF ABSOLUTE PRIVILEGE

**13.50**    **Miscellaneous statutory heads of absolute privilege.** *Add the following to the list of statutory provisions granting absolute privilege to notices, determinations, reports, etc. by regulators, ombudsmen and the like:*

Police, Public Order and Criminal Justice (Scotland) Act 2006, ss.42A and 46A (inserted by s.69 and 70 of the Police and Fire Reform (Scotland) Act 2012. Commissioner for Older People (Northern Ireland) Act 2011, s.22. Legal Services (Scotland) Act 2010, s.115.

CHAPTER 14

# QUALIFIED PRIVILEGE AT COMMON LAW PART I

## SECTION 1. INTRODUCTION

**Arrangement of the material.** *Note 27, add,* It is perfectly possible that a **14.2** communication might be protected under both *Reynolds* and traditional qualified privilege. That a claim to traditional qualified privilege fails would not prevent a court from concluding that the defendant could nevertheless rely on *Reynolds* privilege. However, it has been said on several occasions that where a defendant fails in a *Reynolds* plea in respect of a publication to the general public, it is hard to identify circumstances in which he could succeed on traditional qualified privilege (*Rai v Bholowasia* [2015] EWHC 382 (QB), at [154]*; Starr v Ward* [2015] EWHC 1987 (QB), at [38]; *Hays plc v Hartley* [2010] EWHC 1068 (QB) at [69]; and *Seaga v Harper* [2008] UKPC 9; [2009] 1 A.C. 1, at [15]).

**The limits of privilege for public authorities.** *Note 54, add,* In *Ma v St* **14.5** *George's Healthcare NHS Trust* [2015] EWHC 1866 (QB) Eady J. held that a communication made in a "Paediatric Liaison Health Visitor Referral Form" by a member of nursing staff in A & E about a child safeguarding issue to an on-site health visitor liaison officer whose responsibilities included child safeguarding was protected by qualified privilege. Any reference in such a communication to an adult in a way that damaged his reputation would in all likelihood pass the tests of necessity and proportionality (at [55]). The judge noted that wider publication among persons not having direct responsibilities for child safety and /or safeguarding matters might fall outside the protection of the privilege.

## SECTION 3. DUTY AND INTEREST: PARTICULAR SITUATIONS

### (a) *Communications made in discharge of a duty*

**Inquiries as to credit.** *Note 193, add,* See also the Irish case of *Cagney v* **14.28** *Governor and Company of the Bank of Ireland* [2015] IEHC 288 (HC) in which

Hedigan J. held that a communication by a bank about the financial credit of one of its customers made to the Irish Credit Bureau was made on an occasion of qualified privilege:

> "To do business, whether in the horse and buggy days of 1908 or the cyber world of today, one must be able to find ways to accurately assess the creditworthiness of those with whom one wishes to trade. That is done for financial institutions by the Irish Credit Bureau. The ability of those institutions to rely upon such an agency is crucial to their ability to provide ready, flexible ways for everyone to access credit and thereby use credit and debit cards and the ubiquitous ATM. All of these enhance and convenience many of the essential activities of modern daily life. Needless to say this should be done in a way that respects the privacy and the rights of the people affected. Thus in my judgment the communication of the information that the plaintiff's card was revoked in 2010 and that his account was settled short in 2012 was made on an occasion of qualified privilege" (at [8]).

**14.34**    **Volunteered statements in performance of a duty.** *Note 235, add,* See also, *Ma v St George's Healthcare NHS Trust* [2015] EWHC 1866 (QB) (communication via Paediatric Liaison Health Visitor Referral Form" made by nursing staff in A & E about child safeguarding issues to an on-site health visitor liaison officer whose responsibilities included child safeguarding was held to be protected by qualified privilege).

**14.48**    **Other common interests.** *Note 328, add,* In *Talbot v Hermitage Golf Club* [2014] IESC 57 (Irish Supreme Court), the court held that the trial judge had been correct to conclude that letters of complaint by members of a golf club about the alleged behaviour of another club member were protected by qualified privilege. So too, communication of a defamatory statement by the handicap committee of the club to a computer programmer employed by Genesys, a company responsible for auditing the operation of the handicapping system in the club, was protected by privilege:

> "The evidence established that there are over one thousand members in the Club and that the handicap sub-committee was solely responsible for ensuring that the playing handicap of each such member was constantly reviewed and validated in accordance with the requirements of the Standard Scratch Score and Handicapping System then in force. The work of the sub-committee was subject to random audit by Genesys. In the performance of this exacting and onerous task, the handicap sub-committee needed to constantly refer to the individual records of each playing member of the Club. The evidence established that a failure on the part of the handicap sub-committee to carry out their task efficiently and accurately could result in serious consequences for the Club, including the suspension or loss of handicaps so that members could no longer participate in the game of golf within the CONGU system.
>
>     In these circumstances I find that the third defendant and the other members of the handicap sub committee had a reasonable and a genuine interest in seeking out the computer software system which they considered was best suited to assist them in their task. For this purpose, the third defendant and the other members of the handicap sub-committee of the Club had an interest in communicating with Genesys and, having chosen that particular system, he and they had an interest in ensuring that a complete and accurate database was set up. This, as the minutes record, necessarily involved transferring all existing handicap details of members, including the details relating to the plaintiff, to this new system."

*Note 329, add*, The claim in *Owens v Grose* [2015] EWHC 839 (QB) arose out of a dispute in relation to a deposit paid to letting agents (as stakeholders) by the defendants as security for performance of their obligations under their tenancy agreement with the claimants. Letters containing allegedly defamatory imputations were written by the defendants to the letting agents and a company that was stated in the tenancy agreement to be available for resolving any disputes about deposits by final and binding adjudication. The parties accepted that communications between the tenant and letting agents and stakeholder for the deposit were made on an occasion of qualified privilege. Dingemans J. also held that the dispute resolution company "had a duty or interest in receiving the whole of the letter . . . because they were providing a dispute resolution service relating to the deposit" (at [37]) and consequently communications to them that were in any way related to or connected with the claim for retention of the deposit were protected.

*Note 333, add*, See also *Otuo v Morley and Watch Tower Bible & Tract Society of Britain* [2015] EWHC 1839 (QB) (strong prima facie case that communication during meeting to consider whether Jehovah's Witness who had been disfellowshipped should be reinstated was privileged (at [16])).

#### (d) *Relevance*

**A limited role for relevance.** *Note 471, add*, See also *Owens v Grose* [2015]   **14.64**
EWHC 839 (QB) at [36]-[37].

#### (e) *Excessive publication*

**Publication to uninterested persons.** *Note 507, add*, Cf. *Ma v St George's*   **14.69**
*Healthcare NHS Trust* [2015] EWHC 1866 (QB).

# CHAPTER 15

# PUBLICATION ON A MATTER OF PUBLIC INTEREST

SECTION 1. INTRODUCTION

**15.1**    **Background.** *Add at end of paragraph*: Section 4 of the Defamation Act 2013 is now in force and applies to publications that occurred on or after 1 January 2014. The common law *Reynolds* privilege has been abolished. (See Defamation Act 2013 (Commencement) (England and Wales) Order 2013 SI 2013/3027). In *Yeo v Times Newspapers Limited* [2014] EWHC 2853 (QB); [2015] 1 W.L.R. 971 at [78], Warby J. noted that in cases in which both were applicable, "The interplay between the two defences at common law and under the Act would need attention and seems rife with the potential for complications" on account for example of the possibly divergent positions on applicability to comment.

*Add to note 10*: Referring to the new section 4 defence, in *Barron v Vines* [2015] EWHC 1161 (QB) at [59], Warby J. noted that "It is, in general terms, a matter of high importance to afford political speech protection from the chilling effects which the law of defamation can have . . . this defence is potentially available to meet the need to allow trenchant expression on political matters. The defence can apply in cases where, as here, the defamatory statement contains allegations of fact which cannot be defended as true". See also, *Barron v Collins* [2015] EWHC 1125 (QB) at [54].

SECTION 2. CONCEPTUAL BASIS

**15.4**    **New statutory basis.** *Add*: Section 4 of the Defamation Act 2013 is now in force and applies to publications that occurred on or after 1 January 2014. In accordance with s.4(6), the common law *Reynolds* defence has been abolished.

*Add*: Interestingly, in *Ames v Spamhaus Project Ltd* [2015] EWHC 127 (QB); [2015] 1 W.L.R. 3409 at [109], counsel for the claimant suggested that "the English law public interest defence under s 4 of the Defamation Act 2013 is close to the *Sullivan* public figure defence". Warby J. did not need to determine the point, noting only that "that may or may not be so; that is a large topic".

**Subject matter of public interest.** *Add text following note 79*: Public figures'      **15.6**
knowledge of and failure to address evidence of long-running child sexual abuse
was held to be a matter of public interest in *Barron v Vines* [2015] EWHC 1161
(QB).

**Reasonable belief that publishing is in public interest.** *Add at end of par-*      **15.9**
*agraph*:

The operation of s.4(1) was considered by Warby J. in *Barron v Vines* (above)
with a particular focus on the issue of the subjective state of mind of the
defendant at the time of publishing. The defendant in the case was self-
represented and had offered something of a "muddle" by way of a defence (see
at [38], per Warby J.) In particular, he had emphasised that the meaning pleaded
by the claimant was not that which he had intended to convey. This was accepted
by the judge, but—in terms of its relevance for the determination of meaning—
was described as "plainly wrong in law" ([37]). Warby J. considered, however,
that the publisher's intended meaning—as opposed to that found by the court—
could conceivably be relevant to the s.4 defence. He considered that the criterion
in s.4(1)(b) to the effect that the defendant "reasonably believed that publishing
the statement complained of was in the public interest" is open to two tenable
interpretations. On one hand, it might be said that because he did not intend the
determined meaning the defendant "cannot have believed, let alone reasonably
believed, that it was in the public interest to make 'the statement complained of'"
([63]). Conversely, the judge mooted that because the phrase used in the particular provision was "statement complained of" rather than "imputation" (more
commonly used in the 2013 Act to refer to the determined meaning), it might be
arguable that "a reasonable belief that it is the public interest to make statement
A could be the basis for a defence, even if the words used unintentionally
conveyed meaning B". Warby J. considered that this second approach would
"seem more consistent with the previous law". The judge emphasised that his
reflections were "somewhat tentative and provisional", and that "there is inevitably some room for argument about [the provision's] exact scope and application
to particular facts" ([at 64]. On account of this dichotomy of tenable approaches
to the statutory provision, the judge determined that he would not grant a
summary judgment. Instead, he invited the defendant to take legal advice and to
determine whether he would pursue the possibility of developing the defence (at
[65]-[67]). In the event, the defendant declined to take this opportunity. As the
defence was not pursued further by the defendant, the proper interpretation of the
s.4 defence remains an open question. It is important to note that these observations were not merely obiter, but were offered without the benefit of any
argument, so cannot be seen as authoritative.

**Application to facts and opinion.** *Add at end of paragraph*: In *Barron v*      **15.19**
*Vines*, Warby J. noted that "in principle it seems [the defence] may be capable of
protecting expressions of opinion even though the defence of honest opinion is

not available—though commentators have observed that it is hard to envisage circumstances where this would be so":[2015] EWHC 1161 (QB) at [59].

**15.21**   **Irrelevance of malice.** *Add to note 203*: See also, *Yeo v Times Newspapers Limited (No2)* [2015] EWHC 209 (QB); [2015] 1 W.L.R. 3031 at [25] (per Warby J.): "Although the *Reynolds* defence is a species of privilege it is not the practice to plead malice in answer to a *Reynolds* defence". He was referring to the words of Lord Hoffmann in *Jameel v Wall Street Journal Europe Sprl* [2006] UKHL 44; [2007] 1 A.C. 359 at [46]: "There is no question of the privilege being defeated by proof of malice because the propriety of the conduct of the defendant is built into the conditions under which the material is privileged".

CHAPTER 16

## QUALIFIED PRIVILEGE: STATUTE

SECTION 1. INTRODUCTION

**In general.** *Add*: The Defamation Act 2013 came into force on 1 January **16.1** 2014. It does not affect causes of action which accrued before that date.

**Background.** *Insert the following after the second sentence in the second* **16.2** *paragraph of para.16.2*: The Defamation Act 2013, s.11, abolished the right to trial by jury in defamation cases in England and Wales (for all actions started on or after 1 January 2014). There remains a discretion to order trial by jury, but it is a discretion that will be exercised very rarely. Consequently, any tactical advantage that may previously have been gained by relying on the common law no longer exists.

*Delete the third and fourth sentences of the second paragraph of para.16.2.*

SECTION 2. PRIVILEGE CONFERRED BY SCH.1 TO THE DEFAMATION ACT 1996

**Public concern and public benefit.** *Add*: Defamation Act 2013 s.7 has been **16.5** in force since 1 January 2014 in respect of causes of action that accrued on or after that date. "'Public concern'" in s15(3) of the 1996 Act is therefore now replaced by "'public interest'" (s.7(2)). Juries are most unlikely to have any further role in determining public interest or public benefit, because by s.11 of the 2013 Act the right to trial by jury for defamation cases in England and Wales has been abolished for all actions started on or after 1 January 2014. There remains a residual discretion to order trial by jury, but it is likely to be exercised very rarely.

*Note 64, add*, The Defamation Act 2013, s.7 is now in force.

**Defamation Act 2013—Amendments to s.15 and Sch.1 of the 1996 Act.** **16.7** *Replace para.16.7 with the following*:

The Defamation Act 2013 (which, so far as is material, came into force on 1 January 2014 and affects causes of action that accrued on or after that date) amends in a number of respects s.15 and Sch.1 of the 1996 Act. The main effect of these provisions is to further "internationalise" the existing provisions extending the protection afforded by qualified privilege to reports of the proceedings of various institutions outside the European Union. This change was originally proposed in Lord Lester's Defamation Bill on the footing that there was no good reason why the statutory privilege should be so restricted, as it was, to publications relating to legislatures, governments, courts, public meetings and associations in the European Union. In view of this, and in response to concerns expressed by a number of organisations that they were regularly threatened by libel proceedings for quoting or citing public documents published in non-European Union countries, the government decided that it would be in the public interest to extend the scope of Pt II qualified privilege to publications beyond the confines of the United Kingdom and European Union. Section 7 also "internationalises" the provision relating to reports of proceedings at company meetings so that it covers the meetings of companies worldwide. The current restriction to meetings of UK public companies is also removed and the protection now applies to the meeting of any listed company (*note 73*). In addition to qualified privilege attaching to fair and accurate *copies of or extracts from* various types of publication, subs.(4), (7)(b) and (10) of s.7 of the Act extend the scope of qualified privilege to cover fair and accurate *summaries* of material (*note 74*). In response to concerns raised by the science community, the 2013 Act also introduced specific protection for reports of proceedings of an academic or scientific conference held anywhere in the world (*note 75*). Additionally, a qualified privilege now attaches, by virtue of s.6, to peer-reviewed statements in scientific or academic journals (*note 76*). These changes are considered at the appropriate points below.

(a) *Statements privileged under Schedule 1 without explanation or contradiction*

**16.10**     **Judicial Proceedings.** *Add*: The Defamation Act 2013 is now in force. The definition of 'court' is therefore amended (Defamation Act 2013, s.7(11).

**16.12**     **International organisations or conferences.** *Add*: Defamation Act 2013, s7(9) is now in force: see *note 106*.

(b) *Statements privileged under Schedule 1 subject to explanation or contradiction*

**16.17**     **Notices from governments, etc.** *Add*: Defamation Act 2013, s.7(4) is in force.

**16.18**     **Courts.** *Add*: Defamation Act 2013, s.7(4) is in force.

**16.19**     **Local Authority meetings, inquiries, etc.** *Add*: Defamation Act 2013, s.7(5) is in force.

**Public meetings in Member States.** *Add*: Defamation Act 2013, s.7(6) is in   **16.20**
force.

**Companies.** *Add*: Defamation Act 2013, s.7(7) is in force. "Listed com-   **16.21**
panies" has the same meaning as in Part 12 of the Corporation Tax Act 2009,
s.1005: see s.7(7)(b)(4).

**Associations.** *Add*: Defamation Act 2013, s.7(8) is in force.   **16.22**

**Proceedings of a scientific or academic conference.** *Add*: Defamation Act   **16.23**
2013, s.7(9) is in force.

**Designated bodies, etc.** *Add*: Para.15 of Schedule 1 of the 1996 Act, as   **16.24**
amended by s.7(10), Defamation Act 2013, now extends qualified privilege to a
fair and accurate report or summary of, copy of or extract from, any adjudication,
report, statement or notice issued by a body, officer or other person designated for
the purpose of this paragraph by order of the Lord Chancellor.

Section 3. Peer Reviewed Statements in Scientific or Academic Journals

**Peer-reviewed statements.** *Add*: Defamation Act 2013, s.6 is in force, and   **16.25**
applies to all causes of action that accrued on or after 1 January 2014.

Section 4. Miscellaneous Statutes Conferring Qualified Privilege

**Other statutory provisions.** *Add the following to the list of statutory provi-*   **16.28**
*sions granting qualified privilege to reports, determinations or the issue of*
*material to which the public have a right of access*: Pensions Act 2004, s.89A (as
inserted by Sch.4, para.12 of the Public Service Pensions Act 2013). Scottish
Parliamentary Commissions and Commissioners etc. Act 2010, s.5.
Ethical Standards in Public Life, etc. (Scotland) Act, s.27(1) (as amended by
Scottish Parliamentary Commissions and Commissioners etc. Act 2010, Sch.2,
para.3).

CHAPTER 17

## MALICE

SECTION 1. GENERAL

**17.2** **"Presumed" and "express" malice.** *Note 9, add*, On the pleading of malice, see 28.6 below and *Barry v Butler* [2015] EWHC 447, at [13]-[14].

**17.5** **Matter believed to be true but purpose to injure.** *Note 43, add*, See also *Rai v Bholowasia* [2015] EWHC 382 (QB): the fact that the defendant disliked the person whom he defamed, or was indignant at what he believed to be that person's conduct and welcomed the opportunity of expressing it, is not sufficient for the privilege to be lost if he is acting in compliance with a duty or in protection of a legitimate interest (at [166]).

**17.6** **Improper motive.** *Note 57, add*, The statement in the text above to the effect that it will be a rare case that malice will be established where a report is found to be fair and accurate was accepted as correct by Gillen J. in *Loughran v Century Newspapers Limited* [2014] N.I.Q.B. 26, at [22]. In that case, the words complained of had been found, as a matter of law, to be a fair and accurate copy or extract of matter published by or on the authority of the Northern Ireland Assembly and were therefore protected by statutory qualified privilege pursuant to Defamation Act 1996, s.15 and Sch.1, para.7. Nevertheless, Gillen J. rejected the defendant's application to strike out a pleading of malice. While the judge noted that it would be rare once a report had been shown to be fair for malice to be made out, the court should be wary of taking the issue of malice away from a jury (where there was one) and he could not say at that stage that no jury, properly directed, could justifiably make a finding of malice (at [31]).

**17.11** **Information as to crime.** *Note 83, add*, The decision of the Outer House was upheld on the qualified privilege issue by the Inner House, Court of Session: [2013] CSIH 46.

**17.17** **Untruth, belief and wilful blindness.** *Note 114, add*: See also *Owens v Grose* [2015] EWHC 839 (QB), per Dingemans J., at [40].

*Note 120, add*, For a case in which an allegation of malice failed, see *Ma v St George's Healthcare NHS Trust* [2015] EWHC 1866 (QB). See also *Owens v*

*Grose* [2015] EWHC 839 (QB) in which Dingemans J. reversed Master Kay QC's decision to allow the issue of malice to proceed to trial.

**Malice and variant meanings.** *Add*: In *Cruddas v Calvert* [2015] EWCA Civ **17.20** 171; [2015] E.M.L.R. 16 (discussed at paras.21.5 and 21.8: a malicious falsehood case), the Court of Appeal held that because the test of malice is subjective, knowledge must be assessed by reference to the meaning which the defendant intends to convey (at [111]). Of course, in such a claim the single meaning rule does not apply and more than one meaning of the words complained of may be possible. The court in *Cruddas* held that:

" . . . if (a) an article has one correct meaning which is true but is susceptible to a second incorrect interpretation by some cynical readers which is untrue, (b) the author intends the article to convey its correct meaning but foresees that some cynical readers will place upon it the incorrect interpretation, then that does not constitute malice for the purpose of malicious falsehood" (at [111]).

CHAPTER 18

# EFFECTS OF REHABILITATION

SECTION 1. INTRODUCTION

**18.1**    **The common law.** *Note 1, add*, The Supreme Court in *R v Chief Constable of Greater Manchester Police* [2014] UKSC 35; [2015] A.C. 49 (see below, at para.18.13) concluded that cautions and convictions received by individuals represent an aspect of their private life protected under art.8. A caution, which is given in private, was said to be part of a person's private life from the outset:

> "My receipt of a caution, whenever received, is a sensitive, certainly embarrassing and probably shameful, part of my history, which may have profound detrimental effects on my aspirations for a career; and the unchallengeable fact that I did commit the offence for which I was cautioned makes it no less sensitive but, on the contrary, more sensitive" (at [17]).

A conviction will of course be imposed in public but as it recedes into the past it becomes a part of the person's private life. The point at which the conviction recedes into the past and becomes a part of a person's private life will usually be the point at which it becomes spent under the 1974 Act (at [18]).

In the light of this decision, it is certainly open to a court to conclude that disclosure of a past caution or conviction, even if not technically spent, should give rise to a claim for misuse of private information. (See further para.22.5 below.)

**18.4**    **Reform of the Rehabilitation of Offenders Act.** *Replace final sentence of para.18.4 with the following*:

Legal Aid, Sentencing and Punishment Act 2012, s.139 was brought into force on 10 March 2014 by the Legal Aid, Sentencing and Punishment of Offenders Act 2012 (Commencement No.9, Saving Provision and Specification of Commencement Date) Order 2014.

SECTION 2. SPENT CONVICTIONS

**18.5**    **Conviction needed.** *Insert after fourth sentence in para.18.5*: While a conviction followed by an absolute or conditional discharge is treated as a conviction for the purposes of the Act, s.14 of the Powers of the Criminal Courts (Sentencing) Act 2000 has the effect of rendering the provision of almost no relevance in that it provides that for almost all purposes a conviction for an offence for which an order of conditional or absolute discharge is issued shall not be deemed a conviction for any purpose other than the purposes of the proceedings in which the order is made and of any subsequent proceedings which may be taken against the offender in the event that he commits a further offence.

**Sentences excluded from rehabilitation.** *Replace first sentence of para.18.6*  **18.6**
*with the following*: Some sentences are excluded from rehabilitation; they are (a) imprisonment for life, (*note 21*) (b) imprisonment (or youth custody, detention in a youth offender institution or corrective training for a term exceeding 48 months (*note 22*), and (c) certain equivalent sentences (*note 23*).

*Replace fourth and fifth sentence of para.18.6 with the following*:

Thus if X was convicted in 2005 and sentenced to 30 months' imprisonment (for which the rehabilitation period is seven years: s.139(4) LASPO amending Rehabilitation of Offenders Act s.5(1)(b) and (d)) and in 2011 was convicted again and sentenced to five years imprisonment, he cannot become rehabilitated in respect of either conviction (Rehabilitation of Offenders Act 1974, s.1(1)). If on the other hand, the second conviction is not until 2013, he will have become a rehabilitated person in respect of the first conviction, but cannot become so in respect of the second.

*Note 22, replace existing text with the following:* Section.139(2) LASPO amending Rehabilitation of Offenders Act s.5(2).

*Note 23, replace existing text with the following:* For example, sentence of preventive detention and public protection sentences.

**Rehabilitation period: substantial sentences.** *Replace para.18.7 with the*  **18.7**
*following*:

The rehabilitation period applicable to any conviction is based not on the nature of the offence for which the individual was convicted, but on the nature and length of the sentence imposed. The main periods for both adult offenders and those under the age of 18 at the time of conviction are found in Table A of s.5(2) of the Act which has been significantly amended by s.139(4) LASPO (*new note 26A*). Where the sentence is of imprisonment for a term of more than 30 months and up to, or consisting of 48 months, the period of rehabilitation is seven years beginning with the day on which the sentence (including any licence period) is completed (*new note 26B*). The rehabilitation period where the offender was under 18 at the date of conviction is 42 months. Where the sentence is of imprisonment for a term of more than six months and up to, or consisting of 30 months, the period of rehabilitation is 48 months (*new note 26C*) or 24 months for an offender under the age of 18. Where the sentence of imprisonment is for six months or less, the period of rehabilitation is 24 months (*new note 26D*) or 18 months in the case of an offender under the age of 18. The period of rehabilitation for a person removed from Her Majesty's Service or sentenced to a period of service detention is 12 months (*new note 26E*). There are also provisions in the amended Table for certain sentences confined to young offenders (*new note 26F*).

*New Note 26A:* The Rehabilitation of Offenders Act 1974, s.5(2)(a) provides that the periods of rehabilitation are subject to a reduction by half where the sentence is imposed on someone who is under 18 at the date of conviction.

*New Note 26B:* S.139(4) LASPO amending Rehabilitation of Offenders Act s.5(2)(a) Table A.

*New Note 26C:* S.139(4) LASPO amending Rehabilitation of Offenders Act s.5(2)(a) Table A.

*New Note 26D:* (s.139(4) LASPO amending Rehabilitation of Offenders Act s.5(2)(a) Table A.

*New Note 26E:* S.139(4) LASPO amending Rehabilitation of Offenders Act s.5(2)(a) Table A.

*New Note 26F:* S.139(4) LASPO amending Rehabilitation of Offenders Act s.5(2)(a) Table B)

**18.8**     **Other sentences.** *Replace para.18.8 with the following*:

Following the coming into effect of the Legal Aid, Sentencing and Punishment Act 2012 (LASPO), s.139, there is now no period of rehabilitation for an order discharging a person absolutely (*new note 26G*). The period where a person is conditionally discharged, bound over to keep the peace or be of good behaviour is the period of the order (*new note 26H*)). The same rule applies to certain orders and requirements relating to children and young persons (*new note 26I*). A simple caution is now spent immediately (*new note 26J*), while a period of three months applies to a conditional caution and youth conditional condition (*new note 26K*). Where a probation order or a community service order is made, the period of rehabilitation is now one year (*new note 26L*) except in the case of a person under the age of 18 at the date of conviction, in which case it is six months beginning with the day provided for by or under the order as the last day on which the order is to have effect (*new note 26M*). Where a hospital order is made, the rehabilitation period applicable to the sentence shall be the period of five years from the date of conviction or a period beginning with that date and ending two years after the date on which the hospital order ceases or ceased to have effect, whichever is the longer (*new note 26N*). In the case of any other order, the period of rehabilitation is now the day provided for by or under the order as the last day on which the order is to have effect (*new note 26O*). Where an order is made imposing on the person convicted any disqualification, disability, prohibition or other penalty, the rehabilitation period applicable to the sentence shall be a period beginning with the date of conviction and ending on the date on which the disqualification, disability, prohibition or penalty (as the case may be) ceases or ceased to have effect (*note 38*).

*New Note 26G:* S.139(4) LASPO amending Rehabilitation of Offenders Act s.5(2)(a).

*New Note 26H:* S.139(4) LASPO amending Rehabilitation of Offenders Act s.5(3)(a).

*New Note 26I:* S.139(4) LASPO amending Rehabilitation of Offenders Act s.5(4)(B), 4(C).

*New Note 26J:* S.139(4) LASPO and Sch.2.

*New Note 26K:* S.139(4) LASPO and Sch.2.

*New Note 26L:* S.139(4) LASPO amending Rehabilitation of Offenders Act s.5(4)(A).

*New Note 26M:* s.139(4) LASPO amending Rehabilitation of Offenders Act s.5(4)(A).

*New Note 26N:* Rehabilitation of Offenders Act s.5(7).

*New Note 26O:* s.139(4) LASPO amending Rehabilitation of Offenders Act s.5(4)(A).

*Note 33, add,* and Legal Aid, Sentencing and Punishment Act 2012, s.139(4).

**Period applicable to conviction.** *Note 40, add,* Where two or more sentences   **18.9**
are consecutive, the sentences are added together to calculate the rehabilitation
period. For concurrent periods, the longest applicable rehabilitation period will
apply to all the sentences. (s.139(4) LASPO amending Rehabilitation of Offenders Act s.5(9)).

**Subsequent Offences.** *Replace from second sentence until end of para.18.10*   **18.10**
*with the following*: Thus, if a person was convicted and sentenced to 30 months'
imprisonment in 2005 (for which the period of rehabilitation is seven years) and
was convicted and fined in 2006 (for which the period of rehabilitation is 12
months) both rehabilitation periods would have ended in 2012. If, on the other
hand, he had been fined on the first occasion and sentenced to 30 months on the
second, both periods would have ended in 2013. Where, however, the rehabilitation period applicable to one of the convictions is that applicable to an order
imposing any disqualification, disability, prohibition or other penalty, the period
of the other conviction is to be extended, if at all, only by reference to the longest
period applicable to any other sentence imposed along with the penalty (Rehabilitation of Offenders Act 1974, s.6(8)). Thus, if the person in the first example
above had been disqualified from driving for 10 years on his second conviction
as well as being fined, the rehabilitation period for the first conviction would still
end in 2012, even though that for the second conviction would continue until
2015.

SECTION 3. EFFECTS OF REHABILITATION

**18.12**    **Effects of rehabilitation.** *Note 56, add,* See also *A v B (evidence: spent conviction)* [2013] I.R.L.R. 434.

**18.13**    **Extrajudicial consequences.** *Note 57, add,* Under the Powers of Criminal Courts (Sentencing) Act 2000, 14(1), a conviction for an offence for which an order is made discharging the offender absolutely or conditionally shall be deemed not to be a conviction for most purposes. Consequently, a person who has been absolutely or conditionally discharged following a conviction, does not make a false representation if the answer is "no" when asked if he has ever been "convicted" of an offence (*Omenma* [2014] UKUT 00314 (IAC)). What the position would be if a person was asked whether they had been "found guilty" of an offence is not entirely clear. In *R v Patel (Rupal)* [2007] 1 Cr. App. R12 (CA) Hughes L.J. suggested that the person might have to disclose his guilt but this is surely doubtful. The editors of *Archbold* (2014) at 623 view this latter point as *obiter* and they make the following observation: "This however, must remain open to argument; a conclusion so completely at odds with the purpose and intent of the provision could hardly be justified on the basis of semantics."

*Insert at the end of para.18.13*:

The compatibility of the Rehabilitation of Offenders Act 1974 (Exceptions) order 1975 SI 1975/102 (1975 Order) with the Human Rights Act 1998 has been the subject of judicial review proceedings in *R v Chief Constable of Greater Manchester Police*. The Court of Appeal concluded (*new note 62A*), inter alia, that the 1975 Order was incompatible with art.8 ECHR in so far as it required the disclosure of all convictions and cautions that were recorded on central records on certificates. The court declared the whole Order incompatible with art.8 and ultra vires the Rehabilitation of Offenders Act. The effect of the decision was that the 1975 Order had been incompatible with art.8 since the coming into effect of the Human Rights Act 1998 and consequently any decision to dismiss or not to hire in reliance on disclosures made had been unlawful.

Subsequent to the Court of Appeal decision, the Secretary of State issued an amendment to the 1975 Order—the Rehabilitation of Offenders Act 1974 (Exceptions) Order 1975 (Amendment) (England and Wales) Order 2013 SI 2013/1198 (2013 Order)—in an attempt to bring the disclosure requirements within the protection of art.8 and to clarify the disclosure requirements when an employer in certain categories asks about a conviction or caution. The 2013 Order introduces the concept of "protected cautions" and "protected convictions". A caution is protected if it was given otherwise than for any of 14 listed categories of offence and if at least six years have passed since the date of the caution (or two years if the person was then a minor): art.4. A conviction is protected if it was imposed otherwise than for any of the listed categories; if it did not result in a custodial sentence; if the person has not been convicted of any other offence; and if at least 11 years have passed since the date of the conviction (or five-and-a-half years if he was then a minor): art.4. The effect of the new regime is that cautions and convictions will not have to be disclosed to specified employers when the stated additional rehabilitation period has passed. However, the new regime does not apply when questions are asked in order to assess a person's suitability for a few specified types of employment: art.6.

The Supreme Court (*new note 62B*) agreed with the Court of Appeal that the 1975 Order constituted an interference with art.8 (*new note 62C*) and therefore required justification under art.8(2). While there is a clear public interest in ensuring the suitability of applicants for certain positions (namely the protection of certain vulnerable groups) the court held that 1975 Order operated indiscriminately:

> "There was no attempt to separate the spent convictions and the cautions which should, and should not, then be disclosed by reference to any or all of the following: (a) the species of the offence; (b) the circumstances in which the person committed it; (c) his age when he committed it; (d) in the case of a conviction, the sentence imposed upon him; (e) his perpetration or otherwise of further offences; (f) the time that elapsed since he committed the offence; and (g) its relevance to the judgement to be made by the person making the request" (*new note 62D*).

Accordingly, it could only be concluded that the interference in issue had not been necessary in a democratic society. While the Supreme Court agreed that the 1975 Order, in so far as it applied to the applicants, breached art.8, they held that the Court of Appeal should not have declared the 1975 Order ultra vires as the remedies under Human Rights Act 1998, ss.4 and 8 were not available to them (*new note 62E*). On the facts of the case, the court also held that no further remedy was necessary as the applicant had obtained sufficient just satisfaction by the courts' acceptance that his complaint was well founded and the resultant amendment of the Order (*new note 62F*). Consequently, the decision of the Supreme Court reinstated the 1975 Order as amended by the 2013 Order.

Following the decision of the Supreme Court and 2013 Order, the position with regard to disclosure of convictions and cautions where the Exceptions Order applies is that, subject to exceptions for specified classes of employment (art.4), a person is not under an obligation to disclose spent convictions and cautions where such conviction or caution was not given for an offence listed in art-.2(A)(5) of the 2013 Order, the specified period of time has passed (six years for a caution) and, in the case of a conviction, a sentence other than custody or service detention was imposed, the person has not been convicted of any other offence at any time and, where the person was aged 18 or over at the time of the conviction 11 years or more have passed since the date of conviction. Further, an employer may undertake disciplinary proceedings relating to a caution which is spent but not protected.

*New Note 62A:* [2013] EWCA Civ 25.

*New Note 62B:* [2014] UKSC 35; [2015] A.C. 49.

*New Note 62C:* Ibid, at [16]. See also *Gallagher's Application for Judicial Review* [2015] N.I.Q.B. 63 in which Treacy J. concluded that the automatic disclosure requirements in the Northern Irish equivalent of the Exceptions Order

(Rehabilitation of Offenders (Exceptions) Order (Northern Ireland) 1979 also violated art.8.

*New Note 62D:* Ibid, at [41].

*New Note 62E:* Ibid, at [149]-[150].

*New Note 62F:* Ibid, at [157].

Section 4. Defamation Proceedings

18.16     **Justification.** *Note 68, add*, Defamation Act 2013, s.16(2) is now in force.

*Note 69, add*, Defamation Act 2013, s.16(3) is now in force.

18.18     **Honest Comment** *Note 82, add*, Defamation Act 2013, s.16(2) is now in force.

CHAPTER 19

# OTHER DEFENCES

SECTION 1. THE OFFER OF AMENDS PROCEDURE

**The Defamation Act 1996.** *Add*: A helpful summary of the regime contained  **19.2**
in ss.2-4 of the 1996 Act can be found in the judgment of Sharp L.J. in *Murray
v Associated Newspapers Ltd* [2015] EWCA Civ 488; [2015] E.M.L.R. 21, at
[3]-[4].

**If offer accepted.** *Note 35, add*, In *Murray v Associated Newspapers Ltd*  **19.4**
[2015] EWCA Civ 488; [2015] E.M.L.R. 21 the Court of Appeal agreed (at [5])
with the view expressed in *Winslet v Associated Newspaper* [2009] EWHC 2735
(QB); [2010] E.M.L.R. 11 that a claimant who has accepted an offer of amends
can apply to the court for permission to read out a statement in open court in
accordance with the provisions of CPR Part 53, PD para 6.3. The court emphasised the value of such a statement, as an endpoint to litigation, in providing the
means for more publicity to be given to a settlement and therefore to the
claimant's vindication than might otherwise occur. Any statement in court
(whether unilateral or joint) must be fair and proportionate and should not
misrepresent a party's case, or the nature of any settlement reached (at [31]).
However, because a party making their statement in open court is exercising their
right to freedom of expression, a court should not intervene in a unilateral
statement in the absence of any real or substantial unfairness to the objecting or
other third party and "nit-picks" are to be discouraged (at [27]). No different
approach in this respect should exist where the statement is made after the
acceptance of an offer of amends under ss.2-4 Defamation Act 1996. See further
para.29.10, below.

SECTION 3. CONSENT

**Consent.** *Add*: The defence will not inevitably fail unless the defendant can  **19.10**
prove that the claimant consented to the publication of the precise words. In
*Stocker v Stocker* [2015] EWHC 1634; [2015] E.M.L.R. 24, Warby J. stated that

it would arguably be enough to show that the claimant had procured the publication of the allegations complained of (at [28]).

Warby J. referred in support of this view to *Dar Al Arkan Real Estate Development Company v Al Refai* [2013] EHHC 1630 (Comm) in which Andrew Smith J. had held that it was not necessary, in order to fix a person with joint liability for a publication, to show that the defendant knew the precise words complained of before they were published (at [32]-[34]). See also *R v Cooper* (1846) 8 Q.B. 533 per Lord Denman C.J. at 535-6 and *Parkes v Prescott* (1868-69) L.R. 4 Ex. 169 per Montague Smith J. at 178.

Section 4. Limitation

**19.13**    **Basic principle and history.** *Replace first three sentences of para.19.13 with the following*:

Like any other cause of action in tort, one for defamation is barred by the passage of time (note 88). Under the Limitation Act 1939, re-enacted by the Limitation Act 1980, the period of limitation was the general period in tort, that is to say six years from the date of the accrual of the cause of action (*note 89*). At common law, accrual of the cause of action in libel and in slander actionable per se occurred at the date of publication because at that moment the cause of action was complete (note 90); but in the case of slander actionable only on proof of special damage (*note 91*), the cause of action accrued and time began to run at the time the damage was sustained, for until then the cause of action is incomplete (*note 92*).

Whether the position is the same now that the Defamation Act 2013, s.1 is in force is not entirely straightforward. Under s.1 of the Act, the tort is not complete until serious harm has been caused or serious harm is likely to be caused (*new note 92A*). In other words, s.1 now provides two different and alternative ways of establishing that the tort is complete: either by proving as a fact that serious reputational harm has already been suffered or, alternatively, that it probably will be suffered in future (*new note 92B*).

There may be cases, perhaps involving the most serious libels, where the cause of action will be complete at the moment of publication or at least a short period of time afterwards. If, for example, a public figure is accused in a national newspaper of being a paedophile, it is highly likely that a court would draw an inference of serious harm almost from the moment of publication. (*new note 92C*).

Where, however, a grave allegation is published but the publication is more limited, say on a blog which has a small number of readers, and (for instance) the claimant is not named or is not a public figure, determining the time at which the cause of action is complete may be much more difficult. Obviously, if the claimant could establish he had lost his job as a result of the allegation, that would be sufficient to prove serious harm and time might run from then. What if, however, no such "concrete" harm can be shown? How many unique views of the blog, for example, would have to be established before the threshold was met? Uncertainty about the time of accrual of a cause of action is highly undesirable and likely to give rise to considerable difficulties in advising clients when to issue the claim but this seems to be an inevitable consequence of treating proof of serious harm to reputation as the trigger for the accrual of the cause of action.

Similar difficulties are likely to arise where a claim is based not on serious harm to reputation having been caused but instead on the likelihood of it being caused. The first time at which it may be shown that serious harm is likely to be caused must be the time of publication. It is at that moment that a statement has been put in circulation that has the potential to cause serious harm to the claimant. However, there may of course be cases where it would not be possible to show at that time that serious harm was more likely than not to result from the statement. Where this is so the judge will have to find on the facts of each particular case when the cause of action has accrued.

*New Note 92A:* See further paras.2.5-2.8 above.

*New Note 92B: Lachaux v Independent Print Limited* [2015] EWHC 2242 (QB), [2015] E.M.L.R. 28 at [47].

*New Note 92C:* In *Cooke v MGN Limited* [2014] EWHC 2831 (QB); [2015] 1 W.L.R. 895 Bean J. pointed out at [31] that the Act did not make clear which moment marked the dividing line between past ("has caused") and future ("likely to cause"), and ruled out the moment of publication, since at the time of publication no harm could be said to have been caused. That may be questionable. In many of the most serious cases—such as in the example above— serious harm will surely have been suffered at precisely the moment of publication, which is the moment when the damaging statement is read.

**Defamation Act 2013, s.8—single publication rule and accrual of cause of**   **19.15**
**action.** Section 8, Defamation Act 2013 is now in force. See further, para.2.5 above.

**Concealment.** *Note 117, add,* In *Arcadia Group Brands Ltd. v Visa Inc.* [2015]   **19.19**
EWCA Civ 883 (not a libel case) the Court of Appeal accepted that *C v Mirror Group Newspapers Ltd.* [1997] 1 W.L.R. 131 (CA), *Johnson v Chief Constable of Surrey* (CA, unreported, 23 November 1992) and *AIC Ltd v. ITS Testing Services (UK) Ltd, The "Kriti Palm"* [2006] EWCA Civ 1601 were authority for the following principles applicable to s.32(1)(b) of the 1980 Act:

> "(1) a "fact relevant to the plaintiff's right of action" within s.32(1)(b) is a fact without which the cause of action is incomplete; (2) facts which merely improve prospects of success are not facts relevant to the claimant's right of action; (3) facts bearing on a matter which is not a necessary ingredient of the cause of action but which may provide a defence are not facts relevant to the claimant's right of action" (at [49]).

**Exercise of the discretion.** *Note 131, add,* See also *Otuo v The Watchtower*   **19.21**
*Bible and Tract Society of Britain* [2015] EWHC 509 (QB), at [18].

*Note 132, add,* See also *Bewry v Reed Elsevier UK Ltd* [2014] EWCA Civ 1411; [2015] 1 W.L.R. 2565, at [4].

*Note 144, add,* In *Otuo v The Watchtower Bible and Tract Society of Britain* [2015] EWHC 509 (QB) H.H.J. Parkes Q.C. refused to disapply the primary limitation period even though the claimant was only one day out of time. As a result of a mistake as to the exact date by which he should have issued the claim, the claim was issued a day late. However, the claimant had made no complaint at all until then and consequently the judge refused to exercise the discretion in s.32A.

*Note 145, add,* In *Starr v Ward* [2015] EWHC 1987 Nicol J. refused to disapply the limitation period to a case where the period of delay was a little over ten months and the claimant had offered no explanation at all for the delay after the primary limitation period had expired.

*Note 147, add,* Ignorance of the limitation period will rarely if ever be a factor which carries any weight in the exercise of the discretion: *Bewry v Reed Elsevier UK Ltd* [2014] EWCA Civ 1411; [2015] 1 W.L.R. 2565 at [36]. As Sharp L.J. explained:

> "A claimant is expected to pursue his complaint promptly irrespective of the limitation period and whether he knows about it, for the simple reason that not to do so is inconsistent with a genuine wish to pursue vindication of his character promptly and vigorously, which is what the law requires. Ignorance could only be relevant in the most marginal type of case, where a claimant is actively misled for example, but on its facts this was not such a marginal case."

*Note 151, add,* That the claimant had previously sought advice from lawyers and been told that he did not have a viable claim would presumably also be a matter that a court could take into account in considering whether to exercise the discretion.

*Note 153, add*: In *Starr v Ward* [2015] EWHC 1987, Nicol J. concluded that the effect of prejudice to the claimant in striking out one of the several slander claims was not very great. The claimant would still be able to vindicate his reputation albeit that he would lose some compensation for the claim struck out.

*Note 154, add,* See also *Otuo v The Watchtower Bible and Tract Society of Britain* [2015] EWHC 509 (QB), at [31].

*Insert the following after the final sentence of para 19.21:*

Delay after proceedings have been issued is also a relevant factor in determining whether to exercise the discretion. In *Bewry v Reed Elsevier UK Ltd* [2014] EWCA Civ 1411; [2015] 1 W.L.R. 2565 the claimant knew there were significant limitation problems with his claim from the outset and yet did not issue his application to bring his otherwise time-barred publications into the claim for six and a half months. The Court of Appeal held that s.32A(2)(b)(ii) of the Limitation Act 1980 requires the court to consider "the extent to which [the claimant] acted promptly and reasonably once he knew whether or not the facts in question might be capable of giving rise to an action." This was said to be a question that looks forward to all of the claimant's conduct from the point at which he had the relevant knowledge and consequently encompasses delay after issue of proceedings (at [38]).

<br>

SECTION 5. JUDGMENT RECOVERED AND RES JUDICATA

**The nature of the defence.** *Note 159, add*, In *Building Register Ltd. v Weston*   **19.22**
[2014] EWHC 2361 (QB) Nicola Davies J. refused to allow the defendant to
amend its pleadings on the basis that the proposed amendment constituted an
impermissible attempt to re-litigate a case which one of the defendants had
brought unsuccessfully in related proceedings. Absent special circumstances, the
parties could not return to the court to advance arguments, claims or defences
which they could have put forward for decision on the first occasion but failed to
raise.

By way of contrast, in *Tanner v Filby* [2003] All E.R. (D) 279 Eady J. refused
to strike out defences of justification and fair comment on grounds of abuse and
issue estoppel where some of the issues raised by them had been previously
litigated in the small claims court. The small claims proceedings had not comprised the same parties as the instant action and although there was a degree of
overlap in terms of the raw factual data in both actions there was not a complete
match of factual issues. Further he held that to use the small claims action to
prevent the defendants from criticising the claimant, or from defending themselves in a High Court action which concerned their right to free speech, would
run contrary to established common law principles and the requirements of the
ECHR. In the *Building Register Ltd. v Weston* case, Nicola Davies J was referred
to *Tanner* but concluded that the facts were sufficiently different in the two cases
to justify different conclusions being reached (at [65]). Unlike *Tanner,* in which
a decision that the defendant was barred from raising defences of justification and
fair comment would have prevented them from raising any defence and exercising their right to criticise the claimant, the decision in *Building Register Ltd. v
Weston* permitted continuance of the proceedings upon issues which it was fair to
try and also allowed the defendants the opportunity at trial, to prove the truth of
and justify the remainder of the words of which complaint was made. The
proceedings permitted, if appropriate, the vindication of reputation and did not
deprive the defendants of their rights pursuant to Articles 6 and 10 of the ECHR
(at [66]).

*Note 160, add*, In the Irish case of *O'Hara v ACC Bank PLC* [2011] IEHC 367,
Charlton J. held that the rules of issue estoppel may apply to quasi-judicial
tribunals, even though the jurisdiction which they exercise may be specific to
them and not necessarily exercisable by a court (at [19]).

CHAPTER 21

# MALICIOUS FALSEHOOD

SECTION 2. MALICIOUS FALSEHOOD

**21.4**   **Reference to the claimant.** *Note 33, add*, In *Niche Products Ltd v MacDermid Offshore Solutions LLC* [2013] EWHC 3540 (IPEC); [2014] E.M.L.R. 9 it was held to be plainly arguable that a letter which contained the allegedly false words did sufficiently refer to the claimant even though it was not mentioned by name (at [11]).

**21.5**   **Meaning and malicious falsehood.** *Insert the following at end of 21.5*:

While it is clear that the single meaning rule no longer applies in malicious falsehood claims and that the court should identify all reasonably available meanings, liability in malicious falsehood only exists where the claimant can establish that the defendant was malicious. For that purpose, the mere fact that the defendant foresaw or ought to have foreseen that the words complained of might be found to carry more than one meaning. at least one of which was false, is not without more enough to make him malicious. As Jackson L.J. noted in *Cruddas v Calvert* (*new note 42A*), "To require a journalist to expressly disavow every foreseeable, albeit incorrect and unintended, interpretation of what she or he had written would have an unacceptably chilling effect on free speech while at the same time making newspaper articles tortuous to read" (*new note 42B*). Moreover, to impose liability in such a case would expand unacceptably the ambit of the tort. Consequently, he concluded that liability should only arise in malicious falsehood if the falsehood represented one of the possible correct meanings of the defendant's words and the defendant intended to convey that falsehood: (*new note 42C*).

> "Since the test for malice is subjective, knowledge of falsity must be assessed by reference to the meaning which the Defendant intends to convey. In my view, if (a) an article has one correct meaning which is true but is susceptible to a second incorrect interpretation by some cynical readers which is untrue, (b) the author intends the article to convey its correct meaning but foresees that some cynical readers will place upon it the incorrect interpretation, then that does not constitute malice for the purpose of malicious falsehood" (*new note 42D*).

The court concluded, with regard to the allegation that the claimant had, in return for cash donations to the Conservative Party, offered the opportunity to influence government policy, that reasonable people could interpret this as meaning either that: (1) the claimant had made this offer corruptly; or, (2) the claimant had in making the offer committed the criminal offence of corruption under the Bribery Act 2010. It was common ground that the second meaning was not true. In an earlier appeal on meaning (*new note 42E*) the Court of Appeal had said that they could not be certain that a reasonable number of people would not have understood the articles as making an imputation of criminal corruption and consequently that meaning was available for the purposes of malicious falsehood even though it was "plainly wrong" (*new note 42F*). The question of malice had to be considered against this background.

At trial, Tugendhat J had concluded that it was more probable than not that the journalists knew that cynics would read the article as meaning that the claimant was proposing criminal bribes, even though the article did not mean that and the journalists did not intend it to mean that. The judge nevertheless concluded on these facts that the journalists were malicious. The Court of Appeal disagreed. The test of malice is subjective and where, as here, an article has a correct meaning (the claimant made the offer corruptly) but is also susceptible to a second incorrect interpretation by cynical readers (the corruption was criminal), malice will not exist if the author intends the article to convey the correct meaning albeit that he foresees some cynical readers will place on it an incorrect interpretation.

*New Note 42A:* [2015] EWCA Civ 171; [2015] E.M.L.R. 16.

*New Note 42B:* Ibid, at [112].

*New Note 42C:* Ibid, at [114].

*New Note 42D:* Ibid, at [111].

*New Note 42D:* [2013] EWCA Civ 748; [2014] E.M.L.R. 5.

*New Note 42F:* Ibid, at [31]-[32].

**Malice.** *Note 58, add,* In *Niche Products Ltd v MacDermid Offshore Solutions LLC* [2013] EWHC 3540 (IPEC); [2014] E.M.L.R 9, Birss J. struck out words in Particulars of Claim that suggested that malice could be established on the basis either that the defendant knew or *at least a reasonable person in the position of the defendant would have known* that the report about the defendant's product was misleading (at [61]).     **21.8**

*Note 64, add,* See also *Niche Products Ltd v MacDermid Offshore Solutions LLC*, above, at [55].

*Note 66, add,* See also, *Niche Products Ltd v MacDermid Offshore Solutions LLC*, above, at [57]-58].

*Note 72, add,* See now the decision of the Court of Appeal in *Cruddas v Calvert* [2015] EWCA Civ 171; [2015] E.M.L.R. 16 (which reverses in part the decision of Tugendhat J. [2013] EWHC 2298 (QB)). This is discussed in detail at para.21.5 above and below.

*Note 74, add,* But see *Niche Products Ltd v MacDermid Offshore Solutions LLC,* above, in which the judge refused to strike out an allegation of malice based on the pursuit of self-interest as the defendant's only or dominant motive (at [55]-[60]).

*Note 78, add,* See also *Camurat v Thurrock Borough Council* [2014] EWHC 2482 (QB). This was a malicious falsehood claim arising out of reference given following a compromise agreement. The judge found that the defendant was undoubtedly "glad to see the back of the claimant" but said that he was "satisfied that she would not have been a party to deliberate exaggerations or falsification of allegations. I believe that everything that she did, whether it was right or wrong, was driven by a genuine belief that the Claimant was a risk to children" (at [89]).

The decision of Tugendhat J. in *Cruddas v Calvert* [2013] EWHC 2298 (QB) was appealed by the defendants and the appeal was allowed in part (*Cruddas v Calvert* [2015] EWCA Civ 171; [2015] E.M.L.R.16). So far as the malicious falsehood claims were concerned, the Court of Appeal allowed the defendants' appeal in respect of the first imputation, namely that the claimant had, in return for cash donations to the Conservative Party, offered the opportunity to influence government policy. As is explained above at para.21.5, liability can only arise in malicious falsehood if the falsehood represents one of the possible correct meanings of the defendant's words and the defendant intended to convey that falsehood (at [114]). As the defendant did not intend readers to understand the words in the incorrect, but possible, meaning that the claimant was criminally corrupt in making the offer, malice could not be established (at 111]-[116]). However, so far as the remaining imputations were concerned—the so-called foreign donations allegations—the Court of Appeal upheld the judge's decision. The defendant journalists knew that the articles carried the meanings alleged by the claimant and also knew those meanings to be untrue. In particular, they knew that the claimant had not suggested any breach of the criminal law or shown himself willing to commit an offence in respect of the foreign donations (at 118-125]).

**21.13**  **Damage must be pecuniary.** *Note 98, add,* In *Niche Products Ltd v Mac-Dermid Offshore Solutions LLC* [2013] EWHC 3540 (IPEC); [2014] E.M.L.R. 9 Birss J. struck out a claim for lost management time as speculative: "any allegedly malicious falsehood by a trade rival could always be said to require some management time to be spent "verifying" whether it was true or no" (at [40]). Such a claim will not inevitably fail however. If the claimant can establish lost sales then steps taken (including by management) to mitigate that loss would be recoverable on general principles.

*New Note 100A to be inserted after the word 'reputation' in the second sentence:*

See, for example, *Niche Products Ltd v MacDermid Offshore Solutions LLC,* above, in which the court struck out the element of the claim that sought to recover for damage to reputation: "damage to reputation is not pecuniary damage or damage being capable of being estimated in money (as opposed to being compensated in money as in defamation) and cannot be relied on as a head of damage under s.3". (at [39])

**Damage must be the natural result.** *Note 125, add,* See also *Niche Products* **21.15**
*Ltd v MacDermid Offshore Solutions LLC* [2013] EWHC 3540 (IPEC); [2014] E.M.L.R. 9. A rebuttal letter written by the defendant to existing and potential customers contained a statement that a report prepared by the claimant commenting on MacDermid's products was "misleading" and "erroneous." The letter also commended the defendant's product. The claimant complained about the comments on its report and brought an action for malicious falsehood. The defendant sought to argue that the claim should be struck out because the explicit commendation of its own product, of which the claimant did not complain, was self-evidently the statement in the letter that was potentially most likely to bring about the pecuniary damage which the claimant identified as the basis for its claim for lost sales. Birss J. accepted that the defendant's letter, which was intended to have an effect on the market, was likely to lead to a loss of sales of the claimant's product by increasing the sales of the defendant's product and that statements in the letter commending their own product would be a significant cause of that effect. Nevertheless, the judge refused to strike out the claim because there was a properly arguable claim that some proportion of the likely lost sales was more likely than not to have a been caused by the statements complained of:

> "It seems to me that without a trial, I cannot say that there is no properly arguable claim that a real, as opposed to fanciful, proportion of lost sales of [the claimant's product] would be likely to be caused by the statements complained of. Like all the other statements in the letter, the alleged falsehoods were stated with the objective of influencing the market for these products. To strike out a claim at this stage would be to assume in the defendant's favour that the defendant had failed in its own objective" [at [53].

SECTION 4. DISPARAGEMENT OF GOODS

**Mere puffing not actionable.** Note 158, add, In *Niche Products Ltd v Mac-* **21.19**
*Dermid Offshore Solutions LLC* [2013] EWHC 3540 (IPEC); [2014] E.M.L.R. 9 (see n.125 above) the judge held that had the defendant asserted in the letter of rebuttal that the second version of its own product was the same as the first version, the claim would have been struck out. However, the claim was based on an allegedly false assertion by the defendant that a report issued by the claimant about the defendant's product was false and misleading:

> "Merely referring to a competitor would not risk engaging the law of malicious falsehood. However when a trader expressly makes a statement about something emanating from its competitor, it seems to me that the reasons given in the cases why the law of malicious falsehood should not be engaged do not apply. The trader is not then discussing its own products or services, it is addressing what its competitor is doing. For the law of malicious falsehood to apply to such statements does not seem to me to risk infringing the trader's Art.10 right to freedom of speech" (at [30]).

CHAPTER 22

# MISUSE OF PRIVATE INFORMATION

SECTION 1. INTRODUCTION

**22.1** **Scope of the chapter.** *Add in relation to first paragraph*:

Interestingly, it was argued by the defendant in *Hannon v News Group Newspapers Limited* [2014] EWHC 1580 (Ch); [2015] E.M.L.R. 1 at [25]-[77] that while "reputation is an aspect of private life which is protected by, or engaged by, Article 8 . . . the only legal cause of action which protects reputation is defamation. Damage to reputation is not protected by confidence or privacy claims, but only by defamation. The correct interaction between Article 8's protection of reputation and Article 10, which protects free speech, is achieved by the careful limits on a defamation action, under which (inter alia) justification is a complete defence. That interaction has been forged over the years in the law of defamation and the interests of each side have been balanced by the carefully developed law of defamation. That being the case, the court should not allow a party to sidestep or circumvent the protections provided by the law of defamation (including the reduced limitation period of one year) by framing a claim for damage to reputation in a different cause of action" (at [26]). Mann J. noted that this issue was "a point which turns out not to be covered by a clear statement of principle in the authorities" (at [25]). He considered that he did not need to decide the point as it was not made out with sufficient clarity to justify the striking-out of the action which had been sought; that counsel "[had] an argument, but not a sufficiently conclusive one" (at [76]). Nevertheless, he took the provisional view that the contention was wrong (at [28]). He was "not satisfied that as a matter of principle it is necessary or appropriate, or even in some cases practically possible, to draw a hard line between the element of privacy or confidence claims which go into what might be called the realms of reputation, and other elements"; neither did he consider it clear that "as a matter of principle, damage to reputation of this sort should not be within the sort of thing that privacy rights should protect against" (at [29]). He resolved that "a conclusion about that would depend on a close analysis of the new and developing privacy rights, and their interaction with defamation". The judge considered that arguments put by counsel in the instant application tended to conflate questions of remedies with questions of rights, and/or relied on precedent drawn from contexts other than that of the interface between misuse of private information and defamation. An illustration of the importance that the right to privacy and causes of action that protect it should cover not only informational privacy but also harms attendant upon reputational damage can be in seen in the views expressed by Lord Kerr regarding the alienation of juvenile offenders in *In the matter of an application by JR38 for Judicial Review (Northern Ireland)* [2015] UKSC 42—see para 22.5. It might be added that the "bright-line" rule offered by the defence of truth has been considered by some to secure inadequate protection for Article 8 interests by itself, and that this is compensated only by the simultaneous option of relying on the claim for misuse of private information—see above, para 11.1.

*Add in relation to second paragraph*: In *Google Inc v Vidal-Hall* [2015] EWCA Civ 311; [2015] 3 W.L.R. 409, the Court of Appeal confirmed that this distinct cause of action is tortious in character. This conclusion will likely have ramifications for the future development of the parameters of the claim and remedies available there under. The question as to the nature of the misuse claim arose as the court had to determine whether one of the "jurisdictional gateways" under CPR 6.36 and CPR PD 6B had been satisfied so as to justify the grant of permission by the court to serve the proceedings on the defendant in California. The case itself concerned the implications for user privacy of the operation of the "Safari workaround" that used a combination of cookies to collect internet user data without consent.

At first instance, Tugendhat J. had considered himself bound by the decision of the Court of Appeal in *Kitechnology BV v Unicor GmbH Plastmachinen* [1995] FSR 765 to hold that breach of confidence was not a tort, but held that misuse of private information was a tort for the purposes of the rules governing service out of the jurisdiction. Hence, he held that service out of jurisdiction was permissible in principle. Counsel for the appellant contended that this conclusion was wrong as a matter of law and that the judge should have followed *Douglas v Hello (No 3)* [2005] EWCA Civ 595; [2006] QB 125 in which Lord Phillips MR giving the judgment of the court had asserted that the claim was equitable in character. In *Vidal-Hall*, the Court of Appeal concluded that Lord Phillips' comments had been obiter (at [38]). It explained that against a background of judicial and academic commentary to the effect that it would be preferable for the claim to be understood as a tort, "we cannot find any satisfactory or principled answer to the question why misuse of private information should not be [so] categorised . . . if one puts aside the circumstances of its 'birth', there is nothing in the nature of the claim itself to suggest that the more natural classification of it as a tort is wrong" (at [43]). It concluded that "that misuse of private information should now be recognised as a tort for the purposes of service out the jurisdiction. This does not create a new cause of action. In our view, it simply gives the correct legal label to one that already exists" (at [51]). See also *Vidal-Hall* [2014] EWHC 13 (QB); [2014] 1 W.L.R. 4155 at [54]-[57]. The appellants were refused permission to appeal by the Supreme Court on this theme.

*Add at end of paragraph*: While it has been almost entirely unremarked (although see Moreham, "Beyond information: physical privacy in English law"

(2014) *Cambridge Law Journal*, 73(2), 350-377), in recent years there has been a highly significant shift in the coverage of the claim for misuse of private information so as to encompass not only the disclosure of information but also the means by which it has been obtained. This theme sits outside the scope of this text. It is countenanced, however, where developments in that context—such as in respect of the appropriate quantum of damages—may bear on claims concerned more directly with the publication of private facts.

Judicial concerns over the means by which information had been obtained had previously surfaced in a number of cases focused primarily on other forms of conduct—see, e.g, *R (on the application of Wood)* v *Commissioner of Police of the Metropolis* [2009] EWCA Civ 414; [2010] 1 W.L.R. 123, [34] (per Laws LJ); *Mosley* v *News Group Newspapers Ltd* [2008] EWHC 1777 (QB); [2008] E.M.L.R. 20, [139] (per Eady J). Moreover, in a number of decisions, judges had indicated that the claims for breach of confidence and misuse of private information protect privacy more broadly than in respect of the disclosure of information alone—see, e.g, *CTB* v *News Group Newspapers Ltd* [2011] EWHC 1326 (QB), [23] (per Eady J) [2011] EWHC 1334 (QB), [3] (per Tugendhat J). The origin of this "obtaining" strand of the claim for misuse of private information, however, is the decision of the Court of Appeal in *Tchenguiz* v *Imerman* [2010] EWCA Civ 908; [2011] Fam. 116. Recalling Lord Goff's explanation in *Spycatcher* that a duty of confidence arises "where an obviously confidential document is wafted by an electric fan out of a window . . . or . . . is dropped in a public place, and is picked up by a passer-by", Lord Neuberger asserted that "if confidence applies to a defendant who adventitiously, but without authorisation, obtains information in respect of which he must have appreciated that the claimant had an expectation of privacy, it must, a fortiori, extend to a defendant who intentionally, and without authorisation, takes steps to obtain such information. It would seem to us to follow that intentionally obtaining such information, secretly and knowing that the claimant reasonably expects it to be private, is itself a breach of confidence" (at [68]). With respect, while the first element of this view is obviously correct (the generation of the obligation of confidence), the second—breach by mere dint of the obtaining—arguably involves a non sequitur. Certainly, it conflates the generation of the obligation of confidence with the requirement for action constituting a breach. This aspect of the decision in *Imerman* was acknowledged in passing in the later decision of the Court of Appeal in *Phillips* v *News Group Newspapers Ltd* [2012] EWCA Civ 48; [2012] 2 W.L.R. 848, [64]. It was treated with some circumspection by Tugendhat J, however, in *Abbey* v *Gilligan* [2012] EWHC 3217 (QB); [2013] E.M.L.R. 12, [61]-[63] and *Commissioner of Police of the Metropolis* v *Times Newspapers* [2011] EWHC 2705 (QB); [2014] E.M.L.R.1, [120]. The extended conception of the cause of action subsequently provided a basis for many of the claims that arose from the "phone-hacking scandal". In *Gulati* v *MGN Limited* [2015] EWHC 1482 (Ch), for instance, it was treated as common ground between the parties that the claim for misuse covered invasions of privacy occasioned in the obtaining, as well as the onward disclosure, of information.

**22.3     Other systems of law.** *Add in relation to reference to New Zealand in last paragraph*:

Interestingly, in *C v Holland* [2012] NZHC 2155 the New Zealand High Court recognised the existence of a general "privacy intrusion" tort for the first time (the claim arose out the surreptitious filming of the plaintiff in the shower). The Court of Appeal of Ontario did the same in *Jones v Tsige* (repeated accessing of the claimant's banking records): 2012 ONCA 32.

*Add in relation to reference to Australia in last paragraph*: The Australian Law Reform Commission recently recommended the introduction in that jurisdiction of twin privacy torts, one focused on publication of private facts, the other on intrusion on seclusion (physical invasion of privacy): ALRC, *Serious Invasions of Privacy in the Digital Era* (ALRC Report 123, 2014).

SECTION 2. REASONABLE EXPECTATION OF PRIVACY

**Elements of the First Stage Test.** *Add new note in first paragraph, following*     **22.4**
"*. . . This is an objective question.*":

Whether the reasonable expectation of privacy test is to be understood as the exclusive test on the question of whether Article 8 rights are at issue was considered by the Supreme Court in *In the matter of an application by JR38 for Judicial Review (Northern Ireland)* [2015] UKSC 42.

Lord Kerr, with whom Lord Wilson agreed, contended that the "reasonable expectation of privacy, as a test of whether article 8 is engaged, cannot be accorded a status of unique importance . . . [with the] automatic consequence [that a matter falls outside article 8] in every conceivable circumstance where it can be said that a reasonable expectation of privacy was not present" (at [54]). The majority of their Lordships took the opposite, and more persuasive view on this issue (although the two judgments offered by Lords Toulson and Clarke— Lord Hodge agreeing with both—can be criticised on other grounds—see para 22.5).

While Lord Kerr's view of the case was arguably correct in substance (that article 8(1) rights were indeed at stake on the facts—see para 22.5—albeit that their restriction was justified under article 8(2)), it is submitted that it was inaccurate in its explanation of the relevant legal tests. As was noted by both Lord Toulson (at [98], emphasising the objective nature of the test) and Lord Clarke (at [109]), Lord Kerr's view appeared to be predicated on the understanding that the relevant "reasonable expectation of privacy" in any given case was—at least in part—subjective in character. This understanding was reflected, for example, in the observation that "the concept of a reasonable expectation of a right to privacy, connoting, as it might seem to some, the notion that the individual concerned actually expected that his or her personal circumstances, on the occasion of the invasion of that privacy, ought to have been protected, and that that expectation was "reasonable" (at [36]), and in the reference to "personal expectations" (at [66]). Lord Kerr considered that the more subjective reasonable expectation test as he conceived it could not allow for all of the relevant circumstances to be taken into account, that all the circumstances must be taken into account, and that therefore on occasion such wider factors must be allowed—in addition to the reasonable expectation test—to influence the determination of whether article 8 was relevant to a given case. He insisted that the "reasonable expectation of privacy will often be a factor of considerable weight; it might even be described as "a rule of thumb" but to make it an inflexible, wholly determinative test is, in my opinion, to fundamentally misunderstand the proper approach to the application of article 8 and to unwarrantably proscribe the breadth of its possible scope" (at [56]).

For Lord Kerr, "The test for whether article 8 is engaged is, essentially, a contextual one, involving not merely an examination of what it was reasonable for the person who asserts the right to expect, but also a myriad of other possible factors such as the age of the person involved; whether he or she has consented to publication; whether the publication is likely to criminalise or stigmatise the individual concerned; the context in which the activity portrayed in the publication took place; the use to which the published material is to be put; and any other circumstance peculiar to the particular conditions in which publication is proposed. To elevate reasonable expectation of privacy to a position of unique and inviolable influence is to exclude all such factors from consideration and I cannot accept that this is a proper approach" (at [56]). He considered that "the reasonable expectation of privacy is [therefore] but one of a number of factors which may be relevant to the issue of the engagement of article 8" (at (62]).

The "broader" test expounded by Lord Kerr, however, is very little different to the objective reasonable expectation test that has been developed by the courts over time. Indeed, the aspiration to allow factors beyond the claimant's own subjective expectation to be taken into account was accommodated by their Lordships in the majority straightforwardly through their—it is submitted— more correct appreciation of the breadth of the reasonable expectation test. Having cited the broad explanation offered by Sir Anthony Clarke MR in *Murray v Big Pictures (UK) Ltd* [2008] EWCA Civ 446; [2009] Ch. 481 at [36], for instance, Lord Toulson concluded that "If there could be no reasonable expectation of privacy, or legitimate expectation of protection, it is hard to see how there could nevertheless be a lack of respect for their article 8 rights . . . The fact that [in the instant case] the appellant was a child at the relevant time is not in my opinion a reason for departing from the test whether there was a reasonable (or legitimate) expectation of privacy, but it is a potentially relevant factor in its application" (at [88] and [95]; see also at [98]).

*Add at end of paragraph*:

In addition, it may sometimes be necessary for the claimant to demonstrate that the defendant publisher "knew, or ought to have known" that the claimant held a reasonable expectation of privacy. Whether this requirement forms part of the cause of action was a matter of dispute between the parties in *Weller* v *Associated Newspapers Ltd* ([2014] EWHC 1163 (QB); [2014] E.M.L.R. 24 at [16] and [26]-[38]. Such a requirement would appear to follow from the language used by Lord Nicholls and by Baroness Hale in *Campbell* v *MGN Ltd* [2004] UKHL 22; [2004] 2 AC 457, at [14] and [134] respectively. See also, *Douglas* v *Hello! Ltd (No.3)* [2005] EWCA Civ 595; [2006] QB 125, at [100]; *Murray* v *Big Pictures (UK) Ltd* [2008] EWCA Civ 446; [2009] Ch. 481, at [36]).

Dingemans J. concluded in *Weller* that the "broad test" that takes account of all the circumstances of the case allows the Court to assess what the publishers knew, and what they ought to have known (at [37]). He explained further that this element of the assessment does not prevent publishers from placing reliance on matters that they did not know—and could not have known about—at the time of publication to show that there was no reasonable expectation of privacy. (The judge also suggested that the specific issue regarding the state of the publisher's knowledge may not have arisen directly in earlier cases as, in practical terms, "very little is likely to turn on the point" (at [38]). While this is almost certainly true of claims based upon the disclosure of private facts, it can be envisaged that many cases in which a claimant complains about the means by which information has been *obtained* may turn upon the question as to whether a defendant-publisher knew how the information had been obtained by a third party such that he or she could sensibly be said to have intended to misuse the claimant's private information—see above, para 22.1. This might be especially the case if the information concerned itself appears to be anodyne in nature (but has been obtained by some surreptitious means). Indeed, the seeming mischaracterisation by counsel of the specific complaint in *Weller* as being concerned not only with the publication of the unpixelated faces of children but also the means by which the photographs had been obtained by a paparazzo may explain why the issue became a focus of attention at all in that case.)

**What information is private.** *Add at the end of the paragraph:*          **22.5**

While in many cases it is clear that the tort of misuse of private information is concerned with a claimant's right to control private information relating to himself, this dimension of privacy and hence this conception of the purpose of the tort may not be sufficient. For instance, it is very difficult to conceive of cases that involve publication of the fact of a person's (putative) involvement in criminality (see note 48) as concerning private information that should remain under the control of the individual concerned (absent the availability of some justification for the restriction of such "privacy" under article 8(2)). Rather, such cases involve non-private information the publication of which might have profound ramifications for the reputation of the person concerned, and for that person's future ability to engage in wider society. Harms to reputation and the concomitant impact on individual autonomy, however, also fall within article 8, albeit for reasons other than informational privacy. Very often, the most appropriate cause of action in such cases will be defamation, in which case the falsity of the information at issue will be of central importance. If false information is published about a person's private life, then a claim based on the tort of misuse of private information may also be appropriate (just as it would were the information true). In other cases, however, the publication of true information that does not concern inherently private facts may also warrant protection. Such protection might also be achieved under the tort of misuse of private information.

There is clearly a nominal incongruity in using the tort of misuse of private information in this manner. Indeed, one interpretation of the disagreement between their Lordships in *In the matter of an application by JR38 for Judicial Review (Northern Ireland)* [2015] UKSC 42 highlights this potential duality of purpose of the tort of misuse of private information. The majority of their Lordships refused to recognise the information concerned—photographs depicting a juvenile's putative involvement in criminal activity—as being private in character. Hence, they concluded that there could be no reasonable expectation of privacy that the photographs would not be published.

The position of the majority can be criticised for failing to accommodate the further harm to the interests protected under article 8(1) that would be attendant on publication: harm to reputation. This concern was to the fore in the judgment offered by Lord Kerr (with whom Lord Wilson agreed). Self-evidently, in general, such harms should be covered by the tort of defamation. In *JR38*, however, Lord Kerr emphasised the impact of publication on the juvenile's future life chances. He quoted Morgan LCJ at first instance in highlighting "the risk that [an identified juvenile offender] will become stigmatised with a consequent effect on their reputation and standing within the community . . . their rehabilitation may thereafter be impaired" (at [31]; to support this point he referred to the provisions of domestic law on the protection of juvenile offenders and a number of international conventions (at [47]-[53])).

This reality comprises a powerful reason—in principle—to accommodate such scenarios within the reasonable expectation of privacy (and by extension within the claim for misuse of private information). This would not mean that publication would necessarily be precluded: in the instant case their Lordships were unanimous that the publication of the photographs was justified for public interest purposes. While Lord Kerr himself did not proceed in this manner (see para 22.4), these wider concerns can legitimately be drawn within the reasonable expectation of privacy, not on grounds that they relate to private information per se but on account of the reputational harm and associated detriments that would otherwise flow from publication. It may be preferable for this to be recognised explicitly as an expansion of the concept of the reasonable expectation of privacy (and by extension of the claim for misuse of private information), rather than that such considerations should remain partially obscured as part of the wider "context" to be taken into consideration in the assessment of reasonable expectations.

*Add in note 30*: See also, *Gulati v MGN Limited* [2015] EWHC 1482 (Ch) at [229(i)].

*Add in note 34*: Further illustration of the fact that an individual's "relationship status" is potentially private information can be seen in *CHS v DNH* [2015] EWHC 1214 (Ch) and *ZYT v Associated Newspapers Ltd* [2015] EWHC 1162 (QB). In the latter case, Warby J. noted that "Whether the fact of a relationship is private or confidential information will depend on the circumstances of each case. Very often it will not be confidential or private. The relationship between married people is a public fact and in no way confidential, for example. Other relationships involving less formal, public, or enduring commitments can also be public information and not private or confidential . . . [in other cases] the fact of [the] relationship is . . . an item of information that is both confidential and private . . . [such that] the claimants have a right to choose who they tell about the relationship and when" (at [12]). See also, *Gulati v MGN Limited* [2015] EWHC 1482 (Ch) at [225]-[228].

*Add in note 36*: Further illustration of the fact that the intimate detail of personal relationships is private information can be seen in *BUQ v HRE* [2015]

EWHC 1272 (QB) [41]-[43], and *AMC v News Group Newspapers* [2015] EWHC 2361 (QB) at [15].

*Add in note 37*: See also, *Gulati v MGN Limited* [2015] EWHC 1482 (Ch) at [229(iv)].

*Add in note 40*: See also, *Gulati v MGN Limited* [2015] EWHC 1482 (Ch) at [229(ii)].

*Add in note 45, after "paramount"*:

Clause 6(v) of the *Editors' Code* provides that "editors must not use the fame . . . or position of a parent . . . as sole justification for publishing details of a child's private life". This provision is subject to the public interest exception in the *Code*. The *Code* makes it clear that a very high public interest must be satisfied to justify publication of private information details about children aged under 16 years. A guide to the *Code*, Beales, *The Editors' Codebook* (Rev 2nd edn, London: Pressbof, 2012), explains further that "the Code goes to exceptional lengths to safeguard children by raising the thresholds on disclosure and defining tightly the circumstances in which press coverage would be legitimate . . . The welfare of the child includes the effect publication might have . . . Children of the famous: The rules apply equally to children of parents from all walks of life".

*Add in note 45, after "factor in the analysis"*:

In *ZH (Tanzania) v Secretary of State for the Home Department* [2011] UKSC 4; [2011] 2 AC 166 at [46], Lord Kerr stated that "in reaching a decision that will affect a child, a primacy of importance must be accorded to his or her interests. This is not, it is agreed, a factor of limitless importance in the sense that it will prevail over all considerations. It is a factor, however, that must rank higher than any other. It is not merely one consideration that weighs in the balance alongside other competing factors. Where the best interests of the child clearly favour a certain course, that course should be followed, unless countervailing reasons of considerable force displace them". As an illustration of the fact that this important factor will not always outweigh everything else in the balancing exercise, see *PNM v Times Newspapers Ltd* [2014] EWCA Civ 1132; [2014] E.M.L.R. 30 at [43]-[44]. Note that the Supreme Court has given permission to appeal in *PNM*.

*Add at end of note 45*:

See also, *Weller v Associated Newspapers* [2014] EWHC 1163 (QB); [2014] E.M.L.R. 24; *In the matter of an application by JR 38 for Judicial Review* [2013] NIQB 44, [30].

*Add at end of note 48*:

This question has become a matter of some controversy. Most recently, the putative depiction of the appellant engaged in criminal activity in *In the matter of an application by JR38 for Judicial Review (Northern Ireland)* [2015] UKSC 42 saw the majority of their Lordships conclude that his Article 8 rights were not engaged on the facts of the case, even though he was a juvenile. In *PNM v Times Newspapers Ltd* [2013] EWHC 3177 (QB) and [2014] EWCA Civ 1132; [2014] E.M.L.R. 30, the High Court and Court of Appeal respectively considered an application for an interim order in circumstances where the claimant had been arrested but not charged with involvement in serious sexual offences against children. (Note that the Supreme Court has given permission to appeal in *PNM*). A number of other persons had been convicted of related offences, and the claimant's name and putative involvement had been aired in open court. A reporting restriction imposed under s.4(2) of the Contempt of Court Act 1981 was expected to be lifted. On these facts, the engagement of the claimant's Article 8 right was presumed. Both at first instance and in the Court of Appeal, it was concluded that the public interests in open justice and the reporting of allegations of child abuse outweighed the privacy interest given that members of the public generally understand the difference between suspicion and guilt, and know that a person is presumed innocent unless and until proved otherwise. The position of the claimant was considered to be different to that of a person who had merely been arrested (in light of the general policy of the police not now to publish the names of arrested persons outside of specific circumstances—see College of Policing, *Guidance on Relationships with the Media* (Coventry: College of Policy, 2013)), in that details of his arrest and wider details had been extensively aired in open court. A similar question regarding whether there can exist a reasonable expectation of privacy in the fact of an arrest was at issue in *Hannon v News Group Newspapers Limited* [2014] EWHC 1580 (Ch) at [82]-[103]; [2015] E.M.L.R. 1. Mann J. concluded that the issue was a nuanced one, and that much would fall for determination by reference to the specific facts of any given case. The absence or outweighing of any privacy interest was not sufficiently clear, however, to warrant the striking-out of the actions at hand.

**22.6**      **Limiting factors: public domain in general.** *Add in text at end of 2nd paragraph*: In contrast, in *Weller v Associated Newspapers* [2014] EWHC 1163 (QB); [2014] E.M.L.R. 24, the court was presented with a complaint regarding the publication in a newspaper and online of the unpixelated faces of the children of a well-known musician. Evidence showed that there had previously been an array of publication concerning the children, including limited reference to the children in newspaper and other interviews, personal tweets regarding the family (some of which had been picked up and republished by national newspapers), limited online publication by other members of the family circle, publication of photographs in a book, and a single modelling appearance of one of the children in a teen magazine (at [80]-[118] and [129]-[136]). In the main, however, the family had been assiduous in avoiding publicity for the children. Dingemans J. concluded that the children retained a reasonable expectation of privacy over publication of photographs showing their faces, "one of the chief attributes of their respective personalities" (at [170].)

*Add in note 53*: See, for example, *AMC v News Group Newspapers* [2015] EWHC 2361 (QB) at [31].

*Add in note 54*: In *Weller v Associated Newspapers* [2014] EWHC 1163 (QB); [2014] E.M.L.R. 24 at [63], Dingemans J. described "the particular importance attached to photographs in the decided cases" as "a demonstration of the reality that there is a very relevant difference in the potentially intrusive effect of what is witnessed by a person on the one hand, and the publication of a permanent photographic record on the other hand".

*Add in note 55*: See also, *NNN v D1* [2014] EWHC B14 (QB) at [11].

### SECTION 3. ULTIMATE BALANCNG TEST

**Elements of the second stage exercise.** *Add at end of paragraph*:                    **22.11**

As the ultimate balancing test involves consideration of both sides of the case, and often other rights and interests also, it is "probably a fruitless exercise to try to ascertain where the burden of proof lies" (*YXB v TNO* [2015] EWHC 826 (QB) at [13], per Warby J). Both parties must present such evidence as is available to them to assist the court. See also, *AMC v News Group Newspapers* [2015] EWHC 2361 (QB) at [11], per Laing J: "neither 'side' has a burden to discharge, as such; rather, each has to justify a desired interference with the other's Convention right or freedom".

**Relevant factors: strength of the claimant's privacy interest.** *Add in text at*    **22.12**
*end of paragraph*:

Furthermore, it may be that the fact that a claimant has been the victim of blackmail will see the court afford enhanced weight to the privacy interest at stake. In *BUQ v HRE* [2015] EWHC 1272 (QB) at [46], Warby J. stated that "the claimant's rights are to be accorded significant weight, not merely because they relate to information of an intimate, private and personal nature but also because he is a blackmail victim. As I said in *YXB v TNO* [2015] EWHC 826 (QB) [17]: "victims of blackmail or extortion deserve protection from the court; and the court must adapt its procedures to ensure that it does not provide encouragement or assistance to blackmailers'". The judge also discussed the reduced weight to be afforded to the expression rights of a putative blackmailer (see [46]-[47]). Ultimately, whether such enhanced protection for the victims of blackmail is achieved through an enhanced weighting for the privacy interest, or a down-graded weight to the Article 10 interests of the blackmailer—see 22.15 below—is immaterial.

*Add in note 104*: For this reason, "claimants are expected to speak for themselves unless there is some good reason why they cannot do so . . . ordi-narily . . . at every hearing . . . there should be evidence from the claimant"—see *YXB v TNO* [2015] EWHC 826 (QB) at [18]. In that case, Warby J. heard evidence from a solicitor who in turn had obtained it from the claimant's agent and another representative, and not from the claimant directly. He considered that "the court can hardly be expected to attach great weight to the privacy rights asserted on the claimant's behalf if he fails, without justification, to give any evidence himself", and found "the most remarkable feature of this [to be] the complete absence of any evidence from the claimant"—at [61(iii)(c)]. He con-cluded that the application had been "primarily driven by others", and that there were "strong grounds for inferring . . . that commercial motives play a considerable role . . . [given] the very limited role played by the claimant himself, the extreme weaknesses of the evidence in support of a claim to privacy, and the leading role that has clearly been taken in events by the claimant's Agent on his behalf"—at [61(iii)(d)].

*Add in note 104*: In *Weller v Associated Newspapers* [2014] EWHC 1163 (QB); [2014] E.M.L.R. 24 at [119]-[124], the counsel for the defendant made much of the fact that the parents of the claimants had not previously complained when details of their children's lives had been published in the media. The judge concluded that the absence of previous complaint was not "any sort of consent to the publication in this action" ([136]). Neither could it sensibly be read as a tacit indication of a lack of concern for privacy. As noted in the judgment ([138]), some publishers may adopt a pragmatic approach to their decisions regarding the publication of private information which involves placing weight on the fact that a particular subject either has or has not previously complained. Such insight might reasonably serve as a guide to the likelihood of complaint in the instant case. Such "rules of thumb" should not be elevated to legal presumptions, however, in the absence of wider evidence as to the claimant's own valuation of his or her privacy. On the facts of Weller, the judge found that one of the children and the parents had been genuinely embarrassed, concerned and upset by the publication ([168]).

**22.14** **Relevant factors: interests of third parties.** *Add in note 107*: See also, *BUQ v HRE* [2015] EWHC 1272 (QB) at [49].

*Add in note 110*: See also, *YXB v TNO* [2015] EWHC 826 (QB) at [18] and [61(v)].

**22.15** **Relevant factors: expression rights of the defendant.** *Add in second sentence of first sub-paragraph, in relation to the desire of individuals to* "tell their own story":

The right to speak of one's own life is also an aspect of the autonomy protected by Article 8—see *Re Angela Roddy* [2003] EWHC 2927 (Fam), [2004] EMLR 8; *YXB v TNO* [2015] EWHC 826 (QB) at [12].

*Add at end of second sentence of first sub-paragraph*: In *AMC v News Group Newspapers* [2015] EWHC 2361 (QB) at [23], Laing J. noted that "the fact that most newspapers are run for profit does not deprive them of, or lessen the importance of, their article 10 freedom".

*Add in first paragraph, following* " *. . . There is also a general public interest in freedom of expression . . .* ": In contrast to the position under Article 8 ECHR, there is no "threshold of seriousness" to be overcome such that freedom of expression is engaged in every case involving proposed restriction on publication: *Weller v Associated Newspapers* [2014] EWHC 1163 (QB); [2014] E.M.L.R. 24 at [49].

*Add at end of first line in third paragraph*:

In general terms, the basic interest of a media organisation in freedom of expression is little different to that of any other individual. (In *K v News Group Newspapers* [2011] EWCA Civ 439; [2011] 1 WLR 1827 at [13], Ward L.J. stated "everyone has the right to freedom of expression but the ones with the greatest need for this constitutionally vital freedom are the organs of the media".)

*Add note in third paragraph, after* "The first contention has been rejected by the courts": Interestingly, in *Weller v Associated Newspapers* [2014] EWHC 1163 (QB); [2014] E.M.L.R. 24 at [74]-[76], [145]-[147] and [175], Dingemans J. appeared to seek to revive the generality of this approach. He explicitly "accepted and followed" the position asserted by Lord Woolf in *A v B plc*. Insofar as this thinking was intended merely to recognise the social desirability of "a thriving and vigorous newspaper industry", it is a fair—albeit trite—point. Should it be intended to do more than that in the manner of Lord Woolf's suggestion that the commercial success of the press should be treated as a factor in the ultimate balancing exercise, it is simply wrong-headed. The consideration afforded to the theme in the section of the *Weller* judgment focused on the "ultimate balancing test" indicates that it was so treated in that judgment. The logic of this approach is that it is legitimate for individuals who become—whether by design or happenstance—the subjects of prurient newspaper attention to have their privacy "taxed" non-consensually for the wider benefit. It also accepts uncritically the assertion that there is a meaningful and necessary cross-subsidy afforded to socially important journalism by such publishers from the publication of commercially profitable, privacy-invading content.

*Add in note 119*: See also, *NNN v D1* [2014] EWHC B14 (QB) at [14]; *YXB v TNO* [2015] EWHC 826 (QB) at [17].

*Add at end of final paragraph*: Nevertheless, the court will be assiduous in determining whether allegations of blackmail are sustainable on the facts. (In *YXB v TNO* [2015] EWHC 826 (QB), for instance, Warby J. considered at length evidence presented by the defendant that had not been put before the judge at an earlier hearing at which an interim order was made (notwithstanding the duty of full and frank disclosure at ex parte hearings). He concluded that on a full hearing there was a "strong probability . . . that a court would find that the claimant's representatives decided to buy off the defendant, and sought to persuade her to name her price, and that her conduct did not amount to blackmail". Hence he concluded that "the policy arguments in favour of protecting blackmail victims are [not] a weighty consideration in the circumstances of this case" (at [61(iv)])).

**Relevant factors: matters of public interest generally.** *Add in text, following* **22.16** "*corporate malpractice*" 140,] . . . the ethics of personal relationships within an educational context (*ZYT v Associated Newspapers Ltd* [2015] EWHC 1162 (QB) at [14]).

*Add in text at end of final paragraph* In *AMC v News Group Newspapers*, Laing J. engaged with the general contention that the public interest extends to the exposure of all conduct that is "socially harmful" ([2015] EWHC 2361 (QB) at [27]). She cautioned of the "risk that the phrase 'socially harmful' can become a pretext for judging others by reference to moral positions which those others do not, or might not, share. This is a particular risk for a court in an increasingly secular society in which some issues, especially questions of sexual conduct, do not attract the consensus which they once did. In my judgment, few people, other than adherents to strict religious codes, could rationally consider that this conduct is so fundamentally inconsistent with being a role model of the kind [that the claimant] is that there is a public interest in exposing it".

*Add in note 139:* See also *In the matter of an application by JR38 for Judicial Review (Northern Ireland)* [2015] UKSC 42, at [71] per Lord Kerr: "Clearly, the detection and prevention of crime, the prosecution and rendering to justice of those guilty of criminal offending and the diversion of young people from criminal activities . . . are necessary in a democratic society".

**22.17**     **Relevant factors: role models and the public interest.** *Add in note 143*: In the factually similar case of *AMC v News Group Newspapers* [2015] EWHC 2361 (QB), Laing J. sought to distinguish *McClaren* on the facts (at [29]). It might have been preferable to acknowledge that the decision was over-generous to the defendant-publisher.

*Add in note 144*: Similarly, in *AMC v News Group Newspapers* [2015] EWHC 2361 (QB) at [19]-[20], Laing J. noted that "successful sportsmen necessarily have a prominent position in public life, and because of that, and whether they like it or not, lose control over aspects of their private life. But I do not consider that being a public figure of and by itself makes the entire history of that person's sex life public property . . . it is important to analyse what sort of a role model [the claimant] is or can be. He is a role model for sportsmen and aspiring sportsmen. Any scrutiny of his conduct away from sport ought to bear a reasonable relationship with the fact that he is a sportsman. His position does not turn him into an example in every sphere of his existence. He is not a role model for cooks, or for moral philosophers. The fact that he is a prominent sportsman does not mean that he impliedly pontificates publicly about private morality. In my judgment, a discreetly conducted affair, before he was married, some years ago, is not obviously inconsistent with his public role, even if its conduct involved the breach of team rules".

SECTION 4. DATA PROTECTION

**22.19**     **The Data Protection Act 1998.** *Add*: An important application of European data protection law can be seen in the prodigious litigation and wider activity that has flowed from the decision of the European Court of Justice in *Google Spain SL v Agencia Espanola de Proteccion de Datos (AEPD) and Gonzalez*. (Case C-131/12 13 May 2014. Reported at [2014] Q.B. 1022; [2014] E.M.L.R. 27). The factual background to this preliminary ruling involved the continuing publication of personal data by a Spanish newspaper regarding a Mr Gonzalez in an electronic version made available on the internet. The material had originally been published in two printed issues in 1998. Mr Gonzalez argued that this information should no longer be displayed in the search results presented by the internet search engine operated by *Google* when a search was made of his name. In that context, the national court wished to clarify the territorial scope of application of EU data protection rules, the legal position of an internet search engine service provider and the so-called right to be forgotten and the issue of whether data subjects could request that some or all search results concerning them should no longer be accessible through search engines.

This involves the "right to be forgotten", or more accurately the "right to be de-indexed". The court concluded (i) that a search engine collects, retrieves, organizes, stores and discloses personal information, and thus that it engages in the processing of data; (ii) that a search engine is the controller of the data it has processed; (iii) that the processing of such personal data is carried out "in the context of the activities" of search engines located within the EU, and (iv) that "if the data appear to be inadequate, irrelevant or no longer relevant, or excessive in relation to the purposes for which they were processed, the information and links concerned in the list of results must be erased". Thus, the ruling requires internet search engines to delete links to such material so that it is no longer reflected in search returns. In November 2014, the Working Party under Article 29 of Directive 95/46/EC—an independent European advisory body on data protection and privacy—published guidelines in an effort to clarify the reach of *Gonzalez*. (See Article 29 DP Working Party, *Guidelines on the Implementation of the Court of Justice of the European Union Judgment on "Google Spain and Inc v. Agencia Española De Protección De Datos (Aepd) and Mario Costeja González" C-131/12*, 14/EN WP225).

In a regularly updated "transparency report", *Google* indicated that by August 2015 it had received over 300,000 requests under the ruling and had evaluated almost 1.1 million urls. (See http://www.google.com/transparencyreport/removals/europeprivacy/ (accessed August 2015). By analysing source code in the *Google* report, the *Guardian* newspaper found that 95 per cent of requests made to *Google* emanated from "everyday members of the public" rather than criminals, politicians or other high profile public figures—see Tippmann and Powles, "*Google* accidentally reveals data on "right to be forgotten" requests", *Guardian*, 14 July 2015.) As regards the United Kingdom, the report indicated that approximately 37,500 requests had been received and 146,000 urls assessed in consequence. *Google* delists in around 40 per cent of cases.

**Compensation for non-pecuniary loss.** *Add*: The meaning of "damage" in **22.24** s.13 of the Data Protection Act 1998, and in particular whether there can be a claim for compensation without pecuniary loss, was considered by the Court of Appeal in *Google Inc v Vidal-Hall* [2015] EWCA Civ 311; [2015] 3 W.L.R. 409 at [52]-[105]. The court concluded that s.13 should be disapplied as incompatible with the *EU Charter on Fundamental Rights* to the extent that it prevented the recovery of damages for distress alone.

The court acknowledged that on a literal interpretation of s.13, the claimants would not be entitled to recover damages for distress for the alleged breaches of the data protection principles. The claimants did not allege that they suffered pecuniary loss in addition to their distress, and their claims did not relate to processing for any of the special purposes. The court reflected on whether *Johnson v Medical Defence Union* comprised a binding authority to the effect that the meaning of "damage" in s.13(1) could include only "pecuniary loss", but found that the points made by Buxton L.J. in that case were obiter (at [67]-[68]). The court also took the view that, given the aims of the underpinning Directive as evidenced by the recitals in the preamble and article 1, the concept of "damage" in article 23 includes non-pecuniary loss such as distress (at [76]-[79]). The court considered that "since what the Directive purports to protect is privacy rather than economic rights, it would be strange if the Directive could not compensate those individuals whose data privacy had been invaded by a data controller so as to cause them emotional distress (but not pecuniary damage). It is the distressing invasion of privacy which must be taken to be the primary form of damage (commonly referred to in the European context as "moral damage") and the data subject should have an effective remedy in respect of that damage. Furthermore, it is irrational to treat EU data protection law as permitting a more restrictive approach to the recovery of damages than is available under article 8 of the Convention. It is irrational because . . . the object of the Directive is to ensure that data-processing systems protect and respect the fundamental rights and freedoms of individuals "notably the right to privacy, which is recognized both in article 8 of the [Convention] and in the general principles of Community law". The enforcement of privacy rights under article 8 of the Convention has always permitted recovery of non-pecuniary loss" (at [77]).

The court proceeded to assess whether it was possible to interpret s.13(2) in a way which is compatible with article 23 so as to permit the award of compensation for distress by reason of a contravention of a requirement of the DPA even in circumstances which do not satisfy the conditions set out in s.13(2)(a) or (b) (at [84] et seq). It concluded that the *Marleasing* principle could not be invoked to disapply s.13(2)(a) and (b) (at [92]). It found, however, that s.13(2) could be disapplied on the grounds that it conflicts with the rights guaranteed by articles 7 and 8 of the *EU Charter of Fundamental Rights* (at [95]-[105]).

While he did not determine the issue, the "preliminary view" of the issue reached by Tugendhat J. in *Vidal-Hall* had also been that the concept of damage should include non-pecuniary loss—see *Vidal-Hall* [2014] EWHC 13 (QB); [2014] E.M.L.R. 14 at [103]. The Supreme Court had granted the appellants permission to appeal on this point.

*ADD NEW SECTION 5*

SECTION 5. DAMAGES IN PRIVACY CASES

**22.27**     **Damages for misuse of private information: general.** Final remedies have been awarded in only a small number of claims for misuse of private information. Few cases reach the stage of final determination at a full trial; most are settled or are effectively determined at an interim hearing. For claimants who are successful at a full trial, there is a range of remedies available. A final injunction may serve to prevent further unlawful publication, and perhaps to secure the destruction or return by the defendant of any physical product that encapsulates the confidential or private information. Usually, the claimant will (also) seek a financial remedy. The claimant can elect whether to seek compensatory damages or the gain-based remedy of an account of profits. There has been more debate over whether exemplary damages are, or should be, available. The fact that the claim for misuse has been confirmed to be a tort should entail an end to this debate. (In *Google Inc v Vidal-Hall* [2015] EWCA Civ 311; [2015] 3 W.L.R. 409 at [51], the court expressed itself "conscious of the fact that there may be broader implications from our conclusions [that the claim was a tort], for example as to remedies, limitation and vicarious liability . . . and such points will need to be considered as and when they arise".)

**Damages for misuse of private information: compensatory damages.** The    **22.28** purpose of damages is to compensate the claimant for the loss suffered as a result of the misuse of private information. The claimant is, so far as money can do it, to be placed in the same situation as he or she would have enjoyed had the harm not been commissioned. Clearly, where publication has taken place, there is no prospect of a return to the *status quo ante*. For this reason, it is sometimes said that damages cannot be an adequate remedy for the publication of private facts.

Given the different types of loss that may have occurred (pecuniary, non-pecuniary or aggravated losses), the court must maintain a measure of flexibility in how it undertakes the assessment of damages. In circumstances where the claimant may have preferred the private information never to have been disclosed, damages are likely to be primarily for mental distress (non-pecuniary loss), although there may be some aspect of pecuniary loss. Hence, if the evidence indicates that the claimant has suffered no real distress, no award of damages for non-pecuniary loss will be made. (See, e.g, *AVB v TDD* [2014] EWHC 1442 (QB)). Moreover, the extent of the damage may be claimant-specific in the sense that "a thinner-skinned individual may be caused more upset, and therefore receive more compensation, than a thicker-skinned individual who is the subject of the same intrusion" (*Gulati v MGN Limited* [2015] EWHC 1482 (Ch) at [229(viii)] per Mann J) In other circumstances, the claimant may have preferred him or herself to determine when and how the information was disclosed. An example may be where the claimant intends to publish memoirs or to sell rights to photographs of an event. In such scenarios, damages are likely to focus on pecuniary losses. Such loss is generally assessed by comparing the position in which the claimant has found him- or herself with the counterfactual where it is supposed that the misuse of private information has not occurred. Pecuniary losses can be suffered by a range of different means, and can include actual losses and opportunities affected or extinguished.

**Damages for misuse of private information: compensation for non-**    **22.29** **pecuniary loss.** The precise nature of the non-pecuniary losses for which compensation will be given has been a matter of some dispute before the courts. One form of loss—the causing of distress—is generally accepted (see, e.g, *Applause Stores Productions v Raphael* [2008] EWHC 1781 (QB) at (81)). It has also been suggested that a further dimension of damages awards in claims for misuse of private information should be designed to "vindicate" the claimant's Article 8 right. The phrase was used in *Attorney General of Trinidad and Tobago v*

*Ramanoop* [2005] UKPC 15; [2006] 1 AC 328, while in *Mosley v News Group Newspapers* Eady J. outlined a principled explanation for the availability of damages for non-pecuniary loss that was based on the court's need to be able to vindicate article 8 rights. ([2008] EWHC 1777 (QB) at [214]-[217]. See also *AAA v Associated Newspapers Ltd* [2012] EWHC 2103 (QB) [123]-[127]).

In *Weller v Associated Newspapers*, however, Dingemans J. noted that—following the decision of the Supreme Court in *R (on the application of Lumba) v Secretary of State for the Home Department* [2011] UKSC 12; [2012] 1 AC 245, [97]-[101]—"it is clear that . . . "vindicatory damages" as a separate head of damages should not be awarded for misuse of private information": [2014] EWHC 1163 (QB); [2014] E.M.L.R. 24 at [190]-[191]. He added that while "it is right to say that the cause of action for misuse of private information does accommodate both articles 8 and 10 of the ECHR, the claim is for misuse of private information and not a direct claim for infringement of human rights or infringement of constitutional rights . . . the use of the phrase "vindicatory damages" in this area of law is . . . unhelpful and liable to mislead".

This issue resurfaced in the case of *Gulati v MGN Limited*, in which "the heart of the difference between the parties on damages [was] the question of what the claimants can and should be compensated for" ([2015] EWHC 1482 (Ch) at [108] per Mann J). The claimants maintained that there should be compensation for loss of privacy or autonomy resulting from physical intrusion (hacking or blagging), for "damage or affront to dignity or standing", and for injury to feelings (including distress). The defendant maintained that damages were available only for the last of these categories of harm, and the other forms of harm were relevant only insofar as they caused distress. Mann J. took the view that the underpinning values "are not confined to protection from distress, and it is not . . . apparent why distress (or some similar emotion), which would admittedly be a likely consequence of an invasion of privacy, should be the only touchstone for damages. While the law is used to awarding damages for injured feelings, there is no reason in principle . . . why it should not also make an award to reflect infringements of the right itself, if the situation warrants it . . . If one has lost "the right to control the dissemination of information about one's private life" then I fail to see why that, of itself, should not attract a degree of compensation, in an appropriate case. A right has been infringed, and loss of a kind recognised by the court as wrongful has been caused. It would seem to me to be contrary to principle not to recognise that as a potential route to damages . . . Distress will often be the consequence of the infringement to such a degree as to subsume any potential separate award for the infringement itself; but where appropriate the stated values ought of themselves to be protectable with an award of damages" ([111]). He added, first, that limitation of compensation to distress would render the protection afforded to Article 8 "illusory", contrary to the requirements of Convention jurisprudence ([112]-[113]), and secondly that an exclusive focus on distress could not explain why the younger siblings in *Weller*—who had not themselves been at all distressed—received any measure of damages (albeit a reduced measure compared with their older sibling who had herself been acutely embarrassed by the publication involved in that case) ([116]-[117]). In short, the view of Mann J. was that damages could be awarded for distress; that, in light of *Lumba*, damages could not be awarded to "vindicate" the article 8 right, but that these categories were not dispositive. He considered that there was still room for the award in addition to distress of damages to reflect the fact of misuse ([132]-[145]). The defendant has appealed this conclusion.

**Damages for misuse of private information: aggravated damages.** Com-    **22.29**
pensatory damages may include a measure of aggravated damages; aggravated damages are available in claims for misuse of private information (*Gulati v MGN Limited* [2015] EWHC 1482 (Ch) at [203]. See also, *Commissioner of Police for the Metropolis v Shaw* [2012] ICR 464).

The purpose of such damages remains compensatory; they are not intended to punish the defendant. The courts have been clear that the prospect of aggravated damages must not adversely affect the right of the defendant–publisher to a fair trial under Article 6 ECHR. There is no room for generalised suggestions that the choice to defend the action, even vigorously, should incur increases damages. (*Weller v Associated Newspapers* [2014] EWHC 1163 (QB); [2014] E.M.L.R. 24 at [186].)

CHAPTER 23

## OTHER CAUSES OF ACTION ARISING FROM STATEMENTS

SECTION 1. NEGLIGENCE

**23.5**  **Limits on liability for negligence.** *Note 46, add,* See *Sebry v Companies House* [2015] EWHC 115 (QB) which is discussed at 23.7 below.

**23.7**  **Duties in reference-like situations.** *Note 58, add,* In *AB v A Chief Constable* [2014] EWHC 1965 (QB) Cranston J. held, on the particular facts, that there was no duty of care at common law on a chief constable to send a second reference to a former employee's new employer (a Regulatory Body) when the first reference had not contained full details of the employee's sickness and disciplinary details. It does not follow from this case however that there will never be circumstances in which a common law duty of care will be found to exist where the first reference sent is misleading.

*Note 61, add,* Note however that in *Desmond v Chief Constable Nottingham Police* [2011] EWCA Civ 3, the Court of Appeal held that the police owed no duty of care to a person seeking an Enhanced Criminal Record Certificate (ECRC) when supplying information leading to its issue. In such circumstances:

> "The statutory context in which the Chief Officer was obliged to operate is important. The statutory purpose of ECRCs is to provide a degree of protection to vulnerable young people generally. The Chief Officer acts pursuant to a statutory duty. In so acting he does not assume a responsibility which the statute has not obliged him to undertake. He had no choice. . . . There are no special facts in this case from which the court can conclude that, apart from the statutory duty, this particular Chief Officer is to be taken to have assumed responsibility to Mr Desmond in particular" (at [48]).

In *Camurat v Thurrock Borough Council* [2014] EWHC 2482 (QB), the court held that no duty of care was owed to a employee in respect of information supplied by his former employer to the police for the purposes of issuing an ECRC which, the claimant alleged, had caused him to lose his new employment at another school. Substantially the same considerations applied in this case as had applied in *Desmond v Chief Constable Nottingham Police* [2011] EWCA Civ 3:

"There was no duty discernible from the statute and no assumption of duty by the Defendant . . . It is also worthy of note that the court in *Desmond* at para 51 was fortified in its decision by the fact that the Claimant in that case had other possible remedies potentially available. The same applies to the Claimant in this case. Those included the statutory procedure under s.117 to challenge the reference, and judicial review of any refusal to amend an ECRC (as was indeed successfully deployed in 2014, the rationale of the decision by police to accede to it being that the passage of time since the issue of the certificate without any further problems justified it being quashed.) . . . There is no justification, therefore, in this case for imposing a duty of care on a supplier of information to police, which would discourage those who would in good faith provide assistance to the police on safeguarding issues" (at [78]-[80]).

The court in *Camurat* distinguished *McKie v Swindon College* [2011] EWHC 469 (QB) on the grounds that in *McKie* the former employer had volunteered information without any request for the same, and it was couched in highly unfavourable terms which the judge found to be on the facts entirely without foundation, saying it did not "stand up to any sort of scrutiny at all". There was no statutory duty in play in the case, no safeguarding issue in fact arose and the injured party had no alternative remedy for his losses (at [75]). Moreover, *McKie* was not, according to the judge, a "reference" case at all (at [45]).

*Insert the following at end of para. 23.7:*

In *Sebry v Companies House* [2015] EWHC 115 (QB); [2015] B.C.C. 236, Edis J. held that a duty of care was owed by Companies House to a company in respect of which a winding up order was negligently registered in the company register. The company subsequently went into administration because it had run out of cash, the cash shortage having been caused by the rumour that the company was in financial trouble. Where a Registrar undertakes to alter the status of a company on the register which it is his duty to keep, in particular by recording a winding up order against it, he assumes a responsibility to that company. This special relationship between the Registrar and the company arises because it is foreseeable that if a company is wrongly said on the Register to be in liquidation it will suffer serious harm. Moreover, "fairness, justice and reasonableness" demanded a remedy on these facts. First, unless a remedy is provided by the common law of negligence, a company damaged by carelessness in these circumstances would have no remedy. Any claim in defamation would be likely to fail on the basis that qualified privilege applied to the communication. Second, it was not difficult for the staff of the Registrar to avoid making errors of this kind. Third, there were no aspects of the statutory duty or contractual relationship between the company and Companies House which should operate to limit the nature and extent of the responsibility. Companies Act 2006 s.1080(5) provides "The records kept by the registrar must be such that information relating to a company is associated with that company, in such manner as the registrar may determine, so as to enable all the information relating to the company to be retrieved." This means that the imposition of a duty would tend to reinforce the statute by requiring Companies House to do exactly what it is already required to do. Fourth, given that the system of registration is compulsory because it is designed to benefit the business community and the national economy by enhancing the benefit of limited liability, it does not seem unjust to impose liability on those who benefit from the system (ultimately the public) for harm done by its faulty operation. Finally, the ultimate effect of the imposition of this duty is likely to be to improve the accuracy of the Register, which is plainly in the public interest. ([112]) However, while the judge concluded that a duty of care was owed to the company, he held that such a duty was owed to no one else. Consequently, a creditor of the company which had lost money as a result of the company going into administration would not be owed a duty.

**23.8** **Assumption of responsibility without negligence.** *Note 68, add*, Cf. *Camurat v Thurrock Borough Council* [2014] EWHC 2482 (QB).

*Note 74, add*, Cf. *OPO (a child by BHM his litigation friend) v MLA* [2014] EWCA Civ 1277; [2015] E.M.L.R. 4, in which the Court of Appeal held that no duty of care was owed by a father to his disabled son in respect of psychological harm that might be caused to the son by learning of details of the father's abuse as a child contained in his autobiography. While damage was foreseeable and a sufficient relationship of proximity existed between father and son (at [55]), it was not "fair, just and reasonable to impose a duty of care towards the child" (at 57]). The effect of imposing a duty on a parent whenever he causes a child to be exposed to an unacceptable risk "would lead to liability in a large number of cases because any formulation of the proposition for a duty of care in this case would encompass a whole range of commonplace activities in which a parent is involved in caring for his child." ([57]) There was no appeal on the negligence point: [2015] UKSC 32; [2015] 2 W.L.R. 1373. See further para.23.12 for the Supreme Court's decision on the *Wilkinson v Downton* issue.

Section 2. Harassment

**23.12** **The Protection from Harassment Act 1997.** *Replace first paragraph of para.23.12 with the following*:

Behaviour that amounts to harassment may give rise to liability at common law. Where words or conduct, for which there is no justification or reasonable excuse, are intentionally directed towards the claimant and injury is caused, a claim may exist (*note 93*). Thus, in *Wilkinson v Downton*, the defendant was held liable in damages for communicating a false story to the claimant that her husband had fractured his legs as a result of an accident the consequence of which was that the claimant suffered severe shock to her nervous system. However, while liability at common law may arise for words or conduct that amount to "harassment", the circumstances in which they will do so are likely to be limited, particularly in "publication" cases, following the decision of the Supreme Court in *Rhodes v OPO (by his litigation friend BHM)* (*new note 93A*).

The appellant in *Rhodes* was a concert pianist. He had written an autobiography that he wished to publish which, inter alia, documented the abuse he had been subject to as a child. His former wife was deeply concerned that the disabled child that she and the appellant had had together would be seriously psychologically damaged should he read the book or discover its contents. She therefore sought an injunction preventing publication or alternatively the deletion of a large number of passages. At first instance, Bean J. dismissed the application for an interim injunction. The Court of Appeal (*new note 93B*) reversed Bean J.'s decision in part, finding that the claim for intentionally causing harm under the tort in *Wilkinson v Downton* should go to trial. It held however that the claims for misuse of private information and negligence failed. The Court of Appeal granted an interim injunction restraining the appellant from publishing certain information such as, for example, "graphic accounts of . . . sexual abuse he suffered as a child". The father appealed to the Supreme Court.

The Supreme Court allowed the father's appeal, the judgment of the court being given by Lady Hale and Lord Toulson (with whom Lords Clarke and Wilson agreed). Lord Neuberger, with whom Lord Wilson agreed, gave a concurring judgment. The Court held that the tort in *Wilkinson v Downton* consisted of three elements: (1) a conduct element; (2) a mental element; and, (3) a consequence element, albeit that only the first and second were issues in the case. So far as the conduct element was concerned, this required the claimant to establish that the words or conduct complained of were without justification or reasonable excuse and that they were directed towards the claimant. In this case, the conduct complained of was the intended publication of the book to the general public. That did not fall within the conduct element. There was every justification for publication of what was a true autobiographical account of what had happened to the appellant when he was a child. The appellant had the right to tell his own story and there was a corresponding public interest in others hearing about his life:

> "Freedom to report the truth is a basic right to which the law gives a very high level of protection . . . It is difficult to envisage any circumstances in which speech which is not deceptive, threatening or possibly abusive, could give rise to liability in tort for wilful infringement of another's right to personal safety. The right to report the truth is justification in itself. That is not to say that the right of disclosure is absolute, for a person may owe a duty to treat information as private or confidential. But there is no general law prohibiting the publication of facts which will cause distress to another, even if that is the person's intention" (*new note 93C*).

So far as the mental element was concerned, this required an intention to cause physical harm or severe mental or emotional distress. Recklessness was not enough (*new note 93D*). Whether or not the necessary intention existed was a question of fact and might be inferred in an appropriate case but was not to be imputed as a matter of law (*new note 93E*). In this case, there was no evidence that the father intended to cause psychiatric harm or severe emotional or mental distress to his son. The Supreme Court consequently concluded that there was no arguable case that the publication of the book would constitute the requisite conduct element of the tort or that the appellant had the requisite mental element. The appeal was therefore allowed and the judgment of Bean J. restored.

The final element of the tort was the consequence element. Although not necessary for the decision, the court held that this element required proof that physical harm or recognised psychiatric illness had been caused by the words or conduct complained of. Mere distress was not sufficient (*new note 93F*).

In light of the court's decision in *Rhodes*, the narrow definition of the elements of the tort and the strong emphasis on the importance of freedom of expression, it is likely to be rare for a case involving media publication to give rise to liability under *Wilkinson v Downton*. That said, *Rhodes* was of course a case that involved true speech. While it is likely to be a very rare case indeed where a true statement will give rise to a claim (at [107]), the same may not necessarily be the case with untruths. If, for example, a media outlet or other person published an article containing an untrue and gratuitous (*new note 93G*), inexcusable or unjustified (*new note 93H*) statement intended to distress the claimant and directed at him, there is no reason why liability should not exist if the claimant suffered a psychiatric illness as a consequence. Free speech is of fundamental importance but there is surely little value in a gratuitous, untrue statements intended to distress the claimant.

Apart from *Wilkinson v Downton*, liability may arise under the Protection from Harassment Act 1997. By virtue of s.1 of the Act, a person must not pursue a course of conduct (1) which amounts to harassment of another and (2) which he knows or ought to know amounts to harassment of the other (*note 94*). The question whether he ought to know that his conduct amounts to harassment is determined by asking whether a reasonable person in possession of the information he has would think the course of conduct amounted to harassment (*note 95*).

*Note 93, replace existing text with the following: Wilkinson v Downton* [1897] 2 Q.B. 57; *Rhodes v OPO (by his litigation friend BHM)* [2015] UKSC 32; [2015] 2 W.L.R. 1373. See also, *Janvier v Sweeney* [1919] 2 K.B. 316 CA; *Austen v University of Wolverhampton* [2005] EWHC 1635 (QB).

*New Note 93A:* [2015] UKSC 32; [2015] 2 W.L.R. 1373.

*New Note 93B:* OPO (a child by BHM his litigation friend) v MLA [2014] EWCA Civ 1277; [2015] E.M.L.R. 4.

*New Note 93C:* Ibid, at [77].

*New Note 93D:* Ibid, at [87].

*New Note 93E:* Ibid, at [81]-[82].

*New Note 93F:* Ibid, at [88].

*New Note 93G:* Ibid, per Lord Neuberger at [110]-[111].

*New Note 93G:* Ibid, per Lady Hale and Lord Toulson at [74]-[76].

*Note 98, add*, See also *QRS v Beach* [2014] EWHC 4189 (allegations on a website that solicitors had acted corruptly, improperly, dishonestly and lacked integrity amounted to harassment ([62]) albeit that default judgment against one of the defendants was set aside). It has also been said to be arguable that litigation may, where used for an improper purpose—that is say not to air legitimate grievances but to cause distress to those involved in the process—become unlawful under the Protection from Harassment Act (*Allen v Southwark London Borough Council* [2008] EWCA Civ 1478). For an example where allegations of this nature were made but failed see *Fox v Hall* [2014] EWHC 2747 (QB). Note, however, that in *Crawford v Jenkins* [2014] EWCA Civ 1035 the Court of Appeal held that where a complaint to the police is made immunity from suit applies as much to a claim in harassment as it does to a claim in defamation. See further 13.12 (note 118).

*Note 99, add,* In *Calland v Financial Conduct Authority* [2015] EWCA Civ 192 a claim was brought in respect of alleged harassment by the Financial Services Authority who had contacted the claimant, a retired independent financial adviser, three times, once by letter, once by email and once by telephone in connection with a review into pension mis-selling. The claimant's appeal against a grant of summary judgment against him failed. Lewison L.J. described the boundary between lawful and unlawful conduct for the purposes of the Protection from Harassment Act 1997 as follows:

"The boundary between conduct which is lawful and conduct which is tortious or criminal is crossed when the impugned conduct ceases to be merely unattractive or unreasonable and becomes oppressive and unacceptable: *Majrowski v Guy's and St Thomas's NHS Trust* [2006] UKHL 34. In life one has to put up with a certain amount of annoyance: things have got to be fairly severe before the law, civil or criminal, will interfere: *Ferguson v British Gas Trading Ltd* [2009] EWCA Civ 46. Harassment involves persistent conduct of a seriously oppressive nature targeted at an individual and objectively calculated to cause fear or distress: *R v Smith* [2012] EWCA Civ 2566; *Dowson v Chief Constable of Northumbria Police* [2010] EWHC 2612 (QB), at 142. In deciding whether the boundary has been crossed the context is important; but the touchstone is whether the impugned conduct is of such gravity as to justify the sanctions of the criminal law: *Sunderland City Council v Conn.* Whether the boundary has been crossed is to be judged objectively: *Dowson v Chief Constable of Northumbria Police* at 142. Courts should be astute to separate the wheat from the chaff at an early stage in the proceedings: *Majrowski v Guy's and St Thomas's NHS Trust* at 30" (at [5]).

*Insert the following after the second sentence in the second paragraph of para.23.12:*

To constitute harassment the conduct must be targeted at an individual (*new note 99A*). However, it is not a requirement of the statutory tort that the claimant be the primary or even a target of the defendant's conduct. As Briggs L.J. explained in *Levi v Bates* (*new note 99B*):

"The purpose of [the requirement that the conduct be targeted at an individual as articulated by Lord Phillips M.R. in *Thomas v News Group Newspapers*] . . . was not designed to identify who may complain of harassment, but rather to draw out of the well-known word "harassment" the concept that it is targeted behaviour, by which I mean behaviour aimed at someone, rather than behaviour which merely causes alarm or distress without being aimed at anyone. Lord Phillips' immediate example was stalking, conduct which is plainly targeted at someone" (*new note 99C*).

Provided that the conduct is targeted at someone, any person who was foreseeably likely to be directly alarmed or distressed by it may recover (*new note 99D*) though the alarm or distress suffered must arise out of more than simple sympathy for the targeted victim (*new note 99E*). Thus, the articles in the match programmes in *Levi v Bates* were held, in addition to defaming Mr Levi, to constitute harassment of Mrs Levi. This was so not simply because they defamed her husband but because they invited thousands of club supporters to intervene in a hostile manner, at her home, about a business dispute between her husband and the defendant (*new note 99F*).

*New Note 99A: Thomas v News Group Newspapers Ltd* [2001] EWCA Civ 1233, at [29]-[30].

*New Note 99B:* [2015] EWCA Civ 206; [2015] E.M.L.R. 22.

*New Note 99C:* Ibid, at [27].

*New Note 99D:* Ibid, at [34].

*New Note 99E,* Ibid, at [33].

*New Note 99F:* Ibid, at [37].

*Note 101, add,* See also on "course of conduct", *AVB v TDD* [2014] EWHC 1442 (QB).

*Note 109, add,* While it has been held that the word "person" in the Act does not embrace a corporate entity, representative proceedings may be brought (under CPR 19.6) in cases where employees of the company have been subjected to harassment. Thus, in *Daiichi UK Ltd v Stop Huntingdon Animal Cruelty* [2003] EWHC 2337 (QB), a representative claim was brought successfully by the managing director on behalf of himself and his fellow employees. All shared the same interest in the proceedings, namely not to be harassed by animal rights activists (at [22]). See also, *Harvey Nichols & Company Ltd v Coalition to Abolish the Fur Trade and others* [2014] EWHC 4685 (QB); *Harlan Laboratories UK Limited v Stop Huntingdon Animal Cruelty* [2012] EWHC 3409 (QB); *Novartis Pharmaceuticals UK Ltd. v Stop Huntingdon Animal Cruelty* [2014] EWHC 3429 (QB); *Nursing and Midwifery Council v Nowak* [2014] EWHC 2945 (QB).

**23.14** **Remedies and harassment.** *Note 127, add,* In *Raymond v Young* [2015] EWCA Civ 456 the claimants brought a claim against their neighbours alleging trespass, nuisance and harassment. The Court of Appeal upheld an award of damages for distress and inconvenience and also for the diminution in the value of the property caused by the acts of nuisance and harassment. A claim in nuisance is a claim for injury to a proprietary or other interest in land even where the nuisance causes no physical damage to the claimant's land itself but merely affects its reasonable use and enjoyment (*Hunter v Canary Wharf* [1997] A.C. 655 (HL)). The court in *Raymond* concluded that even though the claim under the Protection from Harassment Act 1997 was different in the sense that it provided a civil remedy for conduct amounting to harassment of another, there was no reason why, in the light of s.3(2), the approach to assessment of damages for diminution in the value of the property should be any different to that in nuisance. The fact that an injunction was also granted in this case did not, on the facts, mean that damages could not be recovered for any residual diminution in value of property. The defendant's conduct could not be described as transitory and therefore a permanent injunction was not likely to be treated by a potential purchaser as a guarantee that they would not be subjected to the same treatment:

"The purchaser will know (or be advised) that the benefit of the injunction is personal to the [claimants] and that on a sale the protection it affords will effectively end. The [claimants] would cease on a sale to have any interest in continuing to enforce it and arguably have no locus to do so once they have parted with ownership of the Farm. Any further repetition of the same sort of conduct towards the incoming purchaser would necessitate fresh proceedings for an injunction with all the cost and trouble which that would involve" (at [34]).

*Insert at end of first paragraph of para.23.14*:

An injunction may also be granted to prevent a repetition of harassment or anticipated harassment and in appropriate cases may be granted ex parte (*Kerner v X and others* [2015] EWHC 128 (QB)) and against persons unknown (*Novartis Pharmaceuticals UK Ltd. v Stop Huntingdon Animal Cruelty* [2014] EWHC 3429 (QB)). In *Al Hamadani v Al Khafaf* [2015] EWHC 38 (QB), Warby J. made clear that for the purposes of injunctive relief it is not necessary to establish that the defendant has already engaged in a course of conduct meeting the requirements of the Act. It is sufficient if he may do so unless restrained (at [49]). However, if the defendant has already engaged in a course of conduct that would justify an award of damages that will tend to strengthen the case for an injunction.

## SECTION 4. PASSING OFF

**Nature of the Tort.** *Note 138, add, Fage UK Ltd. v Chobani UK Ltd* [2014] **23.16** EWCA Civ 5; [2014] F.S.R. 29 (yoghurt being made in America selling in UK under label "Greek Yoghurt").

*Note 142, add*, See also *Starbucks (HK) Ltd v British Sky Broadcasting Group Plc* [2015] UKSC 31; [2015] 1 W.L.R. 2628, at [15]. A claimant in a passing off action has to establish its claim as at the inception of the use complained of (ibid., at [15]).

**Goodwill.** Note 145, add, The tort of passing off involves the striking of "a **23.17** compromise between two conflicting objectives, on the one hand the public interest in free competition, on the other the protection of a trader against unfair competition by others" (Somers J. in *Dominion Rent A Car* [1987] 2 TCLR 91, at 116). In *Starbucks (HK) Ltd v British Sky Broadcasting Group Plc* [2015] UKSC 31; [2015] 1 W.L.R. 2628, Lord Neuberger P.S.C. noted that while there is a temptation to conclude that whenever the defendant copies the claimant's mark or get up, and therefore makes use of the claimant's hard work, there ought to be a claim, it is not the case that copying is enough to ground a claim.

"All developments, whether in the commercial, artistic, professional or scientific fields, are made on the back of other people's ideas: copying may often be an essential step to progress. Hence, there has to be some balance achieved between the public interest in not unduly hindering competition and encouraging development, on the one hand, and on the other, the public interest in encouraging, by rewarding through a monopoly, originality, effort and expenditure" (at [61]).

*Note 154, add*, In *Starbucks (HK) Ltd v British Sky Broadcasting Group Plc* [2015] UKSC 31; [2015] 1 W.L.R. 2628, Lord Neuberger P.S.C. clarified what amounts to a sufficient business to constitute goodwill:

"As to what amounts to a sufficient business to amount to goodwill, it seems clear that mere reputation is not enough ... The claimant must show that it has a significant goodwill, in the form of customers, in the jurisdiction, but it is not necessary that the claimant actually has an establishment or office in this country. In order to establish goodwill, the claimant must have customers within the jurisdiction, as opposed to people in the jurisdiction who happen to be customers elsewhere. Thus, where the claimant's business is carried on abroad, it is not enough for a claimant to show that there are people in this jurisdiction who happen to be its customers when they are abroad. However, it could be enough if the claimant could show that there were people in this jurisdiction who, by booking with, or purchasing from, an entity in this country, obtained the right to receive the claimant's service abroad. And, in such a case, the entity need not be a part or branch of the claimant: it can be someone acting for or on behalf of the claimant" (at [52]).

*Insert the following at end of the third sentence of para.23.17*: The "territoriality" of goodwill has been confirmed by the Supreme Court in *Starbucks (HK) Ltd v British Sky Broadcasting Group Plc* [2015] UKSC 31; [2015] 1 W.L.R. 2628. Lord Neuberger P.S.C. stated (at [47]):

" ... a claimant in a passing off claim must establish that it has actual goodwill in this jurisdiction, and that such goodwill involves the presence of clients or customers in the jurisdiction for the products or services in question. And, where the claimant's business is abroad, people who are in the jurisdiction, but who are not customers of the claimant in the jurisdiction, will not do, even if they are customers of the claimant when they go abroad."

*Note 159, add*, See also, *Fage UK Ltd. v Chobani UK Ltd* [2014] EWCA Civ 5; [2014] F.S.R. 29.

**23.18**   **Misrepresentation and Confusion.** *Note 169, insert at beginning of footnote*: The claims failed in several cases because the claimants were unable to satisfy the sine qua non of the claimant and defendant being commercially involved in the "same field of activity".

*Insert the following new paragraph after note 172 at end of second paragraph*:

The Court of Appeal upheld Birss J.'s decision (*new note 172A*). The judge had had proper regard to the distinction between endorsement and general character merchandising and correctly applied the law by finding that to make good any claim in passing off, "He must show that he has a relevant goodwill, that the activities of the defendant amount to a misrepresentation that he has endorsed or approved the goods or services of which he complains, and that these activities have caused or are likely to cause him damage to his goodwill and business" (*new note 172B*).

He was right to conclude that it is not a necessary feature of merchandising that members of the public will think that the products in issue are in any sense endorsed by the celebrity or creator of the character in issue. However, it must be shown that the claimant has a relevant goodwill and that the impugned activity involves a false representation that there is a connection between the claimant and the goods in issue of a relevant kind, that is to say that the claimant is materially responsible for their quality. Applying these principles, Birss J. was entitled to conclude that passing off was made out.

Use of this image would, in all the circumstances of the case, indicate that the t-shirt had been authorised and approved by Rihanna. Many of her fans regarded her endorsement as important for she was their style icon, and they would buy the t-shirt thinking that she had approved and authorised it. In short, the judge correctly found that the sale of this t-shirt bearing this image amounted to a representation that Rihanna had endorsed it.

*New Note 172*A: [2015] EWCA Civ 3; [2015] 1 W.L.R. 3291.

*New Note 172B:* Ibid, at [43].

*Note 176, add, J.W. Spear & Sons Ltd. v Zynga Inc* [2015] EWCA Civ 290; [2015] F.S.R. 19 (no passing off of well-known game *"Scrabble"* by a games company selling an electronic game called *"Scramble"* and *"Scramble With Friends"*).

CHAPTER 24

# THE INITIAL STAGES

SECTION 1. INTRODUCTION

**24.1**  **General.** *Add at end of second paragraph:* It is now clear that Defamation Act s1(1) does more than raise the bar. Words will not be found to be defamatory unless the claimant can prove that they have caused him serious harm to his reputation or will probably do so. Serious harm may be proved by inference if it is justified. This construction of s.1(1) will undoubtedly add to the difficulties facing a claimant in deciding whether or not to issue proceedings: see *Lachaux v Independent Print Ltd* [2015] EWHC 2242 (QB); [2015] E.M.L.R. 28.

*Add to end of note 2*: On construction of Defamation Act 2013 s.1(1) see also *Cooke v MGN* [2014] EWHC 2831 (QB); [2015] 1 W.L.R. 895; *Ames v Spamhaus Project* [2015] EWHC 127 (QB); [2015] 1 W.L.R. 3409.

*Add new note 2A in 4th para after "at the hands of a jury"*: The point remains valid whatever the tribunal, but jury trials are now a dying, if not extinct, species. Defamation Act 2013 s.11 abolished the right to trial by jury in defamation cases for all actions commenced after 31 December 2013. For the principles that apply to exercise of discretion in favour of jury trial, see *Yeo v Times Newspapers Ltd* [2014] EWHC 2853 (QB); [2015] 1 W.L.R. 971.

**24.2**  **Risks.** *Note 5A at the end of the first sentence of the first paragraph*:
See the addition to the second paragraph of 24.1 above, and *Lachaux v Independent Print Ltd* (above).

*Note 9, line 3*: Delete "prospectively".

*Note 10, line 1*: Delete "prospectively".

**24.3**  **Finding out the actual words.** *Add to end of note 13*:
See now also *Wissa v Associated Newspapers Ltd* [2014] EWHC 1518 (QB) at [29], where Tugendhat J said: "In my judgment the effect of CPR 16, the Practice Direction and the guidance given by the Court of Appeal in *Best*, is that

in a claim for libel it is necessary that the Claimant should set out word for word precisely those words which he alleges defame him, whether that is the whole of the text or, as is more commonly the case, an extract from a much larger text". (And see also *Mole v Hunter* [2014] EWHC 658 (QB)).

**Defences.** *Note 15, line 1*: Delete "prospectively".      **24.4**

*Note 20, line 2*: Delete "prospectively".

*Note 27, line 2*: Delete "prospectively".

*Delete final paragraph, and replace with the following*:

The task of advising prospective claimants will not have been made easier by the abolition of the *Reynolds* defence and its replacement by s.4, Defamation Act 2013, the new statutory defence of publication on a matter of public interest. While the Explanatory Notes to the Act suggest that s.4 is intended to reflect the law as laid down in *Flood*,[35] the conditions for the statutory defence are in different terms. The new defence has not yet been the subject of judicial consideration, except for some tentative observations (without the benefit of argument) in *Barron v Vines* [2015] EWHC 1161 (QB) at [58]ff.

**Information to be contained in letter before action.** *Add*: In the light of the   **24.7** decision in *Lachaux v Independent Print Ltd* [2015] EWHC 2242 (QB); [2015] E.M.L.R. 28, it will also be necessary, or at least highly desirable, to set out the facts relied on in support of the case that the words complained of have caused serious harm to the claimant's reputation or are likely to do so (a requirement introduced by s.1(1), Defamation Act 2013). (See also, in respect of s.1(2), per Nicol J. in *Cartus Corporation Ltd v Siddell* [2014] EWHC 2266 (QB), [32(v)]).

**Compensation.** *Add*: It appears that under the new regime in place under s.1,   **24.12** Defamation Act 2013, a speedy and wholehearted apology is now capable of turning a published statement from one which has caused or is likely to cause serious harm to a claimant's reputation, into one which does not have that effect: see *Lachaux v Independent Print Ltd* [2015] EWHC 2242 (QB); [2015] E.M.L.R. 28 at [68]: "Another consequence (of the judge's construction of s.1) is that a publication may in principle change from being defamatory (and hence not actionable), for instance by reason of a prompt and full retraction and apology". That remarkable result offers an opportunity for a defendant not merely to mitigate damages but actually to transform an actionable publication into one which fails to surmount the s.1 threshold of serious harm to reputation.

SECTION 2. CHOICE OF DEFENDANTS

**Repeated statements.** *Note 60*: Delete "prospectively".      **24.19**

Section 3. Jurisdiction

**24.21**    **Publisher of defamatory statement not present in England or Wales.** *Delete the sentence beginning "Damage is presumed in libel", and substitute the following*:

Until very recently, it was a given that damage is presumed in libel, *(Note 67)* but that appears no longer to be the case. In the light of s.1(1), Defamation Act 2013, and the first instance decision of *Lachaux v Independent Print Ltd* [2015] EWHC 2242 (QB; [2015] E.M.L.R. 28, damage can no longer be said to be presumed in English law. On the contrary, the claimant must prove that the publication complained of has caused serious harm to his reputation, or is likely to do so. If there is damage, it is sustained and the act resulting in the damage is committed at the place or places of publication. *(note 68)*

*Delete the contents of note 67 and replace with the following*: The presumption of damage has been a factor of central importance where a claimant wishes to have his action against a foreign publisher tried in England. The necessity to prove serious damage to reputation in England & Wales, or the likelihood of it in the future, may inhibit such claimants, although it should not be forgotten that damage may be proved by inference: see e.g. *Cooke v MGN* [2014] EWHC 2831 (QB); [2015] 1 W.L.R. 895 at [43].

**24.22**    **Procedure.** *Delete second paragraph and replace with the following*:

It is important to note that the bar has been raised by s.9, Defamation Act 2013 in any case where a claimant wishes to bring an action for defamation against a person not domiciled in the UK, another EU country or a Lugano Convention state (Iceland, Norway and Switzerland). The effect of s.9 is that the court no longer has jurisdiction to determine such a claim unless it is satisfied that of all the places in which the statement complained of has been published, England and Wales is clearly the most appropriate place in which to bring an action.

**24.23**    **The Brussels Regime.** *Insert at end of paragraph 1*:

Note that the Judgments Regulation, or Brussels Regulation, of 2001, has been repealed by Regulation (EU) No 1215/2012 of the European Parliament and of the Council of 12 December 2012. The new Regulation, generally known as the Brussels Regulation (Recast), or as the recast Judgments Regulation, applies to legal proceedings started on or after 10 January 2015, and largely repeals the old Regulation. However, the old Regulation continues to apply to judgments given in proceedings started before 10 January 2015. The jurisdictional rules are essentially unchanged.

*Note 75:* Denmark has also submitted to the recast Judgments Regulation.

**24.25**    **Jurisdictional regime.** *Delete the text of note 77 and replace with the* following: The same holds good for the recast Judgments Regulation (see 24.23 above), except that the numbering of the articles has changed. Art.4(1) sets out the general rule that persons domiciled in a Member State shall, whatever their nationality, be sued in the courts of that Member State, art.5(1) provides that such persons may be sued in the courts of another Member State only by virtue of the rules as to special jurisdiction, and art.7(2) provides by way of special jurisdiction that a person domiciled in a Member State may be sued in the courts of another Member State in matters relating to tort, delict or quasi-delict.

*Note 82, line 10, in reference to s1(2), Defamation Act 2013*: Delete "prospectively".

**Publication by English publisher outside the jurisdiction.** *Note 83, add at* 24.26
*end*: See also art.4(1) recast Judgments Regulation (para 24.23 above).

**The *forum conveniens* principle in defamation cases.** *First paragraph:* 24.28
*delete second sentence (but retain note 93) and replace with the following*:

However, a new test for claims brought against defendants not domiciled in the United Kingdom, the EU or the Lugano Convention states (Norway, Iceland, Switzerland) has been introduced by Defamation Act 2013 s.9, although by s.16(7) it does not apply to any action started before 1 January 2014.

*Second paragraph:* Note that the presumption of damage may be a thing of the past in English law, given that by s.1(1) Defamation Act it is necessary for the claimant to prove that the publication complained of has caused or is likely to cause serious harm to his reputation: see *Lachaux v Independent Print Ltd* [2015] EWCH 2242 (QB); [2015] E.M.L.R. 28 at [60].

*Note 100*: See now *Sloutsker v Romanova* [2015] EWHC 545 (QB); [2015] 2 Costs L.R. 321, where one Russian citizen sued another for internet libels and a libel broadcast on *Radio Liberty*, only a small percentage of which would have been read or heard in this jurisdiction, but which nonetheless, given the claimant's standing here, arguably involved real and substantial torts, and where the only rival jurisdiction was the Russian Federation. However, given the nature of the allegations (which in part alleged bribery by the claimant of a Russian judge) and given the defendant's refusal to accept the legitimacy of the Russian system, Russia was not an appropriate forum. (*Sloutsker* was a pre-Defamation Act 2013 case: see 24.29 below. But given that the only two competing jurisdictions were England and Russia, it seems likely that the result would have been the same under s.9). Similarly, England and Wales was the appropriate forum in which to try a claim in misuse of private information against a defendant registered in Delaware and with a principal place of business in California: *Vidal-Hall v Google Inc* [2014] EWHC 13 (QB); [2014] 1 W.L.R 4155; on appeal (appeal dismissed), [2015] EWCA Civ 311; [2015] 3 W.L.R. 409 (appeal pending before the Supreme Court). See *Hegglin v Persons Unknown* [2014] EWHC 2808 (QB) (Bean J.) and *Mosley v Google Inc* [2015] EWHC 59 (QB) (Mitting J.) to like effect. By contrast, in *Carr v Penman* [2013] EWHC 2679 (QB), where an English businessman sought to sue a defendant resident in Victoria, Australia, in respect of libels published almost entirely in Australia, there was no real or substantial tort in this jurisdiction and no reason why the claimant should not sue in Australia; in *Subotic v Knezevic* [2013] EWHC 3011 (QB), a claim by a Serbian national resident in Geneva against a Montenegrin national resident in

Croatia over libels allegedly published in the Balkans, with minimal publication in this jurisdiction, was dismissed as an abuse; and in *Karpov v Browder* [2014] EWHC 3071 (QB); [2014] E.M.L.R. 8 a claim by a Russian citizen with no connection to or reputation in this jurisdiction was struck out as an abuse.

*Note 102:* Add to end of note 102: See also *Carr v Penman* [2013] EWHC 2679 (QB), shortly summarised at *note 100* above.

**24.29**    **"Libel tourism" and Defamation Act 2013, s.9.** Section 9 of the Defamation Act 2013 is now in force. By s.16(7) and the Defamation Act 2013 (Commencement) (England and Wales) Order 2013, it applies to actions brought on or after 1 January 2014. It appears that the section has not as yet been considered by the courts.

SECTION 4. OTHER COMPLAINTS PROCEDURES

**24.32**    **General.** The Press Complaints Commission closed on 8 September 2014, following the publication of the Leveson Report.

On the same day it was replaced in part by the Independent Press Standards Organisation (IPSO), a press-supported body chaired by a retired judge. IPSO has greater powers than the PCC (for example, it can determine the placing and size of corrections), but certain national newspapers have declined to join it (the *Guardian*, the *Observer*, the *Financial Times* and the *Independent* titles). It considers complaints of breaches of its Editors' Code of Practice.

Meanwhile, the Press Recognition Panel (PRP) has been established under Royal Charter to grant recognition to regulators meeting the requirements in the Charter's recognition criteria.

**24.33**    **Press Complaints Commission.** *Change title to Press Complaints.*

*Delete paragraph and replace with the following*: The Press Complaints Commission closed on 8 September 2014. It has been replaced in part by the Independent Press Standards Organisation (IPSO), which represents the bulk of the press, but not the *Guardian, Observer, Financial Times* or the *Independent* titles. Nor does it cover (for example) the *Huffington Post*, the well-known online news provider. It considers complaints of breaches of its Editors' Code of Practice, which is somewhat reminiscent of the Code of Practice of the Press Complaints Commission. It covers such matters as accuracy (the press must take care not to publish inaccurate, misleading or distorted information, including pictures); opportunity to reply; privacy (including a bar on photographing individuals in private places—defined as public or private property where there is a reasonable expectation of privacy—without their consent); harassment, which proscribes persisting in questioning, telephoning, pursuing or photographing individuals once asked to desist, remaining on their property when asked to leave and not following them; intrusion into grief or shock; the treatment of children; and clandestine devices and subterfuge. In some cases (including privacy, harassment, the treatment of children, and clandestine devices and subterfuge) there is a public interest exception.

**Ofcom's Broadcasting Code.** *Amend the first sentence as follows*: The current **24.35**
Broadcasting Code applies to television and radio programmes broadcast on or
after 1 June 2015.

## Section 5. Issue of Claim Form

**Commencement of Action.** *In the third line, replace "CPR PD 7" with CPR* **24.39**
*PD 7A*

**Damages.** *Note 131: replace first sentence with the following*: By the Civil **24.41**
Proceedings and Family Proceedings Fees (Amendment) Order 2015, S.I. 2015
No. 57, fees for issue of a claim form are now 5% of the value of the claim where
the sum claimed is over £10,000 and up to £200,000 (so that a claim for £100,000
will incur a fee of £5,000), and £10,000 where the sum claimed is over £200,000
or is unlimited. These sums might usefully be compared with the equivalents in
2013 and 2014: for a £100,000 claim, the fees were £685 in 2013 and £910 in
2014; in 2013, the fee for an unlimited claim was £1670, and in 2014 it was
£1920. It might be wondered how such egregious inflation can be compatible
with access to justice. (In that context, it may be worth observing that in *R (On
the Application of Unison) v The Lord Chancellor* [2015] EWCA Civ 935, an
unsuccessful challenge to the Employment Tribunals and the Employment
Appeal Tribunal Fees Order SI 2013/1893, which for the first time imposed fees
for bringing proceedings in employment tribunals and the EAT, Underhill LJ
referred at [75] to the decline in the number of claims in the Tribunals following
the introduction of the Fees Order, which he described as "sufficiently startling
to merit a very full and careful analysis of its causes". He went on: "If there are
good grounds for concluding that part of it is accounted for by claimants being
realistically unable to afford to bring proceedings the level of fees and/or the
remission criteria will need to be revisited".)

CHAPTER 25

# INTERIM INJUNCTIONS

SECTION 1. GENERAL PRINCIPLES

**25.2**    **Delicate nature of jurisdiction.** *Note 5*: Sections 12 and 13, Defamation Act 2013, came into force on 1 January 2014.

*Note 6*: See further *Spelman v Express Newspapers* [2012] EWHC 355 (QB) (a privacy case) per Tugendhat J. for an account of why "[a]pplications for injunctions in defamation are rarely successful", at [57]-[62].

*Note 10*: In *Spelman v Express Newspapers*, above, Tugendhat J. observed at [111] that "the fact that a threatened defamatory publication would be highly distressing has never been considered a good reason for granting an injunction".

*In the penultimate line on p.951 of the Main Text, replace "good" with "compelling" and add new note 11A after the word "reasons".*

*New note 11A*: See *Cartus Corporation Ltd v Siddell* [2014] EWHC 2266 (QB) (Nicol J.) at [32(i)].

**25.6**    **Defence of justification. Change title of paragraph to "Defence of truth".**

*Note 29*: In *O v A* [2015] UKSC 32; [2015] 2 W.L.R. 1373, the Supreme Court in a non-defamation injunction case took the opportunity to reiterate and strongly to reaffirm the right to report the truth. The case concerned an appeal from the grant by the Court of Appeal of an interim injunction on the basis of the *Wilkinson v Downton* tort to restrain publication of a book by a father which, it was said, would if published be seriously damaging to his son. The appeal was allowed. In reaching this conclusion, Baroness Hale and Lord Toulson, with whom Lord Clarke and Lord Wilson agreed, said the following at [77]: "Freedom to report the truth is a basic right to which the law gives a very high level of protection. (See, for example, *Napier v Pressdram Ltd* [2009] EWCA Civ 443; [2010] 1 W.L.R. 934, [42].) It is difficult to envisage any circumstances in which speech which is not deceptive, threatening or possibly abusive, could give rise to liability in tort for wilful infringement of another's right to personal safety. The right to report the truth is justification in itself. That is not to say that the right of disclosure is absolute, for a person may owe a duty to treat information as private or confidential. But there is no general law prohibiting the publication of facts which will cause distress to another, even if that is the person's intention".

**The application of** *Bonnard v Perryman in other jurisdictions.*    25.7

*Insert after* "The position in New Zealand": and in Northern Ireland [*new note 39A*].

*New note 39A*: See *Conway v Sunday Newspapers (t/a Sunday World)* [2014] N.I.Q.B. 22 for the governing principles.

**Other defences which might succeed.** *Add at the end of the paragraph:*    25.8
There may be significant difficulties involved in obtaining an interim injunction in libel against an internet service provider, particularly if it is based in a foreign jurisdiction [*new note 44A*].

*New note 44A*: See generally *Re J (A Child)* [2013] EWHC 2694 (QB); [2014] E.M.L.R. 7 (Sir James Munby P.). Such problems are compounded in libel by the enactment of ss.5 and 10, Defamation Act 2013.

**Evidence of an intention to repeat or publish.** *Note 51*: In *Cartus Corp v*    25.10
*Siddell* [2014] EWHC 2266 (QB), Nicol J. declined to continue an interim injunction because there was no evidence that the defendants intended to publish the publications complained of: see at [21]. The judge also refused to grant an interim injunction that restrained the defendants from publishing certain specified imputations on the ground that the claimants were unable to particularise the precise words that the defendants intended to publish: see at [26]-[29]. As to the latter requirement, see para 25.4 in the Main Text.

**Injunctions based on other causes of action.** *Insert new note 62A after the*    25.14
*phrase "misuse of private information".*

*Insert new note 62B after the phrase "which the publisher maintains is true".*

*New note 62A*: In *Spelman v Express Newspapers*, above, Tugendhat J. observed at [64] that, "[t]here is some uncertainty as to whether, and if so when, a court should refuse an injunction on the basis of *Bonnard v Perryman* when it is sought by a claimant who advances his case only on the basis of privacy" but considered that this "important issue of principle" did not need to be resolved in the case before him.

*New note 62B*: While the material in question was not defamatory, this judicial cautiousness was reflected in the Supreme Court's decision in *O v A*, above, in which Baroness Hale, Lord Clarke, Lord Wilson and Lord Toulson held at [77] that there was no general law prohibiting the publication of facts whose publication would cause distress to another, even if that was the publisher's intention, and in which Lord Neuberger and Lord Wilson observed at [111] that the *Wilkinson v Downton* tort should not be used to extend or supplement the law of defamation.

**25.16**     **Injunctions based on other causes of action.** *Examples (2).* *Note 71*: "In this connection, note *Hannon v News Group Newspapers Ltd* [2014] EWHC 1580 (Ch); [2015] E.M.L.R. 1, a privacy case in which Mann J. rejected the defendants' application to strike out the claims, the argument being that they were if anything claims for defamation and that it was an abuse of process for the claimant to proceed in any other cause of action."

**25.17**     **Protection from Harassment Act.** *Add at the end of the paragraph*: In *Merlin Entertainments Plc v Cave* [*new note 82A*] Elisabeth Laing J. held that where the alleged harassment involved statements which a defendant would seek to justify at trial, an interim injunction might, despite the rule in *Bonnard v Perryman*, be appropriate where the defendant's conduct (as distinct from the content of the statements) had additional elements of oppression, persistence or unpleasantness which marked it out as harassment. Nonetheless, such claims would need to be scrutinised carefully to ensure that any relief sought, while restraining objectionable conduct, went no further than was necessary in interfering with art.10.

Note 79: See also *Brand v Berki* [2014] EWHC 2979 (QB), *QRS v Beach* [2014] EWHC 3057 (QB), *Kerner v WX* [2015] EWHC 128 (QB) and *Kerner v WX (No.2)* [2015] EWHC 1247 (QB). As to final injunctions in harassment restraining speech, see *QRS v Beach* [2014] EWHC 3319 (QB) and *Al Hamadani v Al Khafaf* [2015] EWHC 38 (QB).

New note 82A: [2014] EWHC 3036 (QB); [2015] E.M.L.R. 3, at [40]-[41].

**25.24**     **Discretion.** *Note 110*: As to material non-disclosure, see *new note 113A* below.

Section 2. Practice and Procedure

**25.25**     **Introduction.** *In the final paragraph, insert new note 113A after the phrase "will be dismissed for that reason"*: Or set aside on the application of the respondent. See *YXB v TNO* [2015] EWHC 826 (QB) (Warby J.) for a privacy case in which an interim injunction obtained without notice was set aside for material non-disclosure, and *Cartus Corp v Siddell*, above, in which Nicol J. declined to set aside or to refuse to continue an interim injunction, granted without notice in a libel claim, on such grounds.

CHAPTER 26

# PARTICULARS OF CLAIM

SECTION 1. INTRODUCTION

**Material facts.** *Add to end of note 5*: Similar sentiments were expressed in **26.2** *Tchenguiz v Grant Thornton LLP* [2015] EWHC 405 (Comm), a case in the Commercial Court. Leggatt J. struck out particulars of claim which were 94 pages long and flouted the principles set out in the Commercial Court Guide. The Judge said at [1], *"Statements of case must be concise. They must plead only material facts, meaning those necessary for the purpose of formulating a cause of action or defence, and not background facts or evidence. Still less should they contain arguments, reasons or rhetoric. These basic rules were developed long ago and have stood the test of time because they serve the vital purpose of identifying the matters which each party will need to prove by evidence at trial."*

*Add to note 6:* Section 1(1), Defamation Act 2013 does not allow a claimant to allege that it is "likely" that the defendant has published words to some unknown people on some unknown occasion and that it is "likely" that this has caused serious harm to the claimant's reputation: see *Decker v Hopcraft* [2015] EWHC 1170 at [59]-[61].

*Note 9, first sentence, remove the words in brackets*: "(not yet in force)". Section 1(1), Defamation Act 2013 came into force on 1 January 2014.

[139]

*Last sentence, replace,* "When s.1(2), Defamation Act 2013 comes into force," with "Section 1(2), Defamation Act 2013, came into force on 1 January 2014" [*New note 12A at end of paragraph*].

*New note 12A:* In *Cartus Corporation Ltd v Siddell & Anor* [2014] EWHC 2266 (QB), Nicol J. agreed with the last sentence of this paragraph explaining that s.1(2), Defamation Act 2013 is a new feature of defamation law and claimants will need to address it. He said at [32(v)], "*I note, however, that Gatley at paragraph 26.2 says that "When s.1(2) comes into force, a body that trades for profit will have to set out how the publication has caused or is likely to cause serious financial loss." I agree. By CPR r.16.4(1)(a) Particulars of Claim must include a concise statement of the facts on which the Claimant relies. Paragraph 16.4.1 to the White Book notes that "The claimant should state all the facts necessary for the purpose of formulating a complete cause of action." Those will now have to include the matters to which Gatley refers.*" Where claimants are companies within an international group of companies, there may be a difficulty demonstrating serious harm in respect of the non-local trading company which may not be understood to be referred to in the words complained of: see *Reachlocal UK Ltd v Bennett* [2014] EWHC 3405 (QB); [2015] E.M.L.R. 7 at [34].

SECTION 3. PUBLICATION

**26.5**     **Details of publication: libel.** *In the final sentence, remove the words in brackets* "(when it comes into force)". Section 10, Defamation Act 2013 is in force.

**26.7**     **Publication to persons unknown.** *Add to end of note 36:* see *Decker v Hopcraft* [2015] EWHC 1170 at [59].

SECTION 4. THE WORDS PUBLISHED

**26.11**     **Setting out words complained of: libel.** *Add to end of note 47:*

Setting out in the Particulars of Claim the URL where particular words can be found is insufficient: see *Wissa v Associated Newspapers Ltd* [2014] EWHC 1518 (QB). As Tugendhat J. said at [29], "*In my judgment the effect of the CPR 16, the Practice Direction and the guidance given by the Court of Appeal in Best, is that in a claim for libel it is necessary that the Claimant should set out word for word precisely those words which he alleges defame him, whether that is the whole of the text or, as is more commonly the case, an extract from a much larger text.*" See also *Decker v Hopcraft* [2015] EWHC 1170 at [64], [67].

*Add to note 51:* See also *Cartus Corporation Ltd v Siddell & Anor* [2014] EWHC 2266 (QB) (Nicol J.) at [27].

**Setting out words complained of: slander.** *Add to end of note 60*: and *Wissa*   **26.13**
*v Associated Newspapers*, [2014] EWHC 1518 (QB).


SECTION 5. FOREIGN PUBLICATION


**Foreign publication.** *Final sentence, remove* "it has been held at first instance   **26.19**
that".

*Delete note 83 from* "University" *to* "remained good law" *and replace with*:
In *OPO v MLA* [2014] EWCA Civ 109; [2015] E.M.L.R. 4 the Court of Appeal
held that despite certain doubts and reservations expressed in earlier first instance
authorities (referred to in the main text) the "presumption" that the laws of
foreign countries are the same as domestic law remains valid and applicable: see
in particular the judgment of Arden L.J. at [108]-[111]. The Supreme Court
overturned the decision of the Court of Appeal on other grounds. Although this
point was not argued on appeal Lord Neuberger (with whom Lord Wilson
agreed) specifically accepted that the presumption could be applicable, although
he gave no reasons: *O v A* [2015] UKSC 32; [2015] 2 W.L.R. 1373 at [121]. In
*Brownlie v Four Seasons Holdings Incorporated* [2015] EWCA Civ 665 at [73],
[88], [89] Arden L.J. followed her own judgment in *OPO*. For an application of
the principle, see *Ames v Spamhaus Project Ltd* [2015] EWHC 127 (QB); [2015]
E.M.L.R. 1 at [103]-[111] where *OPO* was applied.

*Add to end of paragraph:* Where foreign publication is not pleaded, the claim
must be taken to be limited to publication in England and Wales [*new note
83A*].

*New note 83A: ReachLocal UK Ltd v Bennett* [2015] EWHC 3405 (QB);
[2015] E.M.L.R. 7 at [19].


SECTION 6. THE MEANING OF THE WORDS


**Pleading meanings.** *Note 84*, Section 1, Defamation Act 2013 is now in   **26.20**
force.

*Note 85, Replace* "However, when s.11, Defamation Act 2013 is brought into
effect" *with*, "Now Section 11, Defamation Act 2013 is in force".

*After* "the courts must consider any meanings that can properly be advanced"
*add*: For further examples where the court has stressed that it is not bound by the
parties' pleaded meanings, see *Johnson v League Publications* [2014] EWHC
874 (QB) at [5]; *Donovan v Gibbons* [2014] EWHC 3406 (QB) at [22]; *Rufus v
Elliott* [2015] EWHC 807 (QB) at [23]; *Mughal v Telegraph Media Group
Limited* [2014] EWHC 1371 (QB) at [3]; *White v Express Newspapers* [2014]
EWHC 657 (QB) at [10]; *RBOS Shareholders Action Group Ltd v News Group
Newspapers Ltd* [2014] EWHC 130 (QB); [2014] E.M.L.R. 15 at [14].

**26.21**     **Surmounting the threshold of seriousness.** *Add to note 91*: For a further application of the principle involving a company, see *Prince Al Saud v Forbes LLC* [2014] EWHC 3823 (QB) at [53]-[55].

*Delete entire paragraph, apart from note 91, and replace as follows*:

Defamation Act 2013 s.1 is now in force. Section 1(1) provides that a statement is not defamatory unless its publication has caused or is likely to cause serious harm to the reputation of the claimant; s.1(2), that harm to the reputation of a body that trades for profit is not "serious harm" unless it has caused or is likely to cause the body serious financial loss.

The following principles applicable to pleading can be discerned from the cases to date. Pleaders must continue to plead the defamatory meaning of the words complained of: CPR 53 PD para. 2.3. For a statement to be defamatory it is now necessary to prove as a fact, on the balance of probabilities, that serious reputational harm has been caused by, or is likely to result in the future from, the publication of the words complained of: *Lachaux v Independent Print Limited)* [2015] EWHC 2242; [2015] E.M.L.R. 28, Warby J. at [45], [65]. The Particulars of Claim should make clear which limb or limbs of Defamation Act 2013, s1, are relied upon: *Ames v Spamhaus Project Ltd* [2015] EWHC 127 (QB); [2015] E.M.L.R. 1 at [102]; *Cartus Corporation Ltd v Siddell & Anor* [2014] EWHC 2266 (QB) at [32(v)].

The test under either limb of s.1(1) can be met by adducing actual evidence of harm having been caused or by inviting the court to draw an inference that harm has been caused or is likely to be caused: *Cooke v MGN Ltd* [2014] EWHC 2831 (QB); [2015] 1 WLR 895, [41]-[43]; *Donovan v Gibbons* [2014] EWHC 3406 (QB) at [6]; *Ames v Spamhaus Project Ltd,* above, at [55]; *Lachaux v Independent Print Limited,* above, at [57], [65]. Since the issue is one of fact which must be proved by evidence or inference, the facts relied upon must be pleaded: CPR 16.4(1)(a); *Cartus Corporation Ltd v Siddell & Anor,* above, at [32(v)]; *Ames v Spamhaus Project Ltd* , above, at [102].

The facts which need to be identified in the pleaded case are the same as those which come into play in assessing whether a tort is real and substantial: *Ames* v *Spamhaus Project Ltd,* above, at [52]. They include: the gravity of the imputation; the extent of publication; the fact that the statement was published by a credible source; the likely readership; the actual reputation of the claimant as at the date of publication; the fact that the statement was believed; the reaction of readers or commentators online to the words complained of ('adverse social media responses' or 'name-calling'); the absence of an apology or withdrawal of the allegations; the republication of the words complained of; and any actual loss or damage caused. (See *Lachaux v Independent Print Limited,* above, at [57]-[59], [74], [86]; *Cooke v MGN Ltd,* above, at [41]-[43]). The position will be the same under s1(2), where the test under either limb can be met by adducing actual evidence of loss having been caused or by inviting the court to draw an inference that loss has been caused or is likely to be caused: *Cartus Corporation Ltd v Siddell & Anor,* above, at [32(v)].

Where the claimant relies upon a statement being 'likely to' cause harm in the future, the time when that issue is to be judged is unresolved [*new note 92*].

*Delete existing note 92 and replace with new note 92 as follows:* In *Cooke v MGN,* above, Bean J. considered at [32] that the relevant time was when the claim form was issued. In *Lachaux v Independent Print Limited,* above, Warby J. preferred the date when the issue was determined, that is to say, at trial: [67]. Pleaders would be well advised to guard against either scenario and to plead the fullest case possible at the time of settling the Particulars of Claim, amending later, if required. It is to be noted that in *Reachlocal UK Ltd v Bennett* [2015] EWHC 3405 (QB); [2015] E.M.L.R. 7 H.H.J. Parkes Q.C. (sitting as a High Court Judge) took into account evidence served of the dissemination of the material complained of on social media sites when assessing damages even though it had not been pleaded: [60].

**Pleading the natural and ordinary meaning**. *Add new sentence at end of* **26.22** *paragraph*: Now that the Defamation Act 2013 is in force and the courts are ordering trials of preliminary issues on meaning, serious harm and whether the words are fact or comment, it may be that pleaded meanings will become more restrained. A meaning which may have been found to be capable for the purpose of opening a case before a jury might not be the correct one by a judge sitting alone and this may impact upon costs.

**Miscellaneous considerations** Add to *note 102*: See also para. 26.20, Note **26.25** 85.

*Note 105: replace* "when the jury ceases to be the presumptive tribunal of fact in defamation cases" *with* "Now that the jury has ceased to be the presumptive tribunal of fact in defamation cases". Section 11, Defamation Act 2013 is in force and applies to proceedings started on or since 1 January 2014.

SECTION 7. IDENTIFICATION OF THE CLAIMANT

**Averment of reference to the claimant.** *Add to note 107, after the second* **26.26** *reference to Fullam v Newcastle*:

See also *Yeo v Times Newspapers Ltd (no3)* [2015] EWHC 2132 (QB) at [38]. Warby J. said, outlining the essential issues at the trial, " . . . *how many of those who read the Sunday Times article of 23 June 2013 had read the articles of 9 June, and recalled enough of what had been published then to identify Mr Yeo as the "select committee chairman" referred to . . . I do not accept that in order to sustain such a case it is necessary for a claimant to adduce evidence from readers in the relevant class. That may be so, if the inference that would otherwise have to be drawn is an inherently improbable one as, for instance, in Fullam v Newcastle Chronicle & Journal Ltd [1977] 1 WLR 651 (CA). But I see no reason why in this case the court may not proceed by way of inference, in the absence of evidence from such readers. This is a national newspaper with a very substantial circulation; it is well-known that newspaper readers are reasonably loyal to a given title; the articles of 9 June were prominent; and only a fortnight passed between the two articles. The inference cannot be said to be fanciful".*

SECTION 8. ACTIONS FOR SLANDER

**26.27**   **Actions for slander.** *Delete second sentence (starting "Similarly, where") and note 113. Replace as follows*: Section 14(1), Defamation Act 2013 has repealed the Slander of Women Act 1891 and s.14(2) will require proof of special damage where the imputation is that a person has a contagious or infectious disease.

SECTION 9. DAMAGES

**26.28**   **General damages.** *Delete whole paragraph and replace with*: Until the coming into force of s1, Defamation Act 2013, a claimant in an action for libel has not needed to allege that actual damage to reputation has resulted from the words complained of. For the position at common law see the authorities cited in this paragraph in the main text. However, in England and Wales for a statement to be defamatory it is now necessary to prove as a fact, on the balance of probabilities, that serious reputational harm has been caused by, or is likely to result in the future from the publication of, the words complained of. Whilst there may be a difference between the concepts of harm and damage, pleaders are well advised at present to repeat the matters pleaded to surmount the threshold of seriousness when addressing the case on damages.

*Add new note 117*: In *Lachaux v Independent Print Limited* [2015] EWHC 2242 (QB); [2015] E.M.L.R. 28, above, Warby J. held at [60] and [86] that upon his construction of s.1, Defamation Act 2013, libel is no longer actionable without proof of serious harm to reputation, and the legal presumption of damage will cease to play any significant role. See para 26.21 above.

*Delete notes 118 to 122.*

**26.29**   **Where damage must be pleaded**. *Add new first sentence*: The effect of s.1 is that serious harm or likelihood of harm to reputation must be pleaded in all cases. *Add new note 122A.*

*New note 122A*: See *Lachaux v Independent Print Limited* [2015] EWHC 2242 (QB); [2015] E.M.L.R. 28, above, at [60] and [86] and para 26.21 above.

*Delete first sentence in main text and replace with:* A claimant must give particulars of the facts and matters relied upon in support of a claim for damages, including details of any conduct by the defendant which it is alleged has increased the loss suffered and of any loss which is peculiar to the claimant's claim.

*Add to end of note 123*: In *Flood v Times Newspapers Ltd* [2014] EWCA Civ 1574 the Court of Appeal upheld Nicola Davies J.'s decision ([2013] EWHC 4075 (QB)) to order the defendant to pay the claimant's costs of the action. There was no appeal from her award of £60,000 in damages, made up of £45,000 general damages and *"£15,000 to represent the aggravation of those damages by reason of the conduct of the defendant and to serve as a deterrent to those who embark upon public interest journalism but thereafter refuse to publish material which in whole, or in part, exculpates the subject of the investigation"*. The Court of Appeal set out in an appendix the passages from the judge's judgment (at [71] to [78]) which identified the matters relevant to aggravated damages which would have to be pleaded (unless they only occurred at trial). The factors identified included the failure of *The Times* to accept the findings of a police investigation vindicating the claimant; the "aggressive and unpleasant" conduct of the then Legal Manager for *The Times*, Alistair Brett; and the manner in which the defence of justification was conducted.

*Add to note 129*: In *Reachlocal UK Ltd v Bennett*, above, [60] evidence of the dissemination of the material complained of on social media sites was taken into account when assessing damages even though it had not been pleaded.

*Add to note 130*: However, regard must be had to proportionality: see *Yeo v Times Newspapers Ltd (no3)*, above, at [42(i)]—[42(ii)].

## SECTION 10. OTHER RELIEF

**Order for a summary of judgment to be published.** *In the first sentence,* **26.37**
*remove* "When it comes into force" *and replace* "will give" *with* "gives".
Section 12, Defamation Act 2013 is now in force.

**Order to remove a statement or cease distribution.** *In the first sentence,* **26.38**
*remove* "When it comes into force" *and replace* "will give" *with* "gives".
Section 13, Defamation Act 2013 is now in force.

## SECTION 12. MALICIOUS FALSEHOOD

**Generally.** *Note 168*: The first instance judgment on meaning in *Cruddas v* **26.42**
*Calvert* is reported at [2014] E.M.L.R. 4. The appeal from that decision is now reported at [2014] E.M.L.R. 5. An appeal from the decision at trial in *Cruddas v Calvert* was allowed in part: see [2015] EWCA Civ 171; [2015] E.M.L.R. 16.

*Add to end of note 168:* The Court of Appeal in the first *Cruddas* appeal held that where an article had one correct meaning which was true but was susceptible to a second incorrect interpretation by some cynical readers which was untrue, and the author intended the article to convey its correct meaning but foresaw that some cynical readers would place upon it the incorrect interpretation, then that did not constitute malice for the purpose of malicious falsehood. The pleader will have to consider carefully whether there is any advantage in pleading alternative meanings.

After the end of the fourth sentence, after "support the allegation of malice", add new note 169A.

*New note 169A*: In *Cruddas v Calvert* [2013] EWHC 1096 (QB) at [15] to [18], Nicol J. refused permission to amend to allow the claimant to include in his case on malice an allegation of intention to injure a third party.

*Add to note 171 after* "speculative case on damage": The Court of Appeal in *Cruddas v Calvert* allowing the appeal in part did not address s.3(1), Defamation Act 1952.

*Add to end of note 171*: See also *Niche Products Ltd v MacDermid Offshore Solutions LLC* [2013] EWHC 3540 (IPEC); [2014] E.M.L.R. 9.

*Add to end of note 172*: See also *Niche Products Ltd v MacDermid Offshore Solutions LLC* [2013] EWHC 3540 (IPEC); [2014] E.M.L.R. 9.

Section 13. Misuse Of Private Information

**26.43**    **Generally.** *Add to note 175:* See also *Vidal-Hall v Google Inc* [2015] EWCA Civ 311; [2015] 3 WLR 409. The Supreme Court gave *Google* permission to appeal on the parts of the decision relating to the Data Protection Act 1998. It refused permission on the question of whether the Court of Appeal was right to hold that the claimants' claims for misuse of private information were claims in tort for the purposes of the rules relating to service out of the jurisdiction.

*Add to note 179*: In *Weller v Associated Newspapers* [2014] EWHC 1163 (QB); [2014] E.M.L.R. 24 (appeal pending) Dingemans J. at [36] followed *Murray v Big Pictures (UK) Ltd* (note 178) and considered that the test for a reasonable expectation of privacy was a broad objective test which allowed publishers to take account of matters which they did not know, and could not have known about, at the time of publication, to order to show that there was no reasonable expectation of privacy. Again, such matters should be pleaded. The majority in the Supreme Court in *In the matter of an application by JR38 for Judicial Review* (Northern Ireland) [2015] UKSC 42 affirmed the *Murray v Express Newspapers* test, finding that the reasonable expectation of privacy test incorporates all the contextual information, and so remains the touchstone of article 8 engagement.

*Add new sentence after* "particularity as in libel and slander", *11 lines from the top of p.1017*:

It is not necessarily an abuse of process to bring a claim for misuse of private information or breach of confidence which involves the protection of reputation. *Add new note 182A.*

*New note 182A*: See *Hannon v News Group Newspapers Ltd* [2015] EWHC 1580 (Ch); [2015] E.M.L.R. 1. This case is an illustration of the potential for overlap between causes of action in privacy and defamation. An earlier examination of this developing area of law can be found in *Terry (LNS) v Persons Unknown* [2010] EWHC 119 (QB); [2010] E.M.L.R. 16 at [96].

Section 14: Amendment of Particulars of Claim

**Permission necessary.** *Add to note 196*: See *Loughran v Century Newspapers*    **26.46**
*Ltd* [2014] NIQB 26, which has a useful summary of the principles governing
amendments to pleadings at [35] to [40].

*Add new note 201A at the end of the first sentence of the third paragraph,*
*ending*: " . . . even after judgment or on appeal".

*New note 201A*: In *Tardios v Linton* [2015] EWHC 1429 (QB), an appeal from
the Master which proceeded as a re-hearing, permission to amend was granted to
allow the claimant to change the name of the defendant after default
judgment.

*Add to end of note 202*: In *Starr v Ward* [2015] EWHC 1987 (QB) Nicol J.
refused an application to amend at trial to include complaint about a further
publication but allowed an application to amend to plead that words complained
about as a slander were actionable without proof of special loss: [65]. The Judge
dismissed an argument from the defendant that permission would cause prejudice. He said at [66], *"While I understand that a legal representative . . . has to*
*make choices as to how to prepare for a trial, an argument based on prejudice*
*has to be rather more clearly particularised. I could not discern in [the defen-*
*dant's] submissions any particular questions which he would have wished to put*
*to any of the witnesses if the Particulars of Claim had stood as [the claimant]*
*wishes to amend them."* In *Moulay Hicham v Elaph Publishing Ltd* [2015]
EWHC 2021 (QB), Dingemans J. noted at [9] that the proposed amendment to
include a Data Protection Act claim was made after there had been an application
to determine whether the article complained of was capable of bearing a defamatory meaning but before a defence had been served, and *"in the general terms of*
*this action the application is not very late."*

*Add to end of note 203*: In *Meadows Care Ltd v Lambert* [2014] EWHC 1226
(QB) the claimant sought to amend the words complained of in a slander action
to substitute a new version of the words attributed to the defendant. Bean J. held
that the revision of the pleaded text of the defendant's remarks did not involve
adding or substituting a new claim within the meaning of CPR 17.4(2) but said
that if he was wrong about that then the new claim arose out of the same or
substantially the same facts: [11].

CHAPTER 27

## DEFENCE

SECTION 1. GENERAL PRINCIPLES

**27.1**   **Defamation Act 2013.** *First sentence, remove* "which is not yet in force." The Defamation Act 2013 is now in force, as from 1 January 2014.

*Final sentence, delete and replace with:* CPR Pt 53 governs defamation actions and sets out the various pleading requirements and is designed to reflect the common law.

*Note 8, delete and replace with:*

In *Barron v Vines* [2015] EWHC 1161 (QB) Warby J. said at [17], "*A Defendant who wishes to advance any of the defences I have mentioned must specifically plead it. The rules as to what needs to be pleaded by way of defence are set out in the Part 53 Practice Direction. This requires a defence of truth to specify the defamatory meaning the Defendant intends to justify and to give details of the matters relied on in support of that allegation: PD53 2.5. Similar requirements apply to the defence of honest opinion (PD53 2.6). The same in principle is true of the defence of publication on a matter of public interest, though the PD has yet to be updated in this respect; it currently refers to "a privileged occasion" (PD53 2.7) reflecting the Reynolds privilege defence.*

*New para: 27.1A* **No need for a defence.** *Add*: Where a defendant proposes to defend a claim on the sole basis that it does not meet the threshold under s.1,

Defamation Act 2013 there may be no need and indeed good reason not to serve a defence. [*new note 9A*]

*New note 9A*: In *Lachaux v Independent Print Limited* [2015] EWHC 2242 (QB); [2015] E.M.L.R. 28 at [168]-[169] Warby J. said that the existence of a substantive defence is immaterial for this purpose and would preclude a defendant who lost on the issue of serious harm from making an offer of amends under ss.2-4, Defamation Act 1996.

*Add*: It should still be necessary to outline the case the defendant intends to run when denying or not admitting that the claim would surmount the s.1, Defamation Act 2013 threshold. This would be in order to allow the claimant to know the basis of the challenge and to accord with the "cards on the table" principle, although it appears that the courts are happy for this to be done in correspondence and not in a formal pleading. It is open to a defendant to plead that the claimant has a bad reputation in the relevant sector of his life to seek to defend a claim that serious harm has been caused or is likely to be caused but this cannot be done by reference to other publications publishing the same or similar allegations [*new note 9B*].

*New note 9B*: *Lachaux v Independent Print Limited,* above, at [74], [84]-[86], [190].

**General denial insufficient Add to note 10**: For the repercussions of failing **27.2** to plead to specific claims raised in a misuse of private information claim, see *Gulati v MGN Ltd* [2015] EWHC 1482 (QB). Mann J. held that it was not open to the defendant to contend at trial that articles admitted to be the result of phone-hacking did not contain private information where it had failed to deal with each allegation of that kind in its defence: see [21] to [23], [222]-[223], [282], [283], [410], [413], [466]. Similarly the Judge held that the defendant could not argue that an article attracted a public interest defence which had not been pleaded: [464], [517]-[518].

**Specific denials.** *Note 14, remove the words* "(not yet in force)". *Section 1,* **27.3** Defamation Act 2013 is now in force. *Add to note 14*: It has been rare for a defendant to defend a claim on the sole basis that the words were not defamatory. However, this may well be how a number of claims are determined in the future. Defendants can apply for trials of preliminary issues seeking to test whether a claimant can overcome the s.1 threshold before or at the same time as serving an affirmative defence, see *Cooke v MGN* [2014] EWHC 2813 (QB); [2015] 1 W.L.R. 895; *Lachaux v Independent Print Limited* [2015] EWHC 915 (QB) at [2]-[3]; *Ames v The Spamhaus Project Ltd* [2015] EWHC 127 (QB), [2015] EMLR 13 [101]; *Lachaux v Independent Print Limited* [2015] EWHC 2242 (QB); [2015] E.M.L.R. 28 at [7].

*Note 19, second sentence:* add: Section 11, Defamation Act 2013 has been in force since 1 January 2014 and bites on actions started on or after that date.

**27.4**     **Substantive defences.** *Add new note 25A at end of first sentence.*

*New note 25A:* In *Meadows Care v Lambert* [2014] EWHC 1226 (QB) Bean J. at [12] expressed the view that *"a defendant cannot sensibly be expected to formulate a defence of honest comment in a slander case until it is proved what words he spoke"*. The Judge went on to say that it was undesirable for a defendant to advance defences in a piecemeal fashion but that it was permissible to keep some or all of his powder dry until after a ruling on meaning.

Section 2. Plea of Justification

**27.6**     **When to plead this defence.** *Add new first sentence*: In England and Wales this defence has now been abolished by the s2(4), Defamation Act 2013 which is addressed later in this chapter at s.3. However, until the courts hold otherwise the law pertaining to the common law defence of justification remains relevant to the statutory defence of truth and the pleading requirements remain the same.

**27.8**     **Justifying the words in their natural and ordinary meaning,** *Add to end of Note 41*: The appeal was allowed in part in *Cruddas v Calvert*: see [2015] EWCA Civ 171; [2015] E.M.L.R. 16. This point was not considered by the Court of Appeal.

*Add to end of Note 46*: See also *Johnson v League Publications Ltd* [2014] EWHC 874 (QB) at [42].

*Note 51, first sentence replace* "when" *with* "now". Section 11, Defamation Act 2013 is now in force.

*Add to end of Note 53*: The appeal was allowed in part in *Cruddas v Calvert*, see [2015] EWCA Civ 171; [2015] E.M.L.R. 16. This point was not considered by the Court of Appeal.

**27.9**     **Partial Justification.** *Add to end of Note 54*: See *Simpson v MGN* [2015] EWHC 77 (QB) at [27(ii)] and *Stocker v Stocker* [2015] EWHC 1634 at [40(ii)].

*Note 59, replace second sentence with*: "Section 2(4), Defamation 2013 has abolished s.5, Defamation Acbut s.2(3) should have a similar effect. See paras 11.16-11.17, above,"

**27.10**    **Justifying an innuendo meaning.** *Add new Note 60A at end of second sentence.*

*New note 60A:* Eady J. disapproved of this statement in *Johnson v League Publications Ltd* [2014] EWHC 874 (QB) and considered that the law was stated correctly at para 3.23 above: see [39]-[41], [44] The Judge said: *[39] Counsel referred to Gatley on Libel & Slander (12th edn) at para 27.10, where the learned editors refer to a claimant's legal innuendo constituting a separate cause of action. They go on to add the comment: "It is submitted that a defendant wishing to meet this separate cause of action with a plea of justification must confine himself to the legal innuendo meaning contended for by the claimant." What seems to me to matter primarily, however, is not the somewhat technical point as to whether the claimant happens to plead separate causes of action, but simply whether there is a defamatory meaning (not separate and distinct from that pleaded by the claimant) which the defendant would be able to justify, thereby depriving the claimant of any right to compensation in respect of that aspect of his reputation: see e.g. Polly Peck v Trelford [1986] 1 QB 1000, at 1032C-D. [40] I note, however, that in a different chapter, at para 3.23, the editors appear expressly to acknowledge a defendant's right to plead extrinsic facts in support of his own innuendo, but they go on to suggest that " . . . he must show that all the persons to whom the words were published knew the facts, since otherwise the claimant will have been defamed to those persons who did not know the facts". The potential impact of this point on the First and Second Defendants' case is considerable. A claimant obviously " . . . need not show that all of the persons to whom the words were published knew the facts" (emphasis added): see Gatley at para 3.22 and the well known cases of Cassidy v Daily Mirror [1929] 2 KB 331, CA, and Hough v London Express [1940] 2 KB 507, CA. As to a defendant's innuendo, the editors refer to a Singapore case: Chiang See Tong v Xin Zhang Jiang Restaurants [1995] 3 SLR 196. They also cite some 19th century cases from various jurisdictions, including Hankinson v Bilby (1847) 16 M&W 422. The principle seems clear, however, despite the dearth of recent English cases. A claimant who can show that the extrinsic facts were known to some of the readers will ex hypothesi have established a defamatory publication to them at least; whereas a defendant who can only show that some readers knew the extrinsic facts he prays in aid will, by the same token, only be able make out a partial defence of justification. It cannot avail him in respect of any readers who were unaware of the relevant facts.*

**Pleading particulars of justification** Add to end of note 64: See Barron v **27.11** Vines [2015] EWHC 1161 (QB) at [17], set out at 27.1 above.

Add to end of note 65: See the discussion in *Johnson v League Publications Ltd* [2014] EWHC 874 (QB) at [41]-[45] and *Karpov v Browder* [2013] EWHC 3071 (QB); [2014] E.M.L.R. 8, where Simon J. held that several paragraphs of the plea of justification were unsustainable. He set out the principles applicable to a plea of justification at [124] before striking out the paragraphs in question because part of the plea focused on the claimant's motive and "*motive alone is not sufficient to support a plea of torture and murder*" and the "*causal link which would one expect from such a serious charge [of involvement in an arrest and imprisonment] is wholly lacking*": [127] to [133]. The Judge also rejected the argument that certain particulars should stay because they were "*part of the story*". Simon J. said at [135], "*The purpose of a pleading is not to tell a story with parenthetical digressions of the story-teller's choosing, but to set out material facts with concision.*" A similar point was made by Leggatt J. in *Tchenguiz v Grant Thornton LLP* [2015] EWHC 405 (Comm) at [1].

*Add to end of Note 68*: See also *Karpov v Browder* [2013] EWHC 3071 (QB); [2014] E.M.L.R. 8.

*Add to note 72 before the final sentence:* In *Stocker v Stocker* [2015] EWHC 1634 (QB) Warby J. declined to apply the *obiter dictum* of Elias L.J. in *Ashcroft v Foley*. The Judge referred to a further decision of Eady J. handed down after the Court of Appeal hearing and reported as *Ashcroft v Foley (no2)* [2012] EWHC 2214 (QB); [2012] E.M.L.R. 32 and said at [26], *"This decision of Eady J was not cited at the hearing, but I refer to it only as reinforcing the view that I would have taken in any event on the basis of the Court of Appeal decision: it is not established law that the pleading of fraud or similarly grave allegations by way of justification is subject to the probability test. I do not, therefore, accept the starting point for Counsel's argument by analogy".*

*Add to note 73 after the reference to Chase v News Group Newspapers Ltd*: The principles applicable to the justification of a *Chase* level 2 meaning were set out in the judgment of Moore-Bick L.J. at [13] in *Miller v Associated Newspapers Limited* [2014] EWCA Civ 39, upholding a decision of Sharp J. at trial.

*Add to end of note 75*: The Court of Appeal upheld the decision of Sharp J. in *Miller v Associated Newspapers Ltd* [2014] EWCA Civ 39.

*Add to end of note 77:* The Court of Appeal in *Miller v Associated Newspapers Ltd* [2014] EWCA Civ 39 made no reference to this paragraph when upholding Sharp J.

*Replace note 78 with*: The Court of Appeal held in *Miller v Associated Newspapers Ltd* [2014] EWCA Civ 39 that explanations given at trial by the defendant about his state of mind at the date of publication should not usually be admissible. Moore-Bick L.J. (with whom Maurice Kay and Lloyd Jones L.L.J. agreed) held at [15], *"In my view, therefore, the claimant's subsequent account of what he thought, believed or intended, even though in one sense it is evidence of a fact subsisting before the date of publication, is not relevant, because it is not itself a primary fact for these purposes. If, however, it is possible to draw an inference about the claimant's state of mind at the time from other primary facts (e.g. that he was aware of a matter that was common knowledge), I see no reason why the reasonable person, or the court acting in that capacity, should not do so."*

**27.13**   **Miscellaneous considerations.** *Add sentence at end of paragraph*: Care should be taken not to plead particulars which are non-justiciable. *[Add new note 84A]*.

*New note 84A*: See *Yeo v Times Newspapers Ltd (no3)* [2015] EWHC 2132 (QB) where parts of the Reply were accepted to infringe Parliamentary Privilege in circumstances where s.13, Defamation Act 1996, has now been repealed. The same point applies to a defence.

SECTION 3. DEFENCE OF TRUTH UNDER DEFAMATION ACT 2013, SECTION 2

**Defence of truth. Replace first sentence with**:  **27.14**

"Section 2 of the Act is now in force and the common law defence of justification has been abolished and replaced with a statutory defence of truth."

*Add new note 87A after* "CPR Pts15 and 16": see *Barron v Vines* [2015] EWHC 1161 (QB) at [17], referred to at 27.1 above.

SECTION 4. HONEST COMMENT

**The name of the defence**. *Replace final sentence with*: CPR Pt 53 PD paras **27.16** 2.6 and 2.8 have now been amended to refer to honest opinion. [*Add new note 90A*].

*New note 90A*: See also *Barron v Vines*, above, at [17], referred to at 27.1 above.

**Defence must be specifically pleaded**. *Add to end of note 91*: In *Meadows* **27.17** *Care v Lambert* [2014] EWHC 1226 (QB) Bean J. at [12] expressed the view that *"a defendant cannot sensibly be expected to formulate a defence of honest comment in a slander case until it is proved what words he spoke."*

**Pleading honest comment**. *Add to end of note 97*: The appeal was allowed in **27.18** part in *Cruddas v Calvert*, see [2015] EWCA Civ 171; [2015] E.M.L.R.16. This point was not considered by the Court of Appeal.

**Pleading particulars**. *Note 102 replace:* "will repeal" with "has now been **27.19** repealed." Section 3(8), Defamation Act 2013 is now in force.

SECTION 5. DEFENCE OF HONEST OPINION UNDER DEFAMATION ACT 2013,
SECTION 3

*Replace first sentence with*: Section 3 of the Defamation Act 2013 has now **27.23** abolished the common law defence of fair or honest comment. Section 3 repeals s.6, Defamation Act 1952 and replaces it with a statutory defence of honest opinion.

*Add new note 111A after*: "CPR Pts 15 and 16".  **27.24**

*New note 111A:* Some further guidance has been provided in *Barron v Vines*, above, at [17], referred to at para. 27.1 above.

SECTION 6. PLEA OF PRIVILEGE

**27.25**    **Defence must be specially pleaded.** *Add to end of note 113*: See *Barron v Vines,* above, at [17].

**27.27**    **Pleading Reynolds qualified privilege.** *Add to note 122: Seaga v Harper* is reported at [2009] 1 A.C. 1 (PC).

SECTION 7. DEFENCE OF PUBLICATION ON A MATTER OF PUBLIC INTEREST UNDER
DEFAMATION ACT 2013, SECTION 4

**27.30**    *In first sentence, replace* "will abolish" *with* "has abolished." *Second sentence, replace* "It will be a defence" *with* "It is a defence". Section 4, Defamation Act 2013 is now in force in respect of causes of action that accrued on or after 1 January 2014.

**27.31**    *Add new note 149A at end of paragraph.*

*New note 149A.* Warby J. briefly considered the s.4 defence in *Barron v Vines,* above, at [58] to [65] on an application for judgment for damages where the defendant was unrepresented. To satisfy the second limb of the s.4(1) defence (that "the Defendant reasonably believed that publishing the statement complained of was in the public interest") requires a pleaded case and evidence.

SECTION 8. DEFENCE FOR PEER-REVIEWED STATEMENTS UNDER DEFAMATION ACT
2013, SECTION 6

**27.32**    *In first sentence, delete* "When it comes into force" *and replace* "will provide" *with* "provides." Section 6 Defamation Act 2013 is now in force in respect of causes of action that accrued on or after 1 January 2014.

SECTION 9. OTHER PLEAS

**27.36**    **Operators of websites defence under Defamation Act 2013, s5.** *First sentence, replace* "There will be" *with* "This is an". Section 5, Defamation Act 2013 is now in force.

SECTION 10. MITIGATION OF DAMAGES

**27.39**    **Mitigation of damages.** *Add to end of note 174:* In *Simpson v MGN Ltd* [2015] EWHC 77 (QB) the defendant's defence of justification was struck out following a ruling on meaning. However, the defendant was entitled to rely in mitigation of damages on the facts which formed directly relevant background context to the publication complained of.

Section 12. Counterclaim

**Pleading the counterclaim.** *Add to end of note 183*: See *Mole v Hunter* [2014]   **27.43**
EWHC 658 (QB) at [74]-[76], [84].

Section 13. Contribution

**Tortfeasors liable for the same damage.** *Note 184, add before final sentence:*   **27.44**
In *Simpson v MGN Ltd* [2015] EWHC 77 (QB) the defendant newspaper applied
to amend to seek a contribution from its source for the story. Warby J. held (see
[43]) that the draft claim form and Particulars disclosed a reasonable basis for a
claim for a contribution.

Section 14. Misuse of Private Information

**Generally** *Add to note 197*: For the repercussions of failing to plead to specific   **27.47**
claims raised in a misuse of private information claim, see *Gulati v MGN Ltd*
[2015] EWHC 1482 (QB). Mann J held that it was not open to the defendants to
contend at trial that articles admitted to be the result of phone-hacking did not
contain private information where it had failed to deal with each allegation of that
kind in its defence: see [21] to [23], [222]-[223], [282], [283], [410], [413],
[466]. Similarly the Judge held that the defendant could not argue that an article
could attract a public interest defence which had not been pleaded: [464],
[517]-[518].

*Add new note 197A after* "he should plead as much."

*New note 197A*: In *Weller v Associated Newspapers* [2014] EWHC 1163 (QB);
[2014] E.M.L.R. 24 (appeal pending) Dingemans J. at [36] followed *Murray v
Big Pictures (UK) Ltd* [2008] EWCA Civ 446; [2009] Ch. 481 and considered
that the test for a reasonable expectation of privacy was a broad objective test
which allows publishers to take account of matters which they did not know, and
could not have known about, at the time of publication, to show that there was
no reasonable expectation of privacy. A defendant therefore can include, in a
response to a claim that a publication was a misuse of private information,
relevant facts and matters that it was not aware of at the time of publication. It
was also said in *Weller* at [70] that "*The reasonable expectation of privacy may
be affected by activities carried out by the person claiming an interference with
their private life or, if the person is a child, their parent.*" The Supreme Court
considered article 8 and the reasonable expectation of privacy test in *In the
Matter of an application by JR38 for Judicial Review (Northern Ireland)* [2015]
UKSC 42. The applicant, a 14 year old boy, complained that the publication of
CCTV images taken of him in the course of a riot and later published in a
newspaper breached his rights under Article 8. The Supreme Court dismissed the
appeal. All the judges agreed that if article 8 was engaged then the interference
with the right was justified but they split over whether it was engaged.

SECTION 16. DEFAULT IN SERVICE OF A DEFENCE

27.50    **Generally.** *Add to note 223*: Examples of applications by a defendant to set aside default judgment include *S v Beach* [2014] EWHC 4189 (QB); [2015] 1 W.L.R. 2701 where the defendant was successful in setting aside judgment in default in a harassment claim, and *Reachlocal UK Ltd & Anor v Bennett & Ors* [2014] EWHC 2161 (QB) where an application for relief from sanctions for filing to serve a defence in an action for libel, slander, malicious falsehood and other causes of action was refused for the first defendant and allowed for the third defendant.

27.52    **Where an injunction is claimed** *Add to note 233*: See *Reachlocal UK Ltd & Anor v Bennett & Ors,* above, at [1] and *Appleyard v Wilby* [2014] EWHC 2770 (QB), where the applicant police officer applied successfully for judgment in default of acknowledgement of service against the defendant and was awarded damages and an injunction.

CHAPTER 28

# REPLY AND DEFENCE TO COUNTERCLAIM

SECTION 3. PLEADING TO A DEFENCE UNDER SECTIONS 2 AND 3, DEFAMATION
ACT 2013

**Admission or denial of facts pleaded in support of a plea under sections 2 28.3
and 3 of the Defamation Act 2013.** *Replace first sentence with:* CPR Pt 53 PD
paras 2.6 and 2.8 have now been amended to refer to honest opinion.

**Pleading an affirmative case.** *Add before final sentence*, Care should be taken 28.4
when responding to a plea of truth or honest opinion not to raise matters which
are non-justiciable and *new note 8A*.

*New note 8A:* see *Yeo v Times Newspapers Ltd (no3)* [2015] EWHC 2132 (QB)
where parts of the Reply were accepted to infringe Parliamentary Privilege in
circumstances where s.13, Defamation Act 1996, has now been repealed.

SECTION 5. MALICE

**Malice** *Add to note 15*: In *Makudi v Triesman* [2014] EWCA Civ 179; [2014] **28.6**
Q.B. 839 the Court of Appeal agreed with the submission of the claimant that it
was not necessary to plead that a defendant had an ulterior motive to establish
malice but re-iterated that a properly particularised case on malice was still
required: [35] to [37].

*Add to end of Note 16:* see also *Cruddas v Calvert* [2013] EWHC 1096 (QB)
at [11]-[12]; *Yeo v Times Newspapers Ltd (No2)* [2015] EWHC 209 (QB); [2015]
1 W.L.R. 3031 at [35].

*Add to note 17 after the first sentence*: The pleading requirements set out in
this paragraph were also endorsed in *Yeo v Times Newspapers Ltd (No2)* [2015]
EWHC 209 (QB); [2015] 1 W.L.R. 3031 at [35] where the court re-iterated the

correct approach to be taken to pleading and proving malice: [30] to [35]. In *Yeo (No2)* Warby J. emphasised that a plea of malice was *"a very different thing"* to a case that journalists had failed to meet the objective standard of responsible journalism: [37]. The Judge struck out the malice plea without prejudice to an application to amend to add a plea of malice, if one could be properly formulated: [42]. See also *Barry v Butler* [2015] EWHC 447 (QB) at [11] to [27] and *Loughran v Century Newspapers Ltd* [2014] NIQB 26 at [11] to [22].

*Add to end of note 18*: see *Niche Products Ltd v MacDermid Offshore Solutions LLC* [2013] EWHC 3540 (IPEC); [2014] E.M.L.R. 9, a malicious falsehood claim, at [55], [61].

*Add to end of note 23*: see also *Abdalla v Transport for London* [2013] EWHC 3916 (QB); [2014] L.L.R. 241, a misfeasance in public office claim, where H.H.J. Moloney QC (sitting as a High Court Judge) said at [20] that *"you do not have to identify by name the individuals [within a corporation] involved, but you have to be satisfied that there were individuals with malicious intent."*

## Section 7. Other Statements of Case

**28.8**     **Other statements of case.** *Add to end of note 27*: See *Yeo v Times Newspapers Ltd (no2)*, above, at [16] where Warby J. was addressing a detailed Reply and said, *"The rules of pleading do not call for any response to a Reply. Even in libel actions, which feature more statements of case than many other kinds of claim, a Rejoinder is extremely rare."* This may have been an example of a case where a rejoinder would have been useful.

CHAPTER 29

# APOLOGY, OFFER OF AMENDS AND COMPROMISE

SECTION 1. APOLOGY

**Apology: mitigation and defence.** *Add at end of paragraph*: Furthermore, a   **29.1**
prompt apology is capable of rebutting the inference that a publication has caused
or is likely to cause serious harm to reputation for the purposes of s.1 of the
Defamation Act 2013 [*new note 5A*].

*New note 5A*: See *Cooke v MGN Ltd* [2014] EWHC 2831 (QB); [2015] 1
W.L.R. 895 at [44] per Bean J. (albeit note that Bean J. granted the claimant
unqualified permission to appeal against his own decision, whereupon the case
settled). See further *Lachaux v Independent Print Ltd* [2015] EWHC 2242 (QB);
[2015] E.M.L.R. 28, per Warby J. at [68].

SECTION 2. SETTLEMENT

**CPR and settlement.** *Note 24: delete reference to CPR r.36.3(2)(a) and*   **29.6**
*substitute:* CPR r.36.7(1).

**Methods of settlement.** *Add to note 31*: An 8th edition of *Foskett, The Law*   **29.8**
*and Practice of Compromise* was published in July 2015.

**Terms incorporated in a judgment.** *Add to note 37*: In *Small v Turner* [2013]   **29.9**
EWHC 4362 (QB) Bean J. held that the claimants were entitled to an injunction
to enforce the terms of a Tomlin order settling defamation proceedings.

**Statements in court.** *Add to note 42*: The Court of Appeal in *Murray v*   **29.10**
*Associated Newspapers Ltd* [2015] EWCA Civ 488; [2015] E.M.L.R. 21 at [5]
approved *Winslet v Associated Newspapers Ltd* [2009] EWHC 2735 (QB);
[2009] E.M.L.R. 11 in confirming that the court had broad powers to permit a
claimant to make a unilateral statement in open court on the settlement of a
defamation claim. It concluded that a claimant who settled a defamation action,
whether by accepting an offer of amends under s.2 Defamation Act 1996 or
otherwise, could expect to be permitted to make a unilateral statement in court

unless the giving of such permission would result in real or substantial unfairness to another party.

**29.12** **Contribution and indemnity.** *Add to note 62*: See further *Simpson v MGN Ltd* [2015] EWHC 77 (QB) in which the defendant newspaper group applied successfully to join the source of the article complained of as a Part 20 defendant.

SECTION 3. PART 36 OFFERS

**29.16** **General.** *Add at end of paragraph*: CPR Part 36 was significantly revised in April 2015, but the summary given in this Section, subject to what follows, remains unaffected.

**29.17** **When an offer or payment may be made. Delete "or payment" from the title of this paragraph.**

*Note 77: Delete reference to CPR r.36.3(2)(a) and substitute:* R.36.7(1).

*Note 79: Delete reference to CPR r.36.14(2) and substitute*: R.36.17(3).

*Note 80: Delete reference to CPR r.36.14(1)(b) and substitute*: R.36.17(1)(b).

*Note 81: Delete the whole note and substitute*: R.36.17(4).

*Note 82: Delete reference to CPR r.36.7(1) and substitute*: R.36.7(2).

**29.18** **Form and content of a Part 36 offer.** *In line 4, delete the reference to CPR r.36.10 and substitute*: CPR r.36.13 or 36.20.

*Note 83: Delete the note and substitute*: "relevant period" is defined in r.36.3(g).

*Note 84: Delete the reference to CPR r.36.2(3) and substitute*: CPR r.36.5(2) (in which case the relevant period is the period up to the end of the trial: see CPR r.36.3(g)(ii)).

*Note 85: Delete the reference to CPR r.36.2(2) and substitute*: R.36.5(1).

**29.19** **Acceptance of offer.** *Note 86: Delete the reference to CPR r.36.9 and substitute:* R.36.11.

*Note 87: Delete the reference to CPR r.36.10(4)(b) and substitute*: R.36.13(4)(b).

*Note 88: Delete the reference to CPR r.36.11(1) and substitute*: R.36.14(1).

*Note 89: Delete the reference to CPR r.36.11(8) and substitute*: R.36.14(8).

*Note 90*: *Delete the reference to CPR r.36.10(1) and (2) and substitute*: R.36.13(1) and (3).

*Note 91*: *Delete the reference to CPR r.36.10(4) and substitute*: R.36.13(4).

**Several defendants.** *Note 93: Delete the reference to CPR r.36.12 and sub-*   **29.20** *stitute*: R.36.15.

**Withdrawal of offer.** *Note 95: Delete the note and substitute the following*:   **29.21** R.36.9. Note the new option of making a time-limited offer provided for by CPR r.36.9(4)(b).

**Statement in Open Court.** *Add to note 96*: and *Associated Newspapers Ltd v*   **29.23** *Murray* [2015] EWCA Civ 488; [2015] E.M.L.R. 21 (as summarised in para 29.10 above).

**Verdict or judgment and costs.** *In the last line of the paragraph, delete the*   **29.25** *reference to CPR r.36.14 and substitute*: r.36.17.

*Note 98: Delete the reference to CPR r.36.14(1) and substitute*: R.36.17(1).

*Note 99: Delete the reference to CPR r.36.14(2) and substitute*: R.36.17(3).

*Note 101: Delete the note and substitute*: R.36.17(4).

*Note 102: Delete the first sentence and substitute*: R.36.17(2). *Amend the second sentence to read as follows*: The purpose of the introduction of the antecedent to r.36.17(2) (r.36.14(1A), added into the CPR with effect from 1 October, 2011).

*In the last line of the note, delete the references to CPR r.36.14(3) and (4) and substitute references to CPR r.36.17(4) and (5).*

*Note 103: Delete the reference to CPR r.36.14(4) and substitute*: R.36.17(5).

**Indemnity costs in favour of defendant.** *Delete the reference to CPR r.36.14*   **29.26** *in the first sentence of the note and substitute*: r.36.17(3).

**Non-disclosure of offer or payment.** *Note 108: delete the reference to CPR*   **29.27** *r.36.13(2) and substitute*: R.36.16(2). *Add at the end of the note*: In proceedings involving a split trial or the trial of preliminary issues, it is now permissible for the judge who has tried a preliminary issue to be informed of the existence but not the terms of a Part 36 offer after judgment has been given (unless the Part 36 offer relates only to the issues that have been decided, in which case the terms of the offer can also be disclosed): see CPR r.36.16(3) and (4).

*Note 109: Delete the reference to CPR r.36.13(3)(c) and substitute*: R.36.16(3)(c).

*Note 113: Delete the reference to CPR r.36.13(1) and substitute*: R.36.16(1).

SECTION 4. OFFER OF AMENDS

**29.29**    **The Offer.** *Add to note 121*: It is worth bearing in mind that a defendant who wishes to defend a claim on the basis that it does not meet the threshold of serious reputational harm erected by s.1, Defamation Act 2013, should not serve a defence before making the s.1 application: *Lachaux v Independent Print Ltd* [2015] EWHC 2242 (QB); [2015] E.M.LR. 28 at [167]. Then, if the s.1 application fails, the defendant can still consider making an offer of amends.

**29.31**    **Consequences of acceptance**. *Add to note 136*: as approved by the Court of Appeal in *Associated Newspapers Ltd v Murray*, above, at [5].

CHAPTER 30

# PRE-TRIAL APPLICATIONS

SECTION 2. RULINGS ON MEANING

**Rulings on meaning: CPR PD 53, paragraph 4.1.** *Replace the last para-*   **30.2**
*graph of para 30.2 with the following*:

The jury ceased to be the presumptive tribunal of fact in defamation cases on
the coming into force of s.11, Defamation Act 2013, on 1 January 2014.
Accordingly there is now no inhibition on judges determining the actual meaning
of words complained of at an early stage in the proceedings. It follows that the
question of whether words are or are not capable of bearing a particular meaning
is liable to become largely an academic one [*new note 5A*]. Where there is a
dispute about meaning, and the defendant also proposes to mount a threshold
challenge to the claimant's case on serious harm under s.1, Defamation Act 2013
(which also came into force on 1 January 2014), it is likely to be preferable for
both issues to be determined at an early stage in the proceedings by way of a trial
of preliminary issues [*new note 5B*]. In the meantime it will generally be
unnecessary for the defendant to serve a defence [*new note 5C*]. A preliminary
ruling on meaning adverse to the claimant may be an end to the claim [*new note
5D*], while a ruling adverse to the defendant may require his defence of truth or
honest opinion to be struck out contingently [*new note 5E*].

*New note 5A*: See in this connection the remarks of Sharp L.J. in *Rufus v Elliott*
[2015] EWCA Civ 121; [2015] E.M.L.R. 17 at [28]: "The defendant wanted the
issue to be determined by the judge, but the claimant would not agree. However,
as this claim arose before the coming into force of the Defamation Act 2013,
meaning could not be determined as a preliminary issue unless both sides
consented, because, theoretically at least, it might usurp the function of a jury. It
may be no comfort for the defendant in the particular circumstances of this case,
but the amendment made by s.11 of the Defamation Act 2013 to the right to trial
by jury provided for in s.69 of the Senior Courts Act 1981, so that defamation
actions will be tried without a jury unless the court otherwise orders, means this

is not a problem that is likely to arise in the future". But note that in *Al Alaoui v Elaph Publishing Ltd* [2015] EWHC 1084 (QB) capability was determined and resolution of the actual meaning was deferred because, on the defendant's case, the actual meaning of the words complained of was tied up with whether they had caused or were likely to cause the claimant's reputation serious harm for the purpose of s.1, Defamation Act 2013. As to the latter, see further *new note 5B* below.

*New note 5B*: See Warby J.'s "comments on procedure" in *Ames v The Spamhaus Project Ltd* [2015] EWHC 127 (QB); [2015] 1 W.L.R. 3409 at [101], as applied by Nicola Davies J. in *Lachaux v Independent Print Ltd* [2015] EWHC 915 (QB) and by Warby J. himself in *Decker v Hopcraft* [2015] EWHC 1170 (QB). Warby J. reiterated his views to this effect in his judgment following the trial of "serious harm" as a preliminary issue in the case of *Lachaux*: [2015] EWHC 2242 (QB); [2015] E.M.L.R. 28, at [167].

*New note 5C*: *Lachaux v Independent Print Ltd* [2015] EWHC 2242 (QB); [2015] E.M.L.R. 28, at [168]-[169] (Warby J.).

*New note 5D*: Subject to amendment, as to the possibility of which, see *Yeo v Times Newspapers Ltd* [2015] EWHC 209 (QB) at [4], per Warby J.

*New note 5E*: As occurred, for example, in *Cruddas v Calvert* [2013] EWHC 1427 (QB); [2014] E.M.L.R. 4 at [123], per Tugendhat J. (the Judge's decision on meaning was later reversed by the Court of Appeal, which had the effect of reinstating the struck out defence of justification: [2013] EWCA Civ 748; [2014] E.M.L.R. 5), and in *Simpson v MGN Ltd* [2015] EWHC 77 and *Yeo v Times Newspapers Ltd* [2015] EWHC 209 (QB), both per Warby J.

**30.5**    **Principles to be applied.** *Amend the penultimate sentence to read as follows*: Furthermore, for words to be defamatory as a matter of common law, the allegation that they comprise must cross a threshold of seriousness, so as to exclude trivial claims.

*Add at the end of the paragraph*: However, that does not mean that art.10 has to be taken into account in some separate or different way in cases involving the defamation of government or local government officials [*new note 30A*].

*Add to note 17*: For a recent authoritative restatement of the principles, see *Rufus v Elliott* [2015] EWCA Civ 121; [2015] E.M.L.R. 17.

*Add to note 21*: "The words 'should not select one bad meaning where other non-defamatory meanings are available' are apt to be misleading without fuller explanation. They obviously do not mean in a case such as this one, where it is open to a defendant to contend either on a capability application or indeed at trial that the words complained of are not defamatory of the claimant, that the tribunal adjudicating on the question must then select the non-defamatory meaning for which the defendant contends. Instead, those words 'are part of the description of the hypothetical reasonable reader, rather than as a prescription of how such a reader should attribute meanings to words complained of as defamatory"': see *McAlpine v Bercow* [2013] EWHC 1342 (QB) paras 63 to 66": *Rufus v Elliott*, above, per Sharp L.J. at [11].

*Add to note 25*: The judgments of Tugendhat J. and the Court of Appeal in *Cruddas v Calvert* referred to in this note are now reported respectively at [2014] E.M.L.R. 4 and [2014] E.M.L.R. 5.

*Note 29*: *Delete the passage* "The principle finds expression in s.1(1) Defamation Act 2013 . . . " *to* " . . . what is defamatory"." *and substitute the following*: This remains a precondition of a defamation action following the enactment of the Defamation Act 2013. Section 1(1) of the Act proceeds on the footing that a statement has been published which is defamatory of the claimant at common law (i.e. applying the principles laid down in *Thornton*): see *Lachaux v Independent Print Ltd* [2015] EWHC 2242 (QB); [2015] E.M.L.R. 28, at [15(5)], [44], [50] and [58] ("The court can still undertake an objective determination of the single meaning of the words, and whether it satisfies the *Thornton* test, before considering whether it has been proved that serious harm has been or is likely to be caused by the publication") (Warby J.). Where it can be shown that no such statement has been published, the court will not need to consider whether the additional requirement of "serious harm" has been made out.

*Add at the end of note 29*: For a more recent application of the principle, see *Briggs v Jordan* [2013] EWHC 3205 (QB) where the words complained of were found to be "disobliging" but not defamatory.

*New note 30A*: Because art.10 has already been taken into consideration in the formulation of the principles in *Jeynes v News Magazines Ltd*: see *Thompson v James* [2014] EWCA Civ 600, at [26]-[28].

**Meaning and the repetition rule.** *Delete the sentence at the start of the* **30.8** *second paragraph beginning "Given that the stated purpose and justification of the repetition rule . . . " and replace with the following:* The repetition rule has apparently survived the Defamation Act 2013 *[new note 45A]*.

*New note 45A*: Sir David Eady in *Lachaux v Independent Print Ltd* [2015] EWHC 620 (QB) observed at [42]: "I see no reason to suppose that the long established (although only relatively recently named) "repetition rule" has been impliedly abrogated by the Defamation Act 2013. Accordingly, in so far as any of the defamatory imputations contained in these articles are attributed to [family members of a witness relied on by the defendants], a defence of truth will still require the substantive allegation to be proved—not merely that the allegation was so made: see e.g. *Gatley on Libel & Slander* (12th edn) at 11.18 and 30.8".

**Malicious falsehood.** *Add to note 63*: The judgments of Tugendhat J. and the **30.13** Court of Appeal in *Cruddas v Calvert* referred to in this note are now reported at [2014] E.M.L.R. 4 and [2014] E.M.L.R. 5 respectively.

SECTION 3. TRIAL OF MEANING AS A PRELIMINARY ISSUE

**30.14** **Meaning and preliminary issue.** *Delete the third sentence and replace with the following*: The trend towards meaning being tried as a preliminary issue continues now that the jury has ceased to be the presumptive tribunal of fact for defamation claims [*new note 66A*]. However, where the claimant's case on serious harm under s.1, Defamation Act 2013 is under challenge, or the defendant contends that he has committed no real and substantial tort (for the purposes of the court's jurisdiction under *Jameel v Dow Jones & Co Inc* [*new note 66B*]), it is likely to be preferable for any disputes as to meaning to be tried together with the "serious harm" and *Jameel* issues at the start of the proceedings [*new note 66C*].

*Add at the end of the paragraph*: In determining the meaning of words, the judge is not bound by the meanings the parties have pleaded or advanced [*new note 76A*]. A ruling on meaning adverse to the defendant, or one which determines the question whether the words complained of are fact or opinion, may require his defence of truth or honest opinion to be struck out contingently [*new note 76B*].

*Add to note 64*: The judgments of Tugendhat J. and the Court of Appeal in *Cruddas v Calvert* referred to in this note are now reported at [2014] E.M.L.R. 4 and [2014] E.M.L.R. 5 respectively.

*Add to note 65*: *Cruddas v Calvert* has been reported: *see note 64 above*.

*Add to note 66*: The relevant judgment in *Lord McAlpine of West Green v Bercow* ([2013] EWHC 981 (QB)) is now reported at [2014] E.M.L.R. 3. In a similar vein, see *RBOS Shareholders Action Group Ltd v News Group Newspapers Ltd* [2014] EWHC 130 (QB); [2014] E.M.L.R. 15.

*New note 66A*: For some recent examples of this procedure being adopted, see *Building Register Ltd v Weston* [2014] EWHC 784 (QB) (Dingemans J.), *Johnston v League Publications Ltd* [2014] EWHC 874 (QB) (Sir David Eady), *Meadows Care Ltd v Lambert* [2014] EWHC 1126 (QB) (Bean J.), *Contostavlos v News Group Newspapers Ltd* [2014] EWHC 1339 (QB) (Tugendhat J.), *Yeo v Times Newspapers Ltd* [2014] EWHC 2853 (QB) (Warby J.), *Donovan v Gibbons* [2014] EWHC 3406 (QB) (H.H. Judge Parkes Q.C., sitting as a High Court Judge), *Hamaizia v Commissioner of Police of the Metropolis* [2014] EWHC 3408 (QB) (H.H. Judge Parkes Q.C.), *Al Saud v Forbes LLC* [2014] EWHC 3823 (QB) (Sir Michael Tugendhat), *Simpson v MGN Ltd* [2015] EWHC 77 (QB) (Warby J.), *Lachaux v Independent Print Ltd* [2015] EWHC 620 (QB) (Sir David Eady), *Rufus v Elliott* [2015] EWHC 807 (QB) (Warby J.), and *Barron v Collins* [2015] EWHC 1125 (QB) (Warby J.).

In the cases of *Johnston, Hamaizia, Al Saud* and *Lachaux*, the court considered both the claimant's suggested meanings and the defendants' proposed *Lucas-Box* meanings; in *Donovan*, the claimant's meaning and the defendant's *Control Risks* meaning. In *Barron v Collins*, the issues of meaning and fact or comment were combined with an issue as to reference.

In *Al Alaoui v Elaph Publishing Ltd* [2015] EWHC 1084 (QB), the defendant sought rulings under CPR PD 53, para.4.1 that the words complained of were not capable of bearing the meanings attributed to them in the particulars of claim or any other meaning defamatory of the claimant. Dingemans J. recorded at [4] that there had been before the court, in the alternative, an application that the actual meaning of the words be tried as a preliminary issue, but it had not been pursued because "whether that meaning [i.e. the actual meaning of the words complained of] was defamatory (as opposed to whether the words were capable of bearing any defamatory meaning) [would] raise issues about whether the statement "*has caused or is likely to cause serious harm*" to the reputation of the Claimant within the meaning of s.1 of the Defamation Act 2013". Although it is not stated as much in the judgment, this approach might be thought to be consistent with Warby J.'s "comments on procedure" in *Ames v The Spamhaus Project Ltd* [2015] EWHC 127 (QB); [2015] 1 W.L.R. 3409 at [101].

*New note 66B*: [2005] EWCA Civ 75; [2005] Q.B. 946.

*New note 66C*: See Warby J.'s (obiter) comments on procedure to this effect in *Ames v The Spamhaus Project Ltd*, above, at [101]. (Previously, in *Cooke v MGN Ltd* [2014] EWHC 2831 (QB); [2015] 1 W.L.R. 895, a preliminary trial of "serious harm" had been ordered with the consent of the parties.) Nicola Davies J. applied Warby J.'s guidance in *Lachaux v Independent Print Ltd* [2015] EWHC 915 (QB) in deciding to order a preliminary trial of issues of serious harm, *Jameel* abuse, meaning, and reference in three inter-related libel actions brought by the same claimant against three publishers, before a case management conference and costs budgeting had taken place, and before one of the defendants (AOL (UK) Ltd) had served a defence. As the judge said at [21]: "It is clear from the Explanatory Note to the 2013 Act that the effect of s.1 and the requirement of "serious harm" is to create a higher hurdle for the claimant and one that is at the threshold of any defamation action. I agree with the approach taken and guidance given by the court in *Cooke v MGN Ltd*, [above,] and *Ames* . . . namely that it is appropriate to determine "serious harm" as a preliminary issue. I regard the issue of "serious harm" as a threshold condition in any action brought pursuant to the provisions of the 2013 Act. It is, moreover, an issue which can be evaluated, in appropriate circumstances without recourse to any pleaded Defence. The claimant brings the action, it is for him to set out his case on this threshold condition". Warby J. took the same approach in similar circumstances in *Decker v Hopcraft* [2015] EWHC 1170 (QB), and again endorsed the approach in his judgment following the trial of "serious harm" as a preliminary issue in *Lachaux v Independent Print Ltd*: [2015] EWHC 2242 (QB); [2015] E.M.L.R. 28 at [167]-[169].

*Add to note 67*: See further *new note 6A* in this Chapter, above. The judgment of Tugendhat J. in *Cruddas v Calvert* is now reported at [2014] E.M.L.R. 4.

*Add to note 68*: The judgment in *Lord McAlpine of West Green v Bercow* is now reported at [2014] E.M.L.R. 3.

*Add to notes 74-76*: The judgments of Tugendhat J. and the Court of Appeal in *Cruddas v Calvert* referred to in this note are now reported at [2014] E.M.L.R. 4 and [2014] E.M.L.R. 5 respectively.

*New note 76A*: See *Johnston v League Publications Ltd*, above, at [5] citing *Slim v Daily Telegraph Ltd* [1968] 2 Q.B. 157.

*New note 76B*: See the authorities cited in *new note 5D* in this Chapter, above.

**30.15** **Preliminary issue: fact or comment.** *Change the title of this paragraph to* **"Preliminary issue: fact or opinion"**.

*Add to note 79*: In *Donovan v Gibbons* [2014] EWHC 3406 (QB) the court determined the issues before it in the following order: (i) words defamatory or not; (ii) fact or comment; and (iii) meaning. In *Meadows Care Ltd v Lambert*, above, Bean J. at [14] held that the fact that the defendant had not pleaded a defence of honest comment did not inhibit the court from determining the issue of fact or comment at the preliminary trial of the issue of meaning.

**30.16** **Appeals.** *Add to notes 82 & 84*: The judgment of the Court of Appeal in *Cruddas v Calvert* is now reported at [2014] E.M.L.R. 5.

SECTION 4. SUMMARY DISPOSAL AND SUMMARY JUDGMENT

**30.31** **The Part 24 rubric. Add to note 143**: It may be noted that in *Barron v Vines* [2015] EWHC (QB), Warby J. dismissed a claimant's application for summary judgment on the basis that the defendant might wish to advance a public interest defence under s.4, Defamation Act 2013 (none had been pleaded: the defendant was a litigant in person).

**30.33** **CPR Part 24 and the right to trial by jury.** *Add at the start of this section*: Section 11, Defamation Act 2013, came into force on 1 January 2014 for actions started on or after that day, thereby abrogating the presumption that defamation claims are to be tried with a jury. The effect of this change must be to render redundant the principles specific to defamation set out in paras 30.33, 30.34 and 30.36 of the Main Work.

**30.35** **Subject matter of applications under Part 24.** *Insert at para 30.35(5) after the word "justification"*: "*Reynolds* privilege, [*new note 167A*]".

*Add to note 160*: See in connection with the issue of responsibility for publication the decision of Sir David Eady at trial in *Bussey Law Firm P.C. v Page* [2015] EWHC 563 (QB).

*Add to note 167*: Now see also *Mireskandari v Centaur Media Plc* [2013] EWHC 3551 (QB) (Tugendhat J.) (application succeeded).

*New note 167A*: *Kneafsey v Independent Television News Ltd* [2013] EWHC 4046 (QB) (Tugendhat J.) (application succeeded).

*Add to note 169*: Now see also *Owens v Grose* [2015] EWHC 839 (QB) (Dingemans J.) (application succeeded).

SECTION 5. STRIKING OUT STATEMENTS OF CASE

**Inadequate or embarrassing statements of case.** *Add to note 252*: For some   **30.45**
recent challenges to particulars of claim (or counterclaim) on grounds of want of particularity and non-compliance with CPR Pt 16, see *Mole v Hunter* [2014] EWHC 658 (QB), *Wissa v Associated Newspapers Ltd* [2014] EWHC 1518 (QB) and *Decker v Hopcraft* [2015] EWHC 1170 (QB). A similar form of attack was made on the claimant's plea of malice in *Barry v Butler* [2015] EWHC 447 (QB).

**The need for finality.** *Add to note 262*: Now see *Krause v Newsquest Media*   **30.46**
*Group Ltd* [2013] EWHC 3400 (QB) in which Tugendhat J. struck out a libel claim as an abuse of process on the ground that it was an attempt by the claimant to re-litigate criminal proceedings that had resulted in her conviction for harassment and a restraining order that she had breached.

*Add to note 264*: In this regard, see *Vaughan v Lewisham London Borough Council* [2013] EWHC 4118 (QB), in which Sir David Eady held that it had been an abuse of process for the claimant to withdraw proceedings in the employment tribunal, which represented the appropriate forum for the adjudication of her claims, and to proceed instead with a defamation claim against her former employer in the High Court.

*Add to note 265*: In *Building Register Ltd v Weston* [2014] EWHC 2361 (QB) (Nicola Davies J.) the defendants were refused permission to amend their defence of justification on the ground that the proposed plea offended against this rule.

*Add to note 267*: But see *note 265*, as modified, above.

**Proceedings which are not "worth the candle".** *Add at end of paragraph*:   **30.48**
The court has started to shed some light on this matter. In *Ames v The Spamhaus Project Ltd* [*new note 295A*] Warby J. held that consideration of "serious harm" under s.1, Defamation Act 2013 should come first, and that if that condition were satisfied, it might be hard for the defendant to establish that the tort alleged failed the "real and substantial tort" test, or that it would be disproportionate to allow it to proceed, having particular regard to the court's costs management powers [*new note 295B*]. It may even be that s.1 has removed the need for a *Jameel* jurisdiction in defamation cases [*new note 295C*].

*Add to note 284* To this list may be added the following: *Carr v Penman* [2013] EWHC 2679 (QB); *Subotic v Knezevic* [2013] EWHC 3011 (QB); *Karpov v Browder* [2013] EWHC 3071 (QB); [2014] E.M.L.R. 8; *Ansari v Knowles* [2013] EWCA Civ 1448; *Bewry v Reed Elsevier UK Ltd* [2014] EWCA Civ 1411, [2015] 1 W.L.R. 2565; *Ames v The Spamhaus Project Ltd* [2015] EWHC 127 (QB); [2015] 1 W.L.R. 3409; *Liberty Fashion Wears Ltd v Primark Stores Ltd* [2015] EWHC 415 (QB); *Sloutsker v Romanova* [2015] EWHC 545 (QB); [2015] 2 Costs W.L.R. 321 and *Lachaux v Independent Print Ltd* [2015] EWHC 2242 (QB); [2015] E.M.L.R. 28. For the approach of the New South Wales court to *Jameel*, see *Bleyer v Google Inc* [2014] NSWSC 897.

*New note 295A*: [2015] EWHC 127 (QB); [2015] E.M.L.R. 13.

*New note 295B*: See at [36], [50]-[51] and [101]. As to the court's costs management powers in the defamation and 'publication torts' context, see *Yeo v Times Newspapers Ltd* [2015] EWHC 209 (QB); [2015] E.M.L.R. 18 per Warby J. (which contains guidance on the matter); *Hegglin v Persons Unknown* [2014] EWHC 3793 (QB); [2015] 1 Costs L.O. 65. (Edis J.); *Simpson v MGN Ltd* [2015] EWHC 126 (QB) (Warby J.); *Lachaux v Independent Print Ltd* [2015] EWHC 915 (QB) (where Nicola Davies J. declined to order costs budgeting before deciding whether to order a trial of 'serious harm' and other matters as preliminary issues); *Stocker v Stocker* [2015] EWHC 1634 (QB); [2015] E.M.L.R. 24 (Warby J.); and *Yeo v Times Newspapers Ltd* [2015] EWHC 2132 (QB) (in which Warby J. refused the claimant's application to revise his approved costs budget).

*New note 295C*: *Lachaux v Independent Print Ltd* [2015] EWHC 2242 (QB); [2015] E.M.L.R. 28 at [50] and [156] (Warby J.).

### Section 6. Stay of Proceedings

**30.52**    **Situations in which stay ordered.** *Add at the end of the paragraph*:

In circumstances where an interim injunction application has been dismissed but there is perceived to be an ongoing risk that the defendant may publish allegations defamatory of the claimant, it may be appropriate for the court to stay the proceedings for a determinate period to cater for the possibility that the risk might materialise. [*new note 326A*]

*Note 325*: *Delete second mention of Shergill v Purewal and insert at that point the following*: "In relation to religious non-justiciability, see also *Otuo v Watchtower Bible and Tract Society of Britain*, unreported, 5 December 2013, per H.H.J. Moloney Q.C. (sitting as a Judge of the High Court).

*New note 326A*: *Cartus Corp v Siddell* [2014] EWHC 2492 (QB) (Nicol J.) at [5].

### Section 7. The Trial of Issues

**30.53**    **Generally.** *Insert after the phrase "a substantial benefit for the litigation" a new note 328A.*

*Delete from "and although unlikely to be made before service of defence ... " to the end of the paragraph, and substitute the following*:

Preliminary trials at an early stage of the proceedings are only likely to become a more commonplace feature of defamation litigation in the post-Defamation Act 2013 era, specifically where the defendant takes a 'threshold' point under s.1 of the Act [*new note 330*]. In such a case, it appears that a defendant ought to apply without delay upon service of the proceedings for an order that the relevant issue or issues be tried; he should not in general serve a defence or await the first case management conference [*new note 330A*]. A claimant who opposes such an application does so at risk of costs [*new note 330B*].

*New note 328A*: For a recent example of the court carrying out this exercise, see *Mitchell v News Group Newspapers Ltd* [2014] EWHC 2615 (QB) in which Warby J. gives his reasons for ordering that certain issues in two inter-related libel claims should be tried as preliminary issues at the same time.

*New note 330*: See *new note 66C* above.

*New note 330A*: See *Lachaux v Independent Print Ltd* [2015] EWHC 2242 (QB); [2015] E.M.L.R. 28, at [168]-[169] (Warby J.).

*New note 330B*: See *Lachaux v Independent Print Ltd* [2015] EWHC 915 (QB) (Nicola Davies J.), where costs were awarded against a claimant who opposed unsuccessfully (on the ground that a decision on the matter ought to await the service of a defence by all the defendants, costs budgeting and a case management conference) the defendants' applications for an order that serious harm, *Jameel* abuse, meaning and reference be tried as preliminary issues.

**Other issues.** *Add to note 344*: The decision of the Court of Appeal in *Cruddas*    **30.55**
*v Calvert* is now reported at [2014] E.M.L.R. 5.

CHAPTER 31

# INTERLOCUTORY MATTERS

SECTION 1. DISCLOSURE

**31.2**     **Disclosure before action.** *Add to note 5*: Similarly, it is not open to a defendant to make a CPR Pt 18 request in order to gauge the strength of his potential defences to a defamation claim: *Stocker v Stocker* [2014] EWHC 2402 (QB), per H.H.J. Parkes Q.C. (sitting as a High Court Judge).

**31.4**     **Norwich Pharmacal orders.** *Add to notes 12 & 16*: The judgment in *Various Claimants v News Group Newspapers Ltd* is now reported at [2014] Ch. 400.

**31.10**     **Non-party disclosure.** *Add to note 58*: See *Mitchell v News Group Newspapers Ltd* [2014] EWHC 1885 (QB) (Tugendhat J.) for a recent example of an application for non-party disclosure that was granted, and (earlier in the same case) *Mitchell v News Group Newspapers Ltd* [2014] EWHC 879 (QB) (Tugendhat J.) for one that was refused (on the basis that the manner in which the applicants—the defendant newspaper publisher and the claimant police officer—had mounted the application had precluded the court from carrying out the necessary balancing act between the rights of the applicants and those of the persons affected by the disclosure sought). See also *Fox v Boulter* [2013] EWHC 4012 (QB) and *Abbas v Yousef* [2014] EWHC 662 (QB) (both per Tugendhat J.) for further applications for non-party disclosure that failed, the former on the ground that the disclosure sought was not necessary for the fair disposal of the action, the latter because it had been made prematurely, prior to the service of the defence.

SECTION 2. FURTHER INFORMATION AND INTERROGATORIES

**31.18**     **Further information before defence. Insert new note 95A after the phrase "for the same reason"**: See *Stocker v Stocker*, n.5 to para 31.2 above (as modified), for a modern application of this principle.

[172]

Section 3. Security for Costs and Maintenance

**Conditional fee agreements.** *Add to note 248*: The court declined to make a    **31.49**
costs-capping order in *Hegglin v Persons Unknown* [2014] EWHC 3793 (QB);
[2015] 1 Costs L.O. 65.

Section 4. Consolidation, Joinder and Severance

**Joinder and severance.** *Add to note 278*: now reported at [2014] E.M.L.R. 2.    **31.61**
But actions against "persons unknown" may be [*new note 278A*].

*New note 278A Brett Wilson LLP v Persons Unknown* [2015] EWHC 2628 (QB)
(Warby J.).

**Addition and substitution of parties.** *Insert new note 280A at the end of the*    **31.62**
*paragraph.*

*New note 280A*: For an example of an actual defendant being substituted for
"persons unknown" after the grant of default judgment in a libel action, see
*Tardios v Linton* [2015] EWHC 1429 (QB) (Dingemans J.).

Section 5. Mode Of Trial

**General.** *Replace paras 31.64 to 31.70 with the following*:    **31.64**

Section 11 of the Defamation Act 2013 was brought into force on 1 January
2014 as regards actions started on or after that day. The court is now very
unlikely to order a claim for defamation to be tried with a jury [*new note 291A*].
In consequence, the principles set out in this Section of the Main Work are no
longer good law so far as concerns actions commenced on or after 1 January
2014.

*New note 291A*: As to the relevant principles, see *Yeo v Times Newspapers Ltd*
[2014] EWHC 2853 (QB); [2015] 1 W.L.R. 971 (Warby J.).

# CHAPTER 32

# THE TRIAL: THE CLAIMANT'S CASE

SECTION 1. COMMENCEMENT OF TRIAL

**32.1**    **Jury.** *Add*: Defamation Act 2013, s.11, which abolishes the right to trial by jury in defamation cases, applies to all actions started on or after 1 January 2014: see s.16(7) and the Defamation Act 2013 (Commencement) (England and Wales) Order 2013, S.I. 2013 No. 3027. There have been no jury trials since 2012, when there were two, and in the wake of s.11 the prospect of any further jury trials in libel or slander cases can safely be said to be very slight.

A consequence of the disappearance of jury trial is that many issues will now be determined as preliminary issues rather than at a full trial of the action—meaning, in particular, and, in the light of s.1 of the 2013 Act and *Lachaux v Independent Print Ltd* [2015] EWHC 2242 (QB; [2015] E.M.L.R. 28, the question of damage to reputation (see 32.24 below). For preliminary issues, see 30.53 above.

*Delete note 1 and replace as follows*:

Section 11 removes the presumption in favour of jury trial in defamation cases. See para.31.64ff, above, for issues arising in respect of mode of trial. For the principles that now apply to the exercise of discretion in favour of jury trial, see *Yeo v Times Newspapers Ltd* [2014] EWHC 2853 (QB); [2015] 1 W.L.R. 971.

**32.2**    **Opening statement.** For trial by jury, see now 32.1 above.

SECTION 2. EVIDENCE FOR THE CLAIMANT: INTRODUCTION

**32.3**    **General.** In principle, the claimant will now have to adduce evidence to prove that the words complained of have caused his reputation serious harm, or that

they are likely to do so (*Lachaux v Independent Print Ltd* [2015] EWHC 2242
(QB; [2015] E.M.L.R. 28). In obvious cases it may be possible to rely on
inference: see *Cooke v MGN Ltd* [2014] EWHC 2831 (QB); [2015] 1 W.L.R. 895
at [43] and *Lachaux* (above) at [57]. However, the issue of serious harm is likely
to have been dealt with at the trial of a preliminary issue, if it is disputed by the
defendant.

### SECTION 3. PROOF OF PUBLICATION

**Inferences.** *Note 26*: s.1, Defamation Act 2013 came into effect on 1 January    **32.8**
2014, but only affects causes of action which accrued on or after that date. As for
its effects, see 6.3 above.

### SECTION 4. IDENTIFICATION OF CLAIMANT

**Claimant not expressly named.** *Insert at line 9, after the words "referred*    **32.19**
*to":*

That proposition is true as far as the common law requirements of reference
are concerned, but it is no longer good enough in the context of consideration of
the "serious harm" threshold set by s.1, Defamation Act 2013. In *Lachaux v
Independent Print Ltd* [2015] EWHC 2242 (QB); [2015] E.M.L.R. 28, Warby J.
stated more than once that he regarded the issue of reference as an objective one
which did not require the claimant to prove that any single individual understood
the words to refer to him. But he suggested at [15] that proof that individuals did
in fact understand the words to refer to the claimant might well be necessary to
satisfy the serious harm requirement, or to overcome a *Jameel* application, or
both. At [100] he stated that the question of how many people in fact understood
the words to refer to the claimant was a question of fact to be determined by
evidence or inference when considering harm.

*Note 76*: *ZAM v CFW* is now reported at [2013] E.M.L.R. 27.

**Evidence of reputation.** *Delete the entire paragraph, and replace with the*    **32.24**
*following:*

Section 1 of Defamation Act 2013, was brought into force with effect from 1
January 2014, and applies to any cause of action that accrues on or after that date.
The construction of s.1 which the judge found in *Lachaux v Independent Print
Ltd* [2015] EWHC 2242 (QB); [2015] E.M.L.R. 28 has the effect that the
claimant must prove that the words complained of have caused (or are likely to
cause) serious harm to his reputation. This is not a matter of the court assessing
whether the words upon publication caused "serious harm" to the claimant's
reputation (i.e. purely as a matter of meaning) as opposed to the "substantial"
harm required at common law: see *Thornton v Telegraph Media Group Ltd*

[2010] EWHC 1414 (QB); [2011] 1 W.L.R. 1985: the claimant's argument to that effect was rejected. The requirement now is to prove as a fact on the balance of probabilities that serious harm to reputation has been caused, or is likely to be caused, by the words complained of. In obvious cases that may be done by inference (*Cooke v MGN Ltd* [2014] EWHC 2831 (QB); [2015] 1 W.L.R. 895 at [43] and *Lachaux* (above) at [57]).

It is surely probable that in many (if not most) cases the fact of serious harm will be so obvious that inference will suffice. The difficulties arise where it will not. It is unclear what devices claimants may have to adopt to prove damage to their reputations. In *Cooke*, counsel for the defendants submitted that reactions in social media, and reader comments in response to media publications, might be relevant: but that would often entail giving weight to the views of the prejudiced, unreasonable or ignorant (and might be unrepresentative of the population of "right-thinking people" generally, as Bean J observed at [43]), and might also run counter to the principle that any given words have one single meaning which is objectively determined by reference to the response of the hypothetical reasonable person. It may be noteworthy that in *Cooke*, Bean J asked the question "How can serious harm be proved?" but did not answer it beyond hinting ([43]) that an opinion poll survey or a selection of comments from the "blogosphere" might in some cases be appropriate. And in *Lachaux* at [86] Warby J said in terms that evidence of adverse social media responses, name-calling or similar events was admissible.

Some guidance is provided by the evidence called by the claimant in *Lachaux* at [101]ff. It is suggested that the relevant evidence is likely to include the extent and nature of publication, including any viral or "grapevine" publication; the sort of people to whom the words were published, including social or professional contacts; any special meaning in which such people might have understood the words; the claimant's response to the libels, including the steps that he took and how fast he took them, as demonstrating both his feelings and the true extent of his desire for vindication (it might be asked how that evidence could be relevant to the objective issue of serious harm to reputation, but it was admitted in *Lachaux*: by contrast, in *Cooke* at [30] Bean J appears to have thought evidence of distress not relevant); if reference is not clear, the extent to which he is likely to have been identified; any responses to the libels of which he became aware, including altered behaviour on the part of people who knew him, and adverse social media responses; and the response of the defendants to his complaints, including the impact of any cessation of publication or of an apology. It is important to remember that the serious harm relied upon may be likely to happen in the future, in which case (unless inference will suffice) the claimant must call evidence which demonstrates that likelihood.

On any view, the long-established presumption of damage in libel appears to have had its day. As Warby J. put it in *Lachaux*, his construction of s.1 means that the legal presumption of damage "will cease to play any significant role" (above, [60]). For a further discussion of the consequences of the decisions in *Cooke* and *Lachaux*, see chapter 2 above.

It should be noted that the question of serious harm to reputation, if it is in issue, is likely to be tried out as a preliminary issue, and not at the full trial of the action.

**Defamation Act 2013, s.1.** Section 1 has been in force since 1 January 2014  **32.25** in relation to causes of action that accrued on or after that date. It appears that its effect is more far-reaching than (as was suggested here) to give statutory effect to a threshold of seriousness recognized by the common law in the shape of the line of authority culminating in *Thornton v Telegraph Media Group Ltd* [2010] EWHC 1414 (QB); [2011] 1 W.L.R. 1985. The presumption of damage in libel appears to have been swept away by s.1. The claimant must now prove on a balance of probabilities that the words complained of have in fact caused his or her reputation serious harm, or that they are likely to do so: *Lachaux*, above.

**Natural and ordinary meaning.** It is unlikely that meaning will in future be  **32.26** determined by a jury: see 32.1 above.

**Damaging nature of a statement.** Section 1 of the Defamation Act 2013 has  **32.31** been in force since 1 January 2014 and bites on all causes of action which have accrued on and since that date. Unless the claimant can rely on inference, he will have to prove on the balance of probabilities that his reputation has been, or is likely to be, caused serious harm by the publication complained of: see 32.24 above.

**Burden of proof.** Burden of proof is not an inapt phrase in the context of  **32.32** damage to reputation. Unless the case is one where serious harm to reputation (or the likelihood of it) can be inferred, the claimant must prove, on the balance of probabilities, that the words complained of have caused, or are likely to prove, serious harm to his reputation: see 32.24 above.

**Introduction.** *Add after existing paragraph*:  **32.33**

*Reynolds* privilege was abolished by s.4(6), Defamation Act 2013. The new statutory defence of publication on a matter of public interest, created by s.4, bites on causes of action that accrued on or after 1 January 2014. It is clear from the Explanatory Notes to the 2013 Act that the statutory defence is based on the common law defence, and is intended to reflect the law as set out in *Flood v Times Newspapers Ltd* [2012] UKSC 53; [2012] 2 A.C. 273. There have as yet been no cases in which the s.4 defence has been authoritatively considered, but the issue of malice will surely be found to be built into the conditions of the privilege, just as it was under the common law. (See e.g. *Yeo v Times Newspapers Ltd (No.2)* [2015] EWHC 209 (QB) at [25]: " . . . it is not the practice to plead malice in answer to a *Reynolds* defence".) Note that one of the two pillars of the defence (s.4(1)(b)) is that the defendant must have reasonably believed that publishing the statement complained of was in the public interest. There might be some difficulty in establishing reasonable belief that publication was in the public interest if the defendant knew that the statement complained of was wholly untrue, or was recklessly indifferent to its truth or falsity. ("The truth is the truth, whether telling it is in the public interest or not. But telling a falsehood would not be in the public interest": *Cruddas v Calvert* [2013] EWHC 2298 (QB), per Tugendhat J. at [3].)

*Add to note 133:* The statutory defence of honest opinion has been in force since 1 January 2014, and by s.16(5) it applies to causes of action accruing on or after that date.

**32.37**    **Sources of evidence.** For trial by jury, see 32.1 above.

**32.45**    **Defendant's conduct in litigation and at trial.** For trial by jury, see 32.1 above.

**32.46**    **Refusal to apologise.** For trial by jury, see 32.1 above.

Section 7. Evidence Directed at Defendant's Case of Privilege

**32.49**    *Reynolds privilege cases (public interest defence). After heading, insert new note 207A:*

The new statutory defence of publication on a matter of public interest, created by s.4, Defamation Act 2013, applies to causes of action that accrued on or after 1 January 2014. See generally Chapter 15 above.

*Insert after penultimate paragraph on p.1254 (concluding words "considered by the House of Lords"):*

Note that the presumption of falsity in libel appears to have been swept away by s.1, Defamation Act 2013: see *Lachaux v Independent Print Ltd* [2015] EWHC 2242 (QB); [2015] E.M.L.R. 28 at [60], and 32.24 above.

*Add at end of final paragraph of this section:* Section 4(1)(b) of the Defamation Act 2013 requires the defendant to show that he or she reasonably believed that publishing the statement complained of was in the public interest. [*Add new note 229A*]

*New note 229A*: It may conceivably be worth the claimant's while to consider whether there is likely to be a disjunction between the meaning advanced by him and the meaning in which the defendant claims to have understood the words. If there is significance in the difference between the words "the statement complained of", used in s.4(1)(b), and the word "imputation" (used elsewhere in the Act to stand for what a practitioner would call the meaning of the words), then even if the court determines that the statement complained of bears meaning A, if the defendant intended his words to bear meaning B, he could still believe that publishing the statement complained of was in the public interest. See the reflections of Warby J. in *Barron v Vines* [2015] EWHC 1161 (QB) at [63]. There was no argument on the point, but it may be that the judge had in mind a line of authority in the context of malice, to the effect that a person cannot have had a dominant intention to injure the claimant in respect of one meaning which he did not intend, when his words were true in the meaning that he did intend: see e.g. *Cruddas v Calvert* [2015] EWCA Civ 171; [2015] E.M.L.R. 16.

## SECTION 8. EVIDENCE TO SUPPORT CLAIM FOR DAMAGES

**Damage presumed.** Section 1 of the Defamation Act 2013 was brought into **32.51** force with effect from 1 January 2014, and applies to any cause of action that accrues on or after that date. The construction of s.1 which the judge found in *Lachaux v Independent Print Ltd* [2015] EWHC 2242 (QB); [2015] E.M.L.R. 28 has the effect that the claimant must prove that the words complained of have caused (or are likely to cause) serious harm to his reputation. In obvious cases that may be done by inference (*Cooke v MGN Ltd* [2014] EWHC 2831 (QB); [2015] 1 W.L.R. 895 at [43] and *Lachaux* (above) at [57]).

There is some uncertainty about what evidence claimants will have to adduce to prove damage to their reputations where inference will not suffice: see 32.24 above. It should be noted that the question of serious harm to reputation, if it is in issue, is likely to be tried out as a preliminary issue, and not at the full trial of the action.

**Extent of publication.** The extent of publication, and the number of people **32.52** who would have understood the claimant (if not named) to have been referred to, are likely to be matters of great importance in proving serious harm to reputation: see *Lachaux* (above) at [15] and [100].

**Injury to reputation.** Evidence of injury to reputation will henceforward be **32.53** essential, especially if the construction of s.1, Defamation Act 2013 reached in *Lachaux* (above) is upheld. For the kinds of evidence that the claimant might wish to consider adducing, see both this paragraph and 32.24 above.

**Slander not actionable per se.** Since Defamation Act 2013 s.1 came into **32.56** force, the claimant must prove that the words complained of have caused serious harm to his reputation, or are likely to do so. That applies to all slanders, whether actionable per se or not. See *Lachaux v Independent Print Ltd* [2015] EWHC 2242 (QB); [2015] E.M.L.R. 28 and *Cooke v MGN Ltd* [2014] EWHC 2831 (QB); [2015] 1 W.L.R. 895. Proof of special damage would be an effective means of showing actual harm to reputation.

**Aggravated damages.** *Add to last paragraph*: **32.57**

Sections 34-39 of the Crime and Courts Act 2013 came into effect on 3 November 2015. (By s.61(7), those sections were to come into force at the end of the period of one year beginning with the day on which a body was established by Royal Charter with the purpose of carrying on activities relating to the recognition of independent regulators of relevant publishers. That body is the Press Recognition Panel, which was established on 3 November 2014.)

**Conduct of case at trial.** *Add to note 275*: The award of £15,000 aggravated **32.59** damages in *Cruddas v Calvert* [2013] EWHC 2298 (QB) (reduced on appeal:

[2015] EWCA Civ 171; [2015] E.M.L.R. 16) seems to have been founded at least in part on the "offensive" conduct of the defendants, both before and during the trial (including in cross-examination).

**32.61**     **Statutory restrictions on awards of exemplary damages.** Sections 34-39 of the Crime and Courts Act 2013 will come into effect on 3 November 2015. The relevant body established by Royal Charter is the Press Recognition Panel, which was established on 3 November 2014.

Section 11. Evidence of Claim in Misuse of Private Information

*Add to note 307*: It is worth noting that claims for misuse of private information may extend to matters which involve an element of damage to reputation: *Hannon v News Group Newspapers Ltd* [2014] EWHC 1580 (Ch); [2015] E.M.L.R. 1. The overlap between the two torts raises some difficult problems: see e.g. *Terry (LNS) v Persons Unknown* [2010] EWHC 119 (QB); [2010] E.M.L.R. 16 at [96].

**32.70**     **Damages.** *Add to note 318*: In *Gulati v MGN Ltd* [2015] EWHC 1482 (Ch), Mann J. rejected the defendant's submissions that damages in the phone-hacking cases were limited to compensation for distress. They extended, in particular, to the acts of invasion of privacy that led to the distress—"blagging"—the process of obtaining information by deception - and the hacking of the claimant's mobile telephones to access their voicemail: [144]. The enormous sums awarded in that case were the product, of course, of the large number of instances of invasion of privacy in respect of which the claims were made. Damages may not be awarded to "vindicate" claimants, even though that might be the effect of an award, and the term "vindicatory damages" is misleading and should not be used: *Gulati* (above) at [132] and *Weller v Associated Newspapers Ltd* [2014] EWHC 1163 (QB); [2014] E.M.L.R. 24.

*Add to note 320*: In *Gulati* (above) at [205], Mann J. followed Underhill J. in *Commissioner of Police for the Metropolis v Shaw* [2012] I.C.R. 464. In Mann J.'s view that case established that aggravated damages were, at least usually, an aspect of injury to feelings: the aggravating factors caused greater hurt, and thus increased the damages. There were typically three aspects of conduct of the defendant which were capable of triggering an aggravated damages award—the manner in which the wrong was committed, motive and subsequent conduct, which could include the manner in which the trial (and a fortiori the litigation as a whole) was conducted by the defendant, including the effect of cross examination.

CHAPTER 33

# THE TRIAL: THE DEFENDANT'S CASE

SECTION 1. SUBMISSION OF NO CASE

**Introductory.** *First paragraph*: Defamation Act 2013, s.11 abolishes the right **33.1**
to trial by jury in defamation cases, and applies to all actions started on or after
1 January 2014: see s.16(7) and the Defamation Act 2013 (Commencement)
(England and Wales) Order 2013, S.I. 2013 No. 3027. There have been no jury
trials since 2012, when there were two, and in the wake of s.11 the prospect of
any further jury trials in libel or slander cases can safely be said to be slight.

*Delete note 1 and replace as follows*:

The law has been amended by s.11 Defamation Act 2013, to remove the
presumption in favour of jury trial in defamation cases. For the principles that
now apply to the exercise of discretion in favour of jury trial, see *Yeo v Times
Newspapers Ltd* [2014] EWHC 2853 (QB); [2015] 1 W.L.R. 971.

*Second paragraph*: Absent a jury, no submissions will be made to the effect
that words are not capable of bearing a particular meaning. Modern practice is
now to determine the question of meaning early on in the proceedings as a
preliminary issue: see 30.2 above. Moreover, words are no longer defamatory
unless their publication has caused serious harm to the claimant's reputation, or
is likely to, and that issue also will have been determined by way of preliminary
issue: *Lachaux v Independent Print Ltd* [2015] EWHC 2242 (QB); 2015
E.M.L.R. 28.

As for honest comment, the common law defence has now been replaced by the statutory defence of honest opinion: s.3, Defamation Act 2013. Public interest is not an element of the s.3 defence.

**33.2**    **Judge's ruling postponed.** Given that the right to trial by jury has been abolished (see 33.1 above), this paragraph is unlikely to have any further relevance to defamation trials.

Section 2. Opening Statement on Behalf of the Defendant

**33.3**    **Defendant's opening speech.** The right to trial by jury has been abolished: see 33.1 above.

**33.7**    **Meaning of words.** Given the abolition of the right to jury trial, meaning will now usually be determined by the judge at a much earlier stage of the proceedings: see 30.2 above.

**33.9**    **Defamation Act 2013, s.1** *Replace existing text as follows*:

Section 1 of the Defamation Act 2013, was brought into force with effect from 1 January 2014, and applies to any cause of action that accrues on or after that date. Section 1(1) has the effect that the claimant must prove as a fact that the words complained of have caused (or are likely to cause) serious harm to his reputation: *Lachaux v Independent Print Ltd* [2015] EWHC 2242 (QB); [2015] E.M.L.R. 28. In obvious cases, that may be done by inference (*Cooke v MGN Ltd* [2014] EWHC 2831 (QB); [2015] 1 W.L.R. 895 at [43] and *Lachaux* (above) at [57]), and no doubt in most cases, especially where the defendant is a mass media publisher, inference will be sufficient. Where it does not suffice, it is not entirely clear how claimants will be expected to prove damage to their reputations. There are some suggestions at 32.24 above, largely prompted by the evidence called by the claimant in *Lachaux* at [101]ff.

A higher corporate threshold applies by virtue of s.1(2), which provides that harm to the reputation of a body that trades for profit is not "serious harm" unless publication has caused or is likely to cause it serious financial loss.

Whether the claimant is caught by s.1(1) or s.1(2), or both, the defendant will wish, if it can, to adduce evidence showing that the claimant's reputation has not suffered serious harm, and is not likely to; and if the claimant is a trading body, to show that serious financial loss has not been and is unlikely to be caused. In *Cooke v MGN Ltd* [2014] EWHC 2831 (QB); [2015] 1 W.L.R. 895, counsel for the defendants submitted that reactions in social media, and reader comments in response to media publications, might be relevant: but that would often entail giving weight to the views of the prejudiced, unreasonable or ignorant (and might be unrepresentative of the population of 'right thinking people' generally, as Bean J observed at [43]). It might also run counter to the principle that any given words have one single meaning which is objectively determined by reference to the response of the hypothetical reasonable person. However, it may be noteworthy that in *Cooke*, Bean J. hinted ([43]) that an opinion poll survey or a selection of comments from the "blogosphere" might in some cases be appropriate. And in *Lachaux* at [86] Warby J said in terms that evidence of adverse social media responses, name-calling or similar events was admissible. If that holds good for the claimant, then presumably the defendant must in principle be able to put in evidence showing that the response to the publication was not adverse to the claimant.

It is not open to the defendant to rely on other publications to a similar effect as bearing on the issue of serious harm: see *Lachaux v Independent Print Ltd* [2015] EWHC 2242 (QB); [2015] E.M.L.R. 28, applying *Dingle v Associated Newspapers Ltd* [1964] AC 371.

### SECTION 4. PROOF OF JUSTIFICATION / TRUTH

*Add to note 33*: Defamation Act 2013, s.2 came into force on 1 January 2014, but does not affect cases in which the cause of action accrued before that date: s.16(5).

**Onus and standard of proof.** *Add to end of note 41*: The Court of Appeal     **33.12**
considered what has to be proved in the case of a "Chase 2" imputation (justification on the objective basis of reasonable grounds to suspect the claimant of guilt) in *Miller v Associated Newspapers* [2014] EWCA Civ 39 at [12]-[22].

*Add to note 42*: Defamation Act 2013, s.2 came into force on 1 January 2014, but does not affect cases in which the cause of action accrued before that date. The repeal of s.5 of the 1952 Act therefore takes effect for all cases in which the cause of action accrued on or after 1 January.

**Evidence before the court on unsuccessful plea of justification or honest**     **33.14**
**comment/opinion** *Add to note 51*: See also *Cruddas v Calvert* [2015] EWCA Civ 171; [2015] E.M.L.R. 16 at [135]-[138], where the *Pamplin* principle was applied. The court found that the defendants had in fact (contrary to the findings of the trial judge) proved the truth of the words complained of in one of three meanings, and reduced the damages accordingly.

*Add to note 61*: The amendment of the 1974 Act became effective from 1 January 2014 in respect of causes of action that accrued on or after that date.

### SECTION 5. PROOF OF FAIR/HONEST COMMENT OR HONEST OPINION

**Supporting facts.** *Add to this paragraph*: The statutory defence of honest     **33.19**
opinion (s.3, Defamation Act 2013) applies to actions where the cause of action accrued on or after 1 January 2014. Under s.3(4)(a), defendants will have to make good their defence by establishing the relevant facts which existed at the time of publication, on the basis of which an honest person could have held the opinion, or alternatively, under s.3.4(b), by establishing the existence of the privileged statement (defined at s.3(7)), published before the words complained of, which contained the facts (or asserted facts) on the basis of which an honest person could have held that opinion.

*Add to note 63*: The statutory defence of honest opinion (s.3, Defamation Act 2013) came into force on 1 January 2014, and applies to actions where the cause of action accrued on or after that date.

*Add to note 67*: And see s.3(5), Defamation Act 2013: the defence is defeated if the claimant shows that the defendant did not hold the opinion.

**33.21**     **Fairness of comment.** *First paragraph*: Section three of the Defamation Act 2013 does not on its face require that the facts on which the opinion was based should have been known to the claimant. S. 3(4) provides that the third condition of the defence is that an honest person could have held the opinion on the basis of any fact which existed at the time the statement complained of was published (and of anything asserted to be a fact in a privileged statement published before the statement complained of). This appears to be the very change in the law which the Supreme Court declined to make in *Joseph v Spiller* [2010] UKSC 53; [2011] 1 A.C. 852: see [108]—[111], where Lord Phillips rejected counsel's submission that the defence should be expanded to embrace facts which were not known to the defendant, or even in existence when he made his comment. "The reforms suggested by (counsel) would radically alter the nature of the defence of fair comment. No longer would it be a personal defence based on the defendant's honest opinion on facts identified by him. The defendant's state of mind would be wholly irrelevant under Mr Price's scheme and almost wholly irrelevant under Mr Caldecott's. Instead fair comment would depend upon an objective test, applied in a similar way to the defence of justification. Did facts exist that might have led a prejudiced and obstinate commentator to express the derogatory opinion expressed by the defendant? I am not persuaded that reforms of this nature would do anything to simplify defamation actions. The scope of the defence of fair comment would be widened, but at the price of continued complexity of process. In any event the proposed reforms go beyond changes that could properly be made by this court in the orderly development of the common law".

**33.22**     **Matter of public interest.** *Add*: Under the statutory defence, which applies to actions founded on causes of actions that accrued on or after 1 January 2014, it is no longer necessary to show that the comment was made on a matter of public interest.

Section 6. Proof of Privilege

**33.23**     **Facts creating privilege must be proved.** *Add*: Defamation Act 2013, s.11 abolishes the right to trial by jury in defamation cases, and applies to all actions started on or after 1 January 2014. There have been no jury trials since the two in 2012, and in the wake of s.11 the prospect of any further jury trials in libel or slander cases can safely be said to be slight.

*Add to note 79*: For recent guidance on the factors relevant to the residual discretion to order jury trial under the new regime, see *Yeo v Times Newspapers Ltd* [2014] EWHC 2853 (QB); [2015] 1 W.L.R. 971.

**Reynolds or public interest privilege.** *Add at end of this section*: While the   **33.25**
Explanatory Notes to the Act suggest that s.4 is intended to reflect the law as laid
down in *Flood*, the conditions for the statutory defence are in different terms. The
new defence has not yet been the subject of judicial consideration, except for
some tentative observations (without the benefit of argument) in *Barron v Vines*
[2015] EWHC 1161 (QB) at [58]ff.

**Reportage.** *Add to note 93*: The statutory successor to the reportage defence,   **33.26**
s.4(3) Defamation Act 2013, came into force in 1 January 2013 for actions in
which the cause of action accrued on or after that date.

SECTION 7. REBUTTAL OF MALICE

**Presumption of good faith.** *Add to end of second paragraph (concluding*   **33.27**
*"opinion expressed")*:

Under the new statutory defence of honest opinion, in force from 1 January
2014 for proceedings in which the cause of action accrued on or after that date,
s.3(5), Defamation Act 2013: the defence is defeated if the claimant shows that
the defendant did not hold the relevant opinion. If the claimant takes the point,
then while the burden will be on him to do so, the defendant is likely to wish to
give evidence to meet it.

**Allegation of express malice.** *Add to this paragraph*: Note that the new   **33.28**
statutory defence of honest opinion (s.3, Defamation Act 2013) came into force
on 1 January 2014 for causes of action that accrued on or after that date. The
scope for a plea of malice under s.3 is very limited indeed. By s.3(5), the defence
is defeated if the claimant shows that the defendant did not hold the relevant
opinion. If the claimant decides to shoulder the burden of proving it, the
defendant is likely to wish to give evidence to show that he or she did indeed hold
the opinion.

SECTION 8. EVIDENCE IN MITIGATION OF DAMAGES

(c) *Evidence properly admitted before the court on some other issue*

**Admissible evidence on some other issue.** *Add to note 173*: The *Pamplin*   **33.47**
principle was applied in *Cruddas v Calvert* [2015] EWCA Civ 171; [2015]
E.M.L.R.16 at [135]-[138], where the court found that the defendants had
(contrary to the findings of the trial judge) proved the truth of the words
complained of in one of three meanings, and reduced the damages
accordingly.

(f) *Apology or other amends*

**Effect of apology.** *Add*: It appears that under the new regime in place under   **33.55**
s.1, Defamation Act 2013, a speedy and wholehearted apology is now capable of

[185]

turning a published statement from one which has caused or is likely to cause serious harm to a claimant's reputation, into one which does not have that effect: see *Lachaux v Independent Print Ltd* [2015] EWHC 2242 (QB); [2015] E.M.L.R. 28 at [68]: "Another consequence (of the judge's construction of s.1) is that a publication may in principle change from being defamatory (and hence not actionable), for instance by reason of a prompt and full retraction and apology". As the judge said, without overstatement, that is a novelty in the substantive law of defamation. However, it offers an opportunity for a defendant not merely to mitigate damages but actually to transform an actionable publication into one which fails to surmount the s.1 threshold of serious harm to reputation.

**33.56**     **Retraction.** *Add*: See 33.55 above on the potential effect of an apology, which must apply with similar force to a retraction.

### (g) *Damages already recovered for same libel*

*Add to note 209*: Similarly, the principle in *Dingle v Associated Newspapers* applies to prevent defendants from arguing that other publications should be taken into account in assessing whether or not the claimant's reputation has been caused, or is likely to be caused, serious harm by the publication of the words complained of (s.1(1), Defamation Act 2013: see *Lachaux v Independent Print Ltd* [2015] EWHC 2242 (QB); [2015] E.M.L.R. 28).

SECTION 9. EVIDENCE IN DEFENCE OF MISUSE OF PRIVATE INFORMATION CLAIM

**33.62**     **Reasonable expectation of privacy.** In *Weller v Associated Newspapers* [2014] EWHC 1163 (QB); [2014] E.M.L.R. 24, Dingemans J. at [36] followed *Murray v Big Pictures (UK) Ltd* [2008] EWCA Civ 446; [2009] Ch. 481 and considered that the test for a reasonable expectation of privacy was a broad objective test which allowed defendants to give evidence not only of matters they knew but also of things which they did not know, and could not have known about, at the time of publication, to show that there was no reasonable expectation of privacy. An appeal is pending against this decision, but in the meantime the Supreme Court has approved the Court of Appeal's characterisation of the test in *Murray*: see *In the matter of an Application by JR38 for Judicial Review* [2015] UKSC 42; [2015] E.M.L.R. [38] [2015] E.M.L.R. 38.

**33.63**     **Damages.** *Add*: Defendants should take care not to aggravate damages by, in particular, the way in which they conduct the trial, including the cross-examination of the claimant: see *Gulati v MGN Ltd* [2015] EWHC 1482 (Ch) at [205]. Once ss.34-39 of the Crime and Courts Act 2013 come into effect, exemplary damages will generally not be awarded against a defendant publisher if it was at the material time a member of an approved regulatory body. Those sections come into effect on 3 November 2015, a year after the establishment by Royal Charter of the Press Recognition Panel.

CHAPTER 34

## THE TRIAL: FUNCTIONS OF JUDGE AND JURY

Defamation Act 2013, s.11 abolishes the right to trial by jury in defamation cases. The section applies to all actions started on or after 1 January 2014: see s.16(7) and the Defamation Act 2013 (Commencement) (England and Wales) Order 2013, S.I. 2013 No. 3027. There have been no jury trials since the two referred to in the main text, which took place in 2012, and in the wake of s.11 the prospect of any further English jury trials in libel or slander cases can safely be said to be very slight. Such utility as this chapter may have had is therefore at an end, at least as far as concerns England and Wales.

For the principles that now apply in England and Wales to the exercise of discretion in favour of jury trial, see *Yeo v Times Newspapers Ltd* [2014] EWHC 2853 (QB); [2015] 1 W.L.R. 971.

# THE TRIAL: THE FINAL STAGES

*Note 1*: Defamation Act 2013, s.11 abolishes the right to trial by jury in defamation cases in England and Wales. It applies to all actions started on or after 1 January 2014: see s.16(7) and the Defamation Act 2013 (Commencement) (England and Wales) Order 2013, S.I. 2013 No. 3027. There have been no jury trials since 2012, when there were two. Trial by jury in defamation will in future be as exceptional in England and Wales as it is in other areas of civil litigation.

Section 2: Summing-Up

*AND*

Section 3. Verdict

These sections are now redundant in England and Wales in the light of the abolition of the right to trial by jury in defamation cases: see *note 1* above.

Section 4. Judgment

**35.10**   **Generally.** *Add*: Jury verdicts are now a thing of the past in England and Wales: see *note 1* above. The first four sentences of this paragraph are therefore redundant.

Section 5. Costs

**35.13**   **Delay in bringing LASPO ss.44, 46 into force in publication and privacy cases.** As at 1 September 2015, the two sections had still not been brought into force in relation to "publication and privacy" cases. The winner's success fee and ATE premium continue to be recoverable from the losing party.

**35.15**   *Add to end of this paragraph*:

See also *Lawrence v Fen Tigers Ltd (No 3)* [2015] UKSC 50; [2015] 1 W.L.R. 3485, where the Supreme Court found that *MGN v United Kingdom* (2011) 53

E.H.R.R. 5; [2011] E.M.L.R. 20 could properly be distinguished on the footing that there was in *Lawrence* no competing interest comparable to freedom of expression.

**Rules for costs management.** *Add to note* 75: The appeal from Master **35.20**
McCloud's draconian order was dismissed: *Mitchell v News Group Newspapers Ltd* [2013] EWCA Civ 1537; [2014] 1 W.L.R. 795. Subsequently *Mitchell* was explained and its effects mitigated in *Denton v TH White Ltd* [2014] EWCA Civ 906; [2014] 1 W.L.R. 3926. For the current approach to relief from sanctions (in a case where the claimant's failure, i.e. to notify of funding arrangements by service of the proper form, was not serious), see e.g. *Yeo v Times Newspapers Ltd* [2014] EWHC 2853 (QB); [2015] 1 W.L.R. 971 at [142ff] and *Sloutsker v Romanova* [2015] EWHC 545 (QB); [2015] 2 Costs L.R. 321, at [27ff].

**Juries' views on costs.** For juries, see *Note 1* above.                **35.21**

**Pt 36: indemnity costs and other sanctions** *Note 121*: The relevant rule is **35.31**
now CPR 36.17.

*Note 123*: The relevant rule is now CPR 36.3(g).

*Note 124*: The relevant rule is now CPR 36.17(3).

*Note 125*: The relevant rule is now CPR 36.17(4).

*Note 126*: The relevant rule is now CPR 36.17(5). The court will also take into account whether the offer was a genuine attempt to settle the proceedings.

*Note 127*: The relevant rule is now CPR 36.17(7).

**Costs in action under Slander of Women Act 1891.** The Slander of Women **35.37**
Act 1891 has now been repealed by s.14(1), Defamation Act 2013. The repeal does not affect causes of action that accrued before 1 January 2014.

CHAPTER 36

# APPEAL

SECTION 1. GENERAL PRINCIPLES

**36.1**    **Application for permission to appeal.** *Add to note 16*: See *Dar Al-Arkan Real Estate Development Company v Al Majid Al-Sayed Bader Hashim Al-Refai* [2014] EWCA Civ 749 refusing an application for permission to appeal the decision of the judge to order split trials.

**36.2**    **Where permission to appeal is granted.** *Add before final sentence of note 23*: see also *Michael Wilson & Partners Ltd v Thomas Sinclair and others* [2012] EWHC 2560 (Comm) at [39].

SECTION 3. WRONG CONCLUSION OF LAW

**36.10**    **Wrongly withdrawing a question from the jury.** *Note 64,* Section 11, Defamation Act 2013 is now in force.

SECTION 4. MISDIRECTION

**36.12**    **Misdirection as to defamatory meaning.** *Note 81:* Tugendhat J.'s decision in *Cruddas v Calvert* is now reported at [2014] E.M.L.R. 4. The Court of Appeal decision is now reported at [2014] E.M.LR. 5.

SECTION 5. UNREASONABLE VERDICT

**36.24**    **Verdict by judge alone.** *Add to Note 142*: see also *Thompson v James* [2014] EWCA Civ 600 at [20] per Longmore L.J.

*Add new note 142A after,* "An appellate tribunal will not lightly interfere".

*New note 142A:* In *Rufus v Elliott* [2015] EWCA Civ 121 Sharp L.J. (with whom McCombe L.J. and Mitting J. agreed) said at [8], *"The judge's task under CPR PD 53 para 4.1 is no more and no less than to "pre-empt perversity": see Jameel v The Wall Street Journal Europe Sprl [2004] E.M.L.R. 6. Though this issue normally arises in the context of rulings made about the meanings pleaded by the parties, it seems to me a similarly high threshold applies to the question whether words are capable of being defamatory of the claimant. The Court of Appeal therefore discourages appeals on such rulings: see Berezovsky v Forbes [2001] EWCA Civ 1251; [2001] E.M.L.R. 45."*

*Note 143:* The Court of Appeal decision in *Cruddas v Calvert* is now reported at [2014] E.M.L.R. 5.

## Appendix 3

## Damages Awards

**Part 1: Awards of libel damages approved or made by the Court of Appeal or the Supreme Court (or formerly the House of Lords) to which reference may be made in other actions.**

Add:
A3.18A *Cruddas v Calvert, Blake and Times Newspapers Ltd* [2015] EWCA Civ 171; [2015] E.M.L.R. 16

**Part 2: Non-jury Damages Awards from 2000**

Note:
A3.65 *Cruddas v Calvert, Blake and Times Newspapers Ltd* [2013] EWHC 2298 (QB)

Add:
A3.65A *Flood v Times Newspapers Ltd* [2013] EWHC 4075 (QB)
A3.65B *Kadir v Channel S Television Ltd* [2014] EWHC 2305 (QB)
A3.65C *Sharma v Sharma* [2014] EWHC 3349 (QB)
A3.65D *Royal Brompton & Harefield NHS Foundation Trust v Shaikh* [2014] EWHC 2857 (QB)
A3.65E *Garcia v Associated Newspapers Ltd* [2014] EWHC 3137 (QB)
A3.65F *ReachLocal UK Ltd v Bennett* [2014] EWHC 3405 (QB); [2015] E.M.L.R. 7
A3.65G *Johnson v Steele* [2014] EWHC B24 (QB)
A3.65H *Rai v Bholowasia* [2015] EWHC 382 (QB)
A3.65I *Asghar v Ahmad* [2015] EWHC 1118 (QB)
A3.65J *Bussey Law Firm PC v Page* [2015] EWHC 563 (QB)
A3.65K *Sloutsker v Romanova* [2015] EWHC 2053 (QB); [2015] E.M.L.R. 27
A3.65L *Tardios v Linton*, unreported, 31 July, 2015

**Part 4: Damages awards in misuse of personal information and harassment cases involving speech (since 2000).**

Add:
A3.88 *Weller v Associated Newspapers Ltd* [2014] EWHC 1163 (QB); [2014] E.M.L.R. 24
A3.89 *Royal Brompton & Harefield NHS Foundation Trust v Shaikh* [2014] EWHC 2857 (QB)
A3.90 *Levi v Bates* [2015] EWCA Civ 206; [2015] E.M.L.R. 22
A3.91 *Gulati v MGN Ltd* [2015] EWHC 1482 (Ch)
A3.92 *Hayes v Willoughby*, unreported, 22 July, 2015 (HHJ Moloney QC, Cambridge County Court)

## Part 1

**Awards of libel damages approved or made by the Court of Appeal or the Supreme Court (or formerly the House of Lords) to which reference may be made in other actions.**

Add:

*Cruddas v Calvert, Blake and Times Newspapers Ltd* [2015] EWCA Civ 171; [2015] E.M.L.R. 16      **A3.18A**

For the facts of the first instance decision see A3.65. The defendants were successful on appeal with their justification plea relating to the first of three meanings the words complained of were ultimately taken to bear. (Namely that, in return for cash donations to the Conservative Party, the claimant offered for sale the opportunity to influence government policy and gain unfair advantage through secret meetings with ministers (the 'cash for access' allegation), which the defendants successfully argued was behaviour that was "inappropriate, unacceptable and wrong", rather than imputing any criminality on the claimant's part.) The Court of Appeal found no basis for overturning the decision on malice in relation to meanings two and three. Having identified what proportion of the general damages award was attributable to each of the pleaded meanings, it proceeded to reduce the respective parts of the award accordingly. The amount of £100,000 relating to the first meaning was set aside in its entirety, and the remaining £65,000, which was attributed to the second and third meanings, was reduced by £22,000 to recognise the defendants' successful justification of the first meaning. General damages were therefore reduced to £43,000 in total and aggravated damages, which had been awarded as a result of the "offensive" way in which the defendants had contested the claims both before and during trial, were reduced from £15,000 to £7,000 (as they were now only apt in relation to the way the defendants had defended the second and third meanings).

## Part 2

**Non-jury Damages Awards (from 2000).**

Note:

*Cruddas v Calvert, Blake and Times Newspapers Ltd* [2013] EWHC 2298 (QB)      **A3.65**

The defendants successfully appealed the rejection of their justification defence in respect of one of the meanings attributed to the words complained of. The damages award was reduced accordingly to £50,000 in total (including aggravated damages). See now A3.18A *Cruddas v Calvert, Blake and Times Newspapers Ltd* [2015] EWCA Civ 171; [2015] E.M.L.R. 16.

Add:

*Flood v Times Newspapers Ltd* [2013] EWHC 4075 (QB)      **A3.65A**

The defendant published an article in *The Times* and on the *TimesOnline* website stating that the police were investigating the claimant on suspicion of taking bribes in return for the unauthorised disclosure of information. The police investigation ultimately concluded that no evidence had been found against the claimant, and the defendant was informed of its findings. Because the parties could not agree on wording for a follow-up article, the defendant did not update the *TimesOnline* website to report the outcome of the investigation until about two years later. The defendant had originally pleaded justification and *Reynolds* privilege in respect of the article. Whilst the Supreme Court (to which the matter ultimately progressed) did uphold its *Reynolds* privilege defence in respect of the print version and the online version of the article, it only did so up to the date the defendant had been informed of the investigation's outcome. The defendant then subsequently abandoned its plea of justification, and therefore it had no defence in respect of the publication which continued after it was notified of the outcome of the investigation. The Court was asked to assess damages in respect of this two-year period. It made a general damages award of £45,000, with an additional £15,000 in respect of aggravated damages "to serve as a deterrent to those who embark upon public interest journalism but thereafter refuse to publish material which in whole, or in part, exculpates the subject of the investigation".

Add:

**A3.65B  *Kadir v Channel S Television Ltd* [2014] EWHC 2305 (QB)**

The first claimant was the director of the second claimant, a money transfer business, both of which had obtained judgment in default against the defendant, a UK based television station broadcasting in the Bengali language. The defendant had published a TV news bulletin that was also subsequently available to some viewers on the internet. Nicol J accepted that the words complained of in the bulletin meant that individuals working for the business were reasonably suspected of having defrauded a large number of customers of substantial sums, but held that they did not actually accuse the first claimant himself of fraud, only that he had dealt with the "suspicions of fraud in a highly evasive and incompetent manner". An award of £40,000 was made in total to the claimants by way of general damages (£20,000 to each). The allegations would have been particularly hurtful to the first claimant due to his position as a religious scholar, and they were likely to have had a seriously detrimental effect on the trading reputation of the business. It was also arguable that the injury to the first claimant's feelings had been aggravated by the defendant's cavalier approach to the litigation. The defendant never apologised to either claimant for its actions.

Add:

**A3.65C  *Sharma v Sharma* [2014] EWHC 3349 (QB)**

The claimant, the General Secretary of the National Council of Hindu Temples UK (NCHT UK), brought a libel action against his predecessor, Dr Sharma, over two emails sent to numerous prominent members of the Hindu community in the UK. The emails linked the claimant to wrong-doing that had in fact been committed by his brother-in-law, and suggested that there were strong grounds to suspect the claimant of having committed fraud and other serious financial criminal offences. The emails were signed off by the defendant in his capacity as Secretary of the NCHT UK. Publication was "probably to be measured in the hundreds": the first email was published to six people, and the second to a much wider audience, including representatives of 28 Hindu organisations, and at least 36 prominent individuals/bodies in total. The claimant sent an email to some of the recipients of the original emails, attempting to explain the situation, which mitigated the damage to a certain extent. The defendant played no active role in the proceedings and judgment in default was entered against him. HHJ Moloney QC held that the allegations were grave, albeit not of the "utmost severity". There was aggravation caused by the defendant's lack of engagement with the process and failure to apologise/withdraw the allegations, but also limited mitigation in the form of the claimant's email. The claimant had also retained his position as General Secretary of the NCHT UK. Damages of £45,000 were awarded in total (£15,000 in respect of the first email, and £30,000 for the second).

Add:

### *Royal Brompton & Harefield NHS Foundation Trust v Shaikh* [2014] EWHC 2857 (QB)

A3.65D

The defendant, a trainee cardiac physiologist, was sued for harassment and libel by five claimants, a hospital trust and four present/former employees of the Trust who had been involved in the defendant's training or disciplinary proceedings against him. He was employed by the Trust at one time, but was subsequently dismissed for gross misconduct, after which he began an intense and lengthy campaign of harassment, consisting of about 120 separate incidents, which included silent phone calls; referring people without justification to regulatory bodies; sending fake letters to patients giving false appointments; fake job applications; anonymous letters; videos; fake phone calls; communications with relations of some of the personal claimants. Much of the harassment consisted in the making of persistent defamatory allegations, which included imputations of lying, fraud, bribery and paedophilia against the claimants. No defence was filed, judgment in default was obtained, and directions were given for the defendant to pay the personal claimants damages for the harassment and libels. In respect of harassment, the second and fourth claimants were awarded £25,000 each, and the third and fifth claimants £20,000 each. In respect of the libels, the second and fourth claimants were awarded an extra £10,000 (making their total awards £35,000 each), and the third and fifth claimants an extra £20,000 (making their total awards £40,000 each). Due to the limitation issue, the libel awards were made only in respect of the allegations published within the twelve months prior to the claim being issued, and were much lower than they would have been but for the harassment awards. HHJ Moloney QC was concerned only to award damages in the libel claims for injury to reputation, and not injury to feelings, as that element had already been accounted for within the harassment awards.

Add:

### *Garcia v Associated Newspapers Ltd* [2014] EWHC 3137 (QB)

A3.65E

The claimant, a qualified Spanish doctor who worked as a GP in the UK, sued the defendant newspaper publisher for libel over an article that appeared in the *Daily Mail* and on the *Mail-Online*. It claimed that he had wrongly reported a patient (who was at the time a bus-driver) to the DVLA for suspected alcohol abuse, despite there being no evidence to support that conclusion, and that he had done so in breach of patient confidentiality obligations owed by him. The article suggested that the claimant's actions were the result of a language barrier, which meant he had misunderstood the patient's reports about his drinking. It was also claimed that he had pretended not to be able to talk to the defendant when he was approached for comment due to confidentiality reasons, despite an appropriate consent form having been signed by the patient. The defendant's pleas of justification and honest comment failed: the Court held that there had been no misunderstanding and the claimant had been justified in acting as he did. An award of £45,000 was made. No award of aggravated damages was appropriate: the defendant was entitled to defend the action in the way it did.

Add:

**A3.65F**   *ReachLocal UK Ltd v Bennett* [2014] EWHC 3405 (QB); [2015] E.M.L.R. 7

The claimants, two companies in an online marketing and advertising agency, sued a rival company and associated individuals *inter alia* for defamation and malicious falsehood over a campaign of phone calls and emails to its customer base (which had been accompanied by press releases and posts on social media) alleging that it had inflated prices and cheated its customers. The campaign resulted in a substantial loss of business, and special damages were claimed. Judgment in default was entered in respect of several of the defendants. The Court was in no doubt that the first claimant (a UK based company) had suffered substantial loss as a direct result of the publications from customers who decided not to continue with cycles of advertising that had been booked, but not paid for, and awarded special damages of £241,945 under this heading (that figure including a 20% discount of the amount claimed to recognise that there were other factors which led to those withdrawals in addition to the defamatory allegations). The sums of £60,728 and £66,600 that the first claimant had spent to fund a remedial PR campaign and to make payments to customers to keep their business in an attempt to mitigate the damage caused were also recoverable. The judgment itself would provide little vindication because it was not a contested decision on the merits, and the allegations were grave and struck at the heart of the first claimant's business credibility. Having only been incorporated in 2008 and being relatively new to its field, the company was more vulnerable to attack. An award of £75,000 in general damages was made on that basis. The second claimant, a Netherlands company that did not trade in the UK, was awarded a nominal sum of £100 in general damages. Nothing was said in relation to damages for the malicious falsehood, as the judge was only asked to determine damages in respect of the libel claim.

Add:

**A3.65G**   *Johnson v Steele* [2014] EWHC B24 (QB)

The defendant launched a sustained attack on the claimant by way of blogs and Twitter accounts, making "allegations of the most serious and distressing kind" including claims of dishonesty, misconduct and criminal behaviour on the claimant's part. The defendant had done everything he could to maximise the damage caused. He had not apologised, nor mitigated the loss in any way; he had started a copycat site in the US after the claimant managed to get some of the UK websites hosting the allegations suspended; he had created fake accounts in the claimant's name; and he had made no attempt to justify or defend the allegations despite their seriousness. The defendant had also put the claimant to the trouble and expense of conducting the litigation and having to respond to his counter-claim. He had attempted to hide or destroy his computers despite being told to preserve them, and made false allegations to the police resulting in the claimant's arrest. An award of £70,000 was made, which included an element of aggravated damages.

Add:

**A3.65H**   *Rai v Bholowasia* [2015] EWHC 382 (QB)

The claimant, a member of the congregation of a Sikh temple, sued the defendants for libel over several articles that appeared in a Sikh community newspaper and online. The articles alleged that he had been caught red-handed stealing money from the temple's donation box whilst counting its contents, that he had conspired to arrange an assault on the man who supposedly saw and reported the theft, and that he was involved in threats to kill that man and his family. The defendants pleaded justification and qualified privilege (including *Reynolds* privilege), both of which were maintained at trial, but which ultimately failed. Hard-copy readership was approximately 80,000. There was no evidence as to online readership. The Court found that the damage was primarily done amongst the claimant's own Sikh community, and made an award of £50,000.

Add:

### *Asghar v Ahmad* [2015] EWHC 1118 (QB)                                           A3.65I

The claimants held appointed management positions on a body responsible for running two Welsh mosques. The first claimant was also a member of the Welsh Assembly and the Conservative Party. The defendants were all supporters of a campaign seeking to bring more transparency and accountability into the management of the mosques, and to have those holding management positions elected, rather than appointed. The claimants succeeded at trial in proving that the fourth defendant had defamed them both on a website and by his publication of a dossier of defamatory documents which included serious allegations of fraud and corruption. His qualified privilege defence failed and, in any event, malice was proved against him. The fourth defendant's conduct of his defence was also noted by the Court: it both attracted further adverse attention in the local media and caused a significant amount of additional distress to the claimants. Awards of £45,000 were made to each of the claimants in respect of those publications. The Court took into account the fact that the claimants had already received awards of £45,000 in a prior libel claim where they had sued the popular Urdu language newspaper, Nawa-i-Jang, for publishing similar serious allegations.

Add:

### *Bussey Law Firm PC v Page* [2015] EWHC 563 (QB)                               A3.65J

The claimants, a US law firm and its principal, brought a libel claim against a UK citizen over a defamatory posting on the law firm's *Google Maps* profile. The posting undermined the effect of other reviews posted, and was viewable for around a year. The defendant denied responsibility despite the post having been made from his *Google* account, but the Court held him responsible. The publication was calculated to cause serious harm to the claimants, and it had caused significant anxiety and distress to the principal as it reflected upon his personal integrity and professional competence. There was never any suggestion the claims were true. Damages were assessed at £45,000 for the principal and £25,000 for the law firm, although the award was capped at £50,000 in total as that was the limit that had been placed on the claim.

Add:

### *Sloutsker v Romanova* [2015] EWHC 2053 (QB); [2015] E.M.L.R. 27              A3.65K

The claimant was a Russian businessman who had been a well-known Senator of the Russian Federation prior to emigrating to Israel in 2011, where he lived since that time. He sued a Russian journalist for libel over several online publications in the UK and in Russia, as well as a radio broadcast, claiming that he had put out a contract to murder her husband (who had previously been employed by one of the claimant's companies) and had bribed court officials who were involved in Russian criminal proceedings against her husband. No defence was filed and judgment in default was entered. The libels were serious and had been published to a relatively wide audience: the Court proceeded on the basis that the online articles could well have reached as many as 60,000 readers in this jurisdiction, and the radio programme would likely have been heard by at least several thousand here, where the claimant had a "substantial and valuable reputation". Damages would only be awarded in respect of those publications that took place in this jurisdiction as per the pleaded claim; the damage caused in Russia was therefore irrelevant for these purposes. A global award of £110,000 was made in respect of all the publications.

Add:

**A3.65L** *Tardios v Linton*, unreported, 31 July, 2015

The claimants, an independent primary school and its headmistress, sued the defendant, a parent of a child who formerly attended the school, over a defamatory petition posted on a US website under a false alias calling for the headmistress' resignation. The petition accused the headmistress of unacceptable treatment and bullying of the children in her care, of being ethically and morally offensive and of causing the children in her care psychological and mental harm. The defendant greatly prolonged the litigation by refusing to admit she was the person behind the posting, thereby considerably aggravating the damage caused by the original publication. For a significant period of time the petition had been the top *Google* search result for the school's name. The school had previously had a strong positive record and the allegations were entirely false. The allegations made against the headmistress had caused her a significant amount of distress, leaving her feeling "destroyed". There was no evidence of mitigating factors, no plea of justification, and extraordinary aggravating factors due to the defendant's conduct in refusing to admit responsibility for the libel. The headmistress was awarded £70,000 in damages, and the company that owned the school (which could only be awarded damages for injury to its reputation) was awarded £25,000.

## Part 4

**Damages awards in misuse of personal information and harassment cases involving speech (since 2000)**

Add:

**A3.88** *Weller v Associated Newspapers Ltd* [2014] EWHC 1163 (QB); [2014] E.M.L.R. 24

The claimants, the children of a famous pop musician, brought a claim through their father for a misuse of private information and a breach of the Data Protection Act following publication of unpixelated photographs of the children enjoying a family day out. The photographs had been taken without their consent whilst they were shopping in a street and relaxing at a café in California. At the time of publication the older child was aged 16, and the younger children, the twins, were 10 months old. The children's facial expressions were visible, and they were identified by their surname. The photographs were published for one day on the *MailOnline* website before they were removed from the internet. The article illustrated by the photographs received 34,000 hits, of which 24,000 were from this jurisdiction. Although the Court held that the twins would not have suffered any "immediate embarrassment from the publication", the older child did. A compensatory award of £5,000 was made to the 16 year old, and £2,500 to each of the twins. Aggravated damages were not appropriate.

Add:

**A3.89** *Royal Brompton & Harefield NHS Foundation Trust v Shaikh* [2014] EWHC 2857 (QB)

See A3.65D above for report.

Add:

*Levi v Bates* [2015] EWCA Civ 206; [2015] E.M.L.R. 22    **A3.90**

The first defendant had controlled Leeds United FC, the second defendant football club. The claimants were husband and wife, known to the first defendant through business dealings connected with the husband's former involvement with the club. The first defendant harboured grievances against the husband. Harassment proceedings were brought by the husband against the first defendant over statements made in a column in the club's match programme, and on the club's radio station, in respect of which damages of £10,000 were awarded to him. However the harassment claim brought by his wife, the second claimant, had been dismissed. It related to statements made in two match programme articles that had included the family's home address and home phone number, inviting thousands of club supporters to intervene in a hostile manner at her home in a business dispute between her husband and the first defendant. The wife successfully challenged the rejection of her claim on appeal. She was awarded £6,000 in damages by the Court of Appeal, having regard to the steps that she and her husband had to take to protect themselves at home, and because of the anxiety she suffered.

Add:

*Gulati v MGN Ltd* [2015] EWHC 1482 (Ch)    **A3.91**

Eight claimants, the majority of whom were well-known celebrities, brought claims for misuse of private information against the defendant newspaper publisher arising from extended campaigns of mobile telephone voicemail hacking. All but one of the claimants also sued for misuse of private information in respect of articles published by the defendant on the basis of information obtained from the hacking. Mann J described the phone hacking as widespread, institutionalised, long-standing and covert. He held that each article published was to be treated separately in terms of an award of damages, and that damages should be awarded to reflect infringements of privacy rights in addition to the distress and injury to feelings suffered. The claimants experienced significant disquiet as a result of not knowing what private information had been listened to or discovered by unlawful means, and the defendant only admitted liability after first indicating it would contest the claims. That was capable of being an aggravating factor. The defendant's apologies were seen by the Court as a sensible tactical move, rather than as being driven by a genuine desire to make amends. The highest award of £260,250 was made to the actress and businesswoman Sadie Frost, said to have suffered a "severe" impact as a result of the misuse of her private information. The remainder of the awards ranged from £72,500 to £201,250. The BBC employee Alan Yentob, about whom no articles had been published, was awarded £85,000.

Add:

*Hayes v Willoughby*, unreported, 22 July, 2015 (HHJ Moloney QC, Cambridge County Court)    **A3.92**

The claimant, a businessman, brought harassment proceedings over a seven-year campaign during which the defendant made various allegations of misconduct concerning the claimant's business dealings, and contacted several law enforcement agencies about his suspicions of fraud and tax evasion. Although the defendant's actions were initially defensible on the basis of s(1)(3)(a) Protection from Harassment Act 1997, because he was pursuing the conduct for the purpose of preventing or detecting crime, his persistence after the claimant had been cleared of the allegations (and knowing that the courts considered his persistence to be irrational) was unlawful harassment. Taking into account the high number of incidents, their nature, the effect on the claimant and the substantial duration of the campaign, a damages award of £30,000 was made. This figure included an amount of £6,000 for aggravated damages, arising in particular from the defendant's persistent and aggressive defence of the claim.